"Dr. Steven Smith is a trusted exegete and accomplished pulpiteer. I read everything he writes, and I encourage you to do the same. All who set out to preach or teach Jeremiah or Lamentations will benefit from consulting this commentary, and as you do, you'll be better equipped to connect these Old Testament prophets to the saving message of Jesus Christ."

Jason K. Allen, Ph.D., president of Midwestern Baptist Theological Seminary & Spurgeon College

"At a time when people refused to hear and obey God, a reluctant prophet named Jeremiah wholeheartedly trusted the Lord and warned others to do the same. This brilliant commentary by Steven Smith demonstrates how grace, mercy, prayer, repentance, and obedience enabled Jeremiah to proclaim and live out the plan of hope that God intended. Smith's rich analysis of Jeremiah's writings, along with carefully crafted sermon outlines and questions for reflection and discussion, will serve as an invaluable resource for pastors laboring so that others might see and embrace the light of the gospel amid a spiritually confused and dark culture similar to that of the prophet Jeremiah."

Todd von Helms, Senior Fellow, Kings College, New York City

"I collect all of these from this Christ-honoring series. Dr Smith has passionately written from the passionate prophet Jeremiah. This commentary will be useful for many years to come."

Johnny Hunt, pastor, First Baptist Church, Woodstock, GA

"As the church continues to contend for the faith, the books of Jeremiah and Lamentations provide invaluable resources and insight for the Christian life. These books remind us of pain, exile, and loss, but most importantly, they remind us of God's redemptive purposes and His commitment to His people. This work by Dr. Smith will help pastors navigate these rich texts with exegetical precision and pastoral nuance, and I cannot recommend it more highly."

J. T. English, pastor, The Village Church Institute

CHRIST-CENTERED

Exposition

OT / COMMENTARY
FEATURING

CSB

AUTHOR **Steven Smith**

SERIES EDITORS **David Platt, Daniel L. Akin, and Tony Merida**

CHRIST-CENTERED
Exposition

EXALTING JESUS IN
JEREMIAH AND LAMENTATIONS

HOLMAN
REFERENCE
NASHVILLE, TENNESSEE

B&H Publishing Group
Nashville, Tennessee
All rights reserved.

ISBN: 978-0-8054-9656-7

Dewey Decimal Classification: 220.7
Subject Heading: BIBLE. O.T. Jeremiah, Lamentations—
COMMENTARIES \ JESUS CHRIST

Printed in the United States of America
1 2 3 4 5 6 7 8 9 10 • 25 24 23 22 21 20 19
BP

TABLE OF CONTENTS

Lamentations

ACKNOWLEDGMENTS

Let me express thanks to Danny Akin for allowing me to participate in the Christ-Centered Exposition series as well as to David Stabnow at B&H for his careful editing and shepherding of this project to completion.

Many thanks to Meagan Lacey, Evan Longo, and Daniel Dickard, who edited many of the chapters. It would have not been complete without their help. Thanks also to Adam Mallette and Deana Loyd for their administrative help during the writing process. I am also grateful to Immanuel Baptist Church, especially as we studied the book of Lamentations together. After five weeks in Lamentations, thank you is the least I can say! Special thanks to my spectacular wife, Ashley. She has helped me understand the ongoing mystery of Lamentations as we walked this path together. It's good to bear down (Lam 3:27).

SERIES INTRODUCTION

Augustine said, "Where Scripture speaks, God speaks." The editors of the Christ-Centered Exposition Commentary series believe that where God speaks, the pastor must speak. God speaks through his written Word. We must speak from that Word. We believe the Bible is God breathed, authoritative, inerrant, sufficient, understandable, necessary, and timeless. We also affirm that the Bible is a Christ-centered book; that is, it contains a unified story of redemptive history of which Jesus is the hero. Because of this Christ-centered trajectory that runs from Genesis 1 through Revelation 22, we believe the Bible has a corresponding global-missions thrust. From beginning to end, we see God's mission as one of making worshipers of Christ from every tribe and tongue worked out through this redemptive drama in Scripture. To that end we must preach the Word.

In addition to these distinct convictions, the Christ-Centered Exposition Commentary series has some distinguishing characteristics. First, this series seeks to display exegetical accuracy. What the Bible says is what we want to say. While not every volume in the series will be a verse-by-verse commentary, we nevertheless desire to handle the text carefully and explain it rightly. Those who teach and preach bear the heavy responsibility of saying what God has said in his Word and declaring what God has done in Christ. We desire to handle God's Word faithfully, knowing that we must give an account for how we have fulfilled this holy calling (Jas 3:1).

Second, the Christ-Centered Exposition Commentary series has pastors in view. While we hope others will read this series, such as parents, teachers, small-group leaders, and student ministers, we desire to provide a commentary busy pastors will use for weekly preparation of biblically faithful and gospel-saturated sermons. This series is not academic in nature. Our aim is to present a readable and pastoral style of commentaries. We believe this aim will serve the church of the Lord Jesus Christ.

Third, we want the Christ-Centered Exposition Commentary series to be known for the inclusion of helpful illustrations and theologically driven applications. Many commentaries offer no help in illustrations, and few offer any kind of help in application. Often those that do offer illustrative material and application unfortunately give little serious attention to the text. While giving ourselves primarily to explanation, we also hope to serve readers by providing inspiring and illuminating illustrations coupled with timely and timeless application.

Finally, as the name suggests, the editors seek to exalt Jesus from every book of the Bible. In saying this, we are not commending wild allegory or fanciful typology. We certainly believe we must be constrained to the meaning intended by the divine Author himself, the Holy Spirit of God. However, we also believe the Bible has a messianic focus, and our hope is that the individual authors will exalt Christ from particular texts. Luke 24:25-27,44-47 and John 5:39,46 inform both our hermeneutics and our homiletics. Not every author will do this the same way or have the same degree of Christ-centered emphasis. That is fine with us. We believe faithful exposition that is Christ centered is not monolithic. We do believe, however, that we must read the whole Bible as Christian Scripture. Therefore, our aim is both to honor the historical particularity of each biblical passage and to highlight its intrinsic connection to the Redeemer.

The editors are indebted to the contributors of each volume. The reader will detect a unique style from each writer, and we celebrate these unique gifts and traits. While distinctive in their approaches, the authors share a common characteristic in that they are pastoral theologians. They love the church, and they regularly preach and teach God's Word to God's people. Further, many of these contributors are younger voices. We think these new, fresh voices can serve the church well, especially among a rising generation that has the task of proclaiming the Word of Christ and the Christ of the Word to the lost world.

We hope and pray this series will serve the body of Christ well in these ways until our Savior returns in glory. If it does, we will have succeeded in our assignment.

David Platt
Daniel L. Akin
Tony Merida
Series Editors
February 2013

Jeremiah

Introduction
The Hope of Judgment

The car edges to the shoulder of the highway; I hear gravel and debris pinging the inside of my wheel well. The siren and lights behind me are like irritating beacons of justice illuminating my guilt. I've been caught speeding. All those who witness this scene are reminded that justice is real, and I have the gnawing feeling that justice will be served.

The reason I was pulled over is because I was guilty. I was speeding. The officer did not trap me, trick me, or treat me differently than others. I knew the law, I knew the risks of breaking the law, I took those risks, and I will pay. Yet, while I know this intellectually, some small part of me wants to blame the officer. Now, I don't yell and scream. No, I simply blame him covertly in the act of trying to be excused. When we beg for mercy, it is a subtle way of saying, "If you were not so good at your job, I would not be in this position. Frankly, this whole thing is partly your fault." Yet, in reality, he is not the one giving me justice. The state in which I live is bringing justice on me. He is not the law; he is the agent of the law. He is in the unenviable position of telling me that judgment is coming from a power higher than both of us. He did not create the situation. He simply enforced it.

This analogy, weak as it is, helps us understand the role of the prophet. Jeremiah might identify with being the enforcer. He was just a man, yet this man had the unenviable position of being called to deliver the message of pending justice, and because he was the agent of the law, some people treated him terribly.

Understandably, he was reluctant to embrace his call. God had to command him to obey the call and not be afraid of people's scowling faces (Jer 1:6-10). And not unlike the resentment we all feel toward the messenger of the bad news, he faced the wrath of many who wanted to kill the messenger for bringing bad news (Jer 38). It never has been easy to enforce the law, and it made for a tough life for Jeremiah. But we are getting ahead of ourselves. Let's start at the beginning—the very beginning.

Context

God created Adam and Eve in the garden of Eden. He activated the faith of Noah, destroyed the rest of the world by a flood, and started over with a new race. This new race also rebelled against its Creator, and God decided to start over yet again, activating the faith of Abraham. This time the human race would not be new physically, but he would create another kingdom within the human race. They were a race of people set apart by nationality, yes, but more specifically by a promise that he would make to them, a promise that contained three things: land, offspring, and blessing.

Abraham was prosperous, but a famine would take this family into Egypt, where they would eventually become slaves. God led them out of Egypt, activating the faith of Moses. All of this was the outworking of God keeping his promise to Abraham. They were a blessed people; they had a large population; however, they had no land. After letting them wander for years, God eventually gave them the land, activating the faith of Joshua.

Their first form of government was a theocracy ruled by judges, but eventually they had the king they always wanted, King Saul. Saul was followed by David, and David was followed by his son Solomon, but Solomon's heart was divided, and at the end of his rule so was the kingdom. The ten northern tribes formed the nation of Israel, and Judah remained as the southern kingdom.

Divided, the kingdoms were vulnerable, and the northern kingdom fell to Assyria in 722 BC. However, Assyria slowly lost power and was overrun by the Babylonians in 612 BC. Judah leveraged this transition to grow in power, and in 641 BC God blessed Judah with the godly king Josiah. He turned the hearts of the people back to God, and by the end of his reign in 609 BC, he established a greater national power. Yet Josiah was never able to completely reform the nation. When he died the hearts of the people turned back to all the practices that evoked God's judgment. In a downward spiral of leadership, Josiah's godly rule was followed by his heavy-handed son Jehoiakim and then the ugly reign of Zedekiah. While Jeremiah was probably Josiah's age, he prophesied during the reign of all three kings.

The Babylonians eventually captured Jerusalem, and God's people became exiles in Babylon. Jeremiah was exiled to Egypt where he died.

Remember, it was the good king Josiah who discovered the books of the law in the temple, leading to a national renewal of the covenant

(2 Chr 34:6-7). Derek Kidner notes that the national renewal Josiah implemented had three effects on Jeremiah (*Message of Jeremiah*, 15–18).

First, he was sent on a preaching tour proclaiming the implications of the newly rediscovered covenant. This led Jeremiah to be beyond unpopular and eventually persecuted and hated by many. Second, this led to a personal struggle with God (chs. 11–20). Jeremiah's message was being rejected, he was persecuted, and at many times he would wonder why he was even called. Jeremiah lamented,

> Why has my pain become unending,
> my wound incurable, refusing to be healed?
> You truly have become like a mirage to me—
> water that is not reliable. (15:18)

Finally, Jeremiah realized that any reformation was short-lived. Reminding one of Israel leaving Egypt and breaking God's law as it was being given to them, Jeremiah's audience was returning to the same sins Josiah worked so hard to eradicate. This reality makes the promise of a new covenant, a covenant written on the heart (31:33), critically relevant. All of the attempts to keep the old covenant made explicitly clear that no external rule can motivate obedience. The presence of a law does not generate love for the lawgiver. Those under the law must be motivated by their own hearts.

Perhaps the three effects of reform—preaching, personal suffering, and lament over lack of reform—correspond to the three major genres of literature in the book: Jeremiah's sermons, Jeremiah's journal, and Jeremiah's songs.

The Book

Themes

Judgment: Jeremiah is about the judgment of God on a specific nation. The book is like one long divorce suit (Dever, *Promises Made*, 594). God is leveling charge after charge against his people.

So, why is God so angry with his own people? There are lots of reasons. They were putting their confidence in the wrong people (2:36-37; 17:5-8). They were putting their confidence in things instead of God (9:23-24; 48:7; 7:8-14). They were acting in ways that were contrary to the nature of their faith. They were guilty of idolatry (10:1-16;

44:1-30); adultery (5:7-9; 7:9); oppressing the aliens, orphans, and widows (7:5-6); lying and slander (9:4-6); and breaking the Sabbath (17:19-27). To make matters worse, they were hypocrites about it all (7:1-11; 9:2-9; 10:1-16).

In a word, God is judging them for being unfaithful—unfaithful to a God who is always faithful. This is why the painful metaphor of an unfaithful bride was so bitingly accurate. There is nothing more devastating to a marriage than unfaithfulness. Jeremiah explains it this way in Jeremiah 3:1-3:

> If a man divorces his wife
> and she leaves him to marry another,
> can he ever return to her?
> Wouldn't such a land become totally defiled?
> But you!
> You have prostituted yourself with many partners—
> can you return to me?
>   This is the LORD's declaration.
> Look to the barren heights and see.
> Where have you not been immoral?
> You sat waiting for them beside the highways
> like a nomad in the desert.
> You have defiled the land
> with your prostitution and wickedness.
> This is why the showers haven't come—
> why there has been no spring rain.
> You have the brazen look of a prostitute
> and refuse to be ashamed.

Another biting metaphor is that of a rebellious child. This is exactly how Judah is responding to their heavenly Father who is trying to parent them. In 3:4-5 Jeremiah writes,

> Haven't you recently called to me, "My Father.
> You were my friend in my youth.
> Will he bear a grudge forever?
> Will he be endlessly infuriated?"
> This is what you have said,
> but you have done the evil thing
> you are capable of.

The rest of chapter 3 continues the theme of judgment coming on Judah for all of their rebellion. Reading chapter 3 will give us a good sense of the flow of the entire book. Look at 3:6-10:

> In the days of King Josiah the LORD asked me, "Have you seen what unfaithful Israel has done? She has ascended every high hill and gone under every green tree to prostitute herself there. I thought, 'After she has done all these things, she will return to me.' But she didn't return, and her treacherous sister Judah saw it. I observed that it was because unfaithful Israel had committed adultery that I had sent her away and had given her a certificate of divorce. Nevertheless, her treacherous sister Judah was not afraid but also went and prostituted herself. Indifferent to her prostitution, she defiled the land and committed adultery with stones and trees. Yet in spite of all this, her treacherous sister Judah didn't return to me with all her heart—only in pretense."
> This is the LORD's declaration.

Hope: In the midst of this judgment is a ray of hope. This is the promise amid the judgment. Let's continue reading in chapter 3.

> The LORD announced to me, "Unfaithful Israel has shown herself more righteous than treacherous Judah. Go, proclaim these words to the north, and say,
>
> 'Return, unfaithful Israel.
>   This is the LORD's declaration.
> I will not look on you with anger,
> for I am unfailing in my love.
>   This is the LORD's declaration.
> I will not be angry forever.
> Only acknowledge your guilt—
> you have rebelled against the LORD your God.
> You have scattered your favors to strangers
> under every green tree
> and have not obeyed me.
>   This is the LORD's declaration.
>
> "Return, you faithless children—this is the LORD's declaration—for I am your master, and I will take you, one from a city and two from a family, and I will bring you to Zion. I will give you shepherds who are loyal to me, and they will shepherd you with knowledge and skill.

*When you multiply and increase in the land, in those days—this is
the* LORD*'s declaration—no one will say again, "The ark of the* LORD*'s
covenant." It will never come to mind, and no one will remember or
miss it. Another one will not be made. At that time Jerusalem will be
called The* LORD*'s Throne, and all the nations will be gathered to it,
to the name of the* LORD *in Jerusalem. They will cease to follow the
stubbornness of their evil hearts. In those days the house of Judah will
join with the house of Israel, and they will come together from the land
of the north to the land I have given your ancestors to inherit."'*

*I thought, "How I long to make you my sons
and give you a desirable land,
the most beautiful inheritance of all the nations."
I thought, "You will call me 'My Father'
and never turn away from me."
However, as a woman may betray her lover,
so you have betrayed me, house of Israel.*
        This is the LORD*'s declaration.*
*A sound is heard on the barren heights:
the children of Israel weeping and begging for mercy,
for they have perverted their way;
they have forgotten the* LORD *their God.
Return, you faithless children.
I will heal your unfaithfulness.
"Here we are, coming to you,
for you are the* LORD *our God.
Surely, falsehood comes from the hills,
commotion from the mountains,
but the salvation of Israel
is only in the* LORD *our God.
From the time of our youth
the shameful one has consumed
what our fathers have worked for—
their flocks and their herds,
their sons and their daughters.
Let us lie down in our shame;
let our disgrace cover us.
We have sinned against the* LORD *our God,
both we and our fathers,*

from the time of our youth even to this day.
We have not obeyed the LORD our God." (3:11-25)

Jeremiah is about hope provided by judgment. That sounds like an odd statement, but it should be comforting. Every sin that has ever been committed is apparent in the eyes of God. He knows each one. And, as a perfect God, he will execute justice on every sin that has ever been committed. Yet that God would *announce* judgment is itself an act of mercy. If God had intended no mercy, he would have simply acted. He allows the judgment to be a means by which people can repent. So in this way the judgment is also discipline. When a parent disciplines a child, the child, no matter how mature, has difficulty seeing the good in it. My four-year-old child needs to have a course correction from time to time. He gets in a rut of rebellion and disobedience. I recognize his need for this because I see it in myself. I need a course correction. I need my direction "righted." If I, a sinful parent, know to discipline my children, how much more does the heavenly Father know how to discipline us (Heb 12:3-11)?

Structure

The book is not really structured like a book. It is not like a novel that develops a story line chronologically to its rising climax and then conclusion. Mark Dever identifies two major sections to the book and offers this outline:

Justice for God's People (Chapters 1–45, 52)
    The Cause of Judgment
    The Promise of Judgment
    The Priority of Judgment
    The Herald of Judgment
Justice for Babylon and the Nations (Chapters 46–51) (*Promises Made*, 590)

An easy way to think about it is this: *The story of God's judgment is told in Jeremiah and Lamentations through Jeremiah's sermons, his journal, and his songs.* The chronology is less important to the author. The sermons extract his message, the songs express his weeping, and the journals expose the private thoughts of a public man.

Feel

Jeremiah is a prophet, but not as much in the foretelling sense as in the forth-telling. His primary focus is not directing us to coming events as much as directing us to the heart of God. He wants us to know how God feels about certain things. Jeremiah loves a good metaphor. In fact, he describes the rebellious people of God as a bride (2:32), someone who slips and falls (8:4-5), birds that do not migrate (8:7), and melting snow (18:13-17). There are dozens of such metaphors in the book.

Strategy

There are many ways to preach through a book of the Bible. One strategy is to preach through each verse in the book (e.g., Ryken, *Jeremiah*). Our strategy here will be to combine *macro* exposition (looking at the major movements of the book) with some micro exposition (looking at individual verses and words). The result is different from sermons preached through an epistle. Not every verse is covered.

This commentary represents consecutive sermons developed canonically through Jeremiah and Lamentations.

This strategy is not unlike trying to understand a historical event. To understand the history of a world war or a nation rising and falling, you could examine every day. Yet to look at every single day would be so granular that you might miss the actual sweep of the historical significance of the individual events. This volume is text driven inasmuch as the major themes of the books will be covered in proportion to how they are covered in the book.

The Real Message

The reason this is all so critical goes back to the beginning. After restarting with Noah, God promised to create a new people, a spiritual race through Abraham. This was his covenant, his promise. Jeremiah marks a devastating time in the trajectory of a fulfilled promise. The nation was scattered in rebellion against this covenant-keeping God. It seemed that hope was lost and that the nation would not survive. Yet it would survive. This is not because of the hearts of the people; they were horribly turned away from God. Their survival would not be because Jeremiah was a great communicator or dynamic leader. His hearers tortured and abused him! What makes all of this work out in the end is that God kept his promise.

The real promise of Jeremiah is found in Jeremiah 31:31, the promise of a new covenant. This is a shocking prophecy! No prophet had as yet discussed the new covenant so explicitly. This promise is fulfilled in the person of Jesus Christ. The entry of Jesus into the world was a direct fulfillment of this promise.

At the end of Jesus's life, he took his disciples in close and, in the context of the Passover, connected the message of the prophet Jeremiah to his work. Luke records it this way in Luke 22:20: "In the same way he also took the cup after supper and said, 'This cup is the new covenant in my blood, which is poured out for you.'"

God was instituting something completely new. The blood in the cup was a metaphor for his spilled blood, when spikes were driven through his hands and feet. This was not simply a man going to his death for us as an example of goodness. It was bigger than that. The reason Jesus died has everything to do with the message of Jeremiah, the message of hope through justice. In this way there is so much gospel in Jeremiah.

Conclusion

When the police officer gives a ticket, he does not ask me to pay on the spot. He does not ask for money, lock me in jail, or punch me in the face. He gives me a little piece of paper. That's all. He has the whole weight of the local government behind him, he has hundreds of hours of training, thousands of dollars invested in that training, and the best tactical gear, yet all of that power and authority is expressed in a little slip of paper. In that moment all I am required to do is accept it and then pay it. Sounds lite. Trivial. I can lose the paper. I can throw it away. I can rip it to shreds. It is, after all, just a piece of paper! It's as momentary and fleeting as, well, this sermon.

Of course, the little piece of paper is not the point. The point is the power behind the paper. The paper is a warning of pending judgment. If I do not pay the ticket, I will feel the whole weight of justice that is behind that paper.

In that way the paper ticket is hope! The existence of the paper tells me that I do not have to have my license revoked, I do not have to have a warrant out for my arrest, and I do not have to go to jail. While all those things will happen if I ignore the paper, the paper is the wonderful news that if I pay it, I can avoid judgment. The new covenant is the even greater news that Jesus paid my penalty for me. God's judgment is real; the sacrifice of Christ is real. The judgment pronounces guilt I cannot reconcile and leads me to grace I do not deserve. In this way Jeremiah leads us to Jesus.

A warning of judgment is always hopeful for those with hearts to repent. That's the gospel truth.

The Anatomy of the Call

JEREMIAH 1

Main Idea: Obedience to the call is a God-sized risk for God-sized results.

I.   **God Calls Jeremiah (1:5).**
II. **When God Calls, We Might Object (1:6).**
III. **God Responds to Our Reasons (1:7-10).**
  A. God commands (1:7).
  B. God cares (1:8).
  C. God commissions (1:9-10).
IV. **What Does This Mean for Jeremiah (1:11-19)?**
  A. A promise: God will honor his word (1:11-12).
  B. A prediction: disaster is coming (1:13-16).

The dimly lit dorm room was filled with a warm breeze. Outside my window was the shadow of the Appalachian foothills. I did not realize what it meant, but outside that window was where I would experience my first East Coast fall. Outside, it was glorious.

Inside, I was alone. Dropped off at college, I opened the box that contained the present my mom left me. It was a Bible in which she had marked every Bible "promise" she had for me. In her heart this was God's way of encouraging, comforting, and committing to her that he was going to take care of her boy.

As I perused that Bible, the one promise that stood out to me, like no other, was the promise of Jeremiah 1:7:

Do not say, "I am only a youth,"
for you will go to everyone I send you to
and speak whatever I tell you.

I was eighteen years old and a few months away from preaching my first sermon in church. Yet in that moment I felt steel in my blood. I felt a resolve that all things would be taken care of by God if only I would act in obedience to him. His call was just that real, but my obedience was just that fragile. Perhaps Jeremiah's awareness of his own frailty is what made him contest God's call.

God used those verses to help me clarify my own call to ministry—what it would look like. For Jeremiah this was a specific call to a specific task. We are not all called to be a prophet, but we are all called.

The Bible describes a call to salvation. God calls us out to be saved. You have to come to grips with the reality of your own salvation. Once we come to Christ, there is a call to holiness. God has never called someone to ride the bench. There is a specific call to live a holy life, which means we are called to do specific things: husbands are called to lead their families and be willing to die for their wives; wives are called to respond to that leadership and manage their homes well; if you are single, you are called to purity and to a life devoted to the gospel; if you are a child, you are called to obey your parents; we are called to live in harmony with one another; and we are called to be good citizens of our country while we wait for our true kingdom. These are specific calls that express what it means to live a holy life.

Yet God will put his hand on some persons specifically and set them apart to have a prophetic word for a situation. This is the call to speak.

Like the other calls, this call has a general and specific expression. We are all called to open our mouths and speak. This means sharing the gospel with others. There are no professional Christians you can pay to do this for you. When a church member tells the pastor, "There is someone who needs a visit," the pastor's best response is, "I will go with you." We cannot outsource our call to share our faith, to speak up for justice, or to right certain wrongs.

Yet this has a specific expression as well. God has always set aside those who will have a full-time vocational life of service to God. So those who are not called to ministry cannot ignore this text either; it applies to all of us. Yet, at the risk of alienating some, it is extremely important that churches not neglect "calling out the called." This means that in this place, at this moment, God has a specific call on your life, and the call cannot be ignored. This was the case for Jeremiah.

God Calls Jeremiah
JEREMIAH 1:5

Jeremiah's call went down something like this:

Before I formed you in the womb I knew you, and before you were born I consecrated you; I appointed you a prophet to the nations.

This had to be a little shocking for Jeremiah to hear. No enlistment. No job fair. No career counseling. No, God told him that as the raw genetic material was being composed in his mother's womb, he was being set apart for this purpose.

The purpose of this passage is not to make a statement about the current abortion debate, but it does nonetheless. God's sonogram did not reveal tissue but a person, a person who was called for a specific purpose. It would seem right for parents to pray for the life, the calling, and the future of their babies as each mother cradles a child in the womb.

There are three driving verbs here: God *knew* him, *consecrated* him, and *appointed* him. God's tone is that this was "done and done." God had this all arranged, but Jeremiah has an objection.

When God Calls, We Might Object
JEREMIAH 1:6

Jeremiah complains that he is too young. While we do not know how young he is, we can imagine him as a late teenager when he is called. He is not so much concerned with his age but that his age prohibits him from being a good public speaker. We see a hint of the call of Moses here. "God, I cannot hold an audience. Not a good speaker, God. Give me some time" (Wright, *Message of Jeremiah*, 54).

The difference is that, unlike Moses, Jeremiah really was young.

His dismay at his call, and his later struggles to keep silent (20:9), gave their own witness to the divine, not human compulsion he was under. And unlike Moses, whose protestations rang a little hollow, Jeremiah *really was* young, it seems, and inexperienced. (Kidner, *Message of Jeremiah*, 26)

God had in mind on-the-job training. By the way, if God called him before he formed him, you would think God could take care of the timing. It's almost as if God anticipated this response and dealt with it before Jeremiah ever made it. It is God's way to answer our objections before we make them. Perhaps this is lost on Jeremiah.

Jeremiah is now facing the pivotal decision of his life. It is the decision to obey. There is no reason to believe that if he passes on this call, it will come back to him later. There is no, "I'll think about this at the next service, at the next camp—next year." There is no next time. There is no tomorrow. Perhaps God calls the young because they are just wise enough to obey. Jeremiah is in the position of simple obedience.

When God sets someone apart for ministry, there is generally a time when he or she knows it. If we reject that call, we may have another moment to respond. As someone said, big moments swing on tiny hinges of obedience. This is true even when, or especially when, we do not know what the next step is. George McDonald said it this way:

> Men would *understand*; they do not care to *obey*. They try to understand where it is impossible they should understand except by obeying. They would search into the work of the Lord instead of doing their part in it. . . . It is on them that do his will that the day dawns. To them the day star arises in their hearts. Obedience is the soul of knowledge. (*Knowing*, 5)

Yet, over the course of years, I have met many, many people who, in a moment of transparency, will confess that at some moment in life they felt a compulsion, a yearning to obey God in a full-time call to ministry. They passed. They took another career path, another job, another degree. That simple decision, not to disobey but to postpone obedience, was the defining moment of their life. That decision led to another, and as days became years, they found that their decision to ignore the voice of God was not just a denial, but it was a trajectory. The soft voice of God being quenched once made it so much easier to do it the next time and the next, and now a life's course has been set on the casual but radical turns away from the voice of God.

So if God is calling you, simply obey.

God responds to Jeremiah's response, countering Jeremiah's counter in three parts.

God Responds to Our Reasons
JEREMIAH 1:7-10

God Commands (v. 7)

This is clear enough. His call was corrective, "Don't say I am only a youth." The point is not small. Everything Jeremiah will do will be accomplished in God's power. There is not even a hint that he is called based on his ability or giftedness.

God Cares (v. 8)

The most frequent divine command in Scripture is simply, "Do not be afraid." The comfort God gives Jeremiah is based on the reality that he will be with him to deliver him. That God is calling him to act based on God's comfort helps us understand true courage. Courage is not an act of character; it is an act of faith. Being brash, taking risks, and throwing caution to the wind—these are not often acts of faith; they are acts of bravado. True courage has an object: faith in the character of God.

God's encouragements are repeated toward the end of the chapter (vv. 17-19).

God Commissions (vv. 9-10)

God's commission is specific. God puts his words in Jeremiah's mouth. God still uses preachers with a prophetic voice, yet God does not use prophets today in the same way he did in the time of Jeremiah. The difference is that we have the complete witness of Scripture. We have in writing what God wants to say to us today and for all future days.

The act of a modern prophet is not retrieving direct revelation from God but rather "re-presenting" what God has already said. As preachers we are not seeking revelation so that we tell others what God is telling us; rather, we are taking his already revealed revelation and speaking it. We are not waiting for "a word" to speak; we are speaking the word God has given to us. This is a critically important distinction. To say it another way, we are speaking God's word today when we re-present the word that is given to us through Jeremiah.

It is interesting that God appointed him to be over this nation. This was not a political office, but there is a ring of stewardship here. It was his responsibility to offer spiritual guardianship for this people. This is an interesting contrast to the shepherds of Israel who did not keep the stewardship God had entrusted to them (Jer 2:8; 10:21).

In the moment of God's call to Jeremiah, God has something specific in mind for him. He was to "pluck up and to break down, to destroy, and to overthrow, to build and to plant." Notice that there are four negatives and two positives. God has promised that he will rebuild and replant Jerusalem. This will happen. But first God will break down and destroy. This is a metaphor he will return to again and again.

Yet even in this destruction God is preparing the way for something new. This is always the point with God. "God's purpose in history—ancient, modern, or eschatological—is that when God brings catastrophic endings it is to prepare the way for unimaginable new beginnings" (Wright, *Message of Jeremiah*, 56). This idea is perfectly summed up in Jeremiah's call. He will be used to both tear down and to build.

What Does This Mean for Jeremiah?
JEREMIAH 1:11-19

A Promise: God Will Honor His Word (1:11-12)

This word picture is a play on words. The Hebrew word for "almond" sounds identical to the word for "watch." God is taking specific care over his word to accomplish it. God's will is that which will be accomplished. Jeremiah can speak with confidence. What God says will be accomplished—every promise fulfilled. Every ministry of the church is a ministry of the word. Counseling is bringing God's word to difficult situations; children's ministry is bringing God's word to a child; women's ministry is bringing God's word to bear on the issues women face. If we are called to be holy, then ministry is a call to act holy. All of life is a response to a God who has already spoken (Adams, *Speaking God's Word*, 59–60).

Preachers today must deal with this. We live in a world that wants suggestions and thoughts but not directives. However, what God has said will absolutely come true. What he promises is true.

A Prediction: Disaster Is Coming (1:13-16)

The historical backdrop to this chapter is that God is going to bring judgment on his people when the enemy comes from the north. The invading enemy will be Babylon. While Babylon lay to the east, when it invades, it will need to come to Jerusalem from the only real access: the north.

This prophecy would come true. Despite Josiah's attempt at reform, ultimately God would use foreign nations to discipline Israel.

Conclusion

I know a sermon like this will cause some to wonder whether they are called. It might make you wonder, and some might feel confused: "Am I called to full-time vocational ministry?" God never writes confusion. So if you are confused about a call, take someone into your confidence and talk through the call to ministry. Those of us in vocational ministry have all been there, and it is important to talk through this to sense how God might be moving in your life and heart. But let's end by talking about this practically. There are both a general call and a specific call.

We Are All Called

The general call is for all of us to be prophets. Every Christian, in one sense, is called to be a prophet. God never gives Miranda rights: you do not have the right to remain silent.

To what is God calling you? Some need to take up the mantle of being a man. God is calling you to stop taking the role of father and husband from cultural cues and lead like a godly man, for ladies to stop listening to the ambient culture about what femininity is and start listening to and obeying God, for students to humble themselves before parents and teachers and learn to be wise. These are God's specific calls. He is not silent. He does not stutter. This is exactly what he is calling you to. It is in his Word. He. Is. Calling. You.

You are called to look at our culture—its government, its values, its entertainment, its way of thinking—and speak to it. Mothers need to be prophets so their children understand what God values. Fathers need to be prophets so families will be able to evaluate culture. It is wise to avoid a movie because of its rating; it is also wise to watch a family- or faith-oriented film and think critically with our children about why the writer and director painted characters in certain ways. Since we knowingly allow movie producers to be the storytellers of our culture, and therefore of our lives, we are obligated to speak to how these stories affirm, deny, or shade biblical truth. Let's be honest. The church does not have equal time with our children. The church can't right in one morning the message the world gives in six days, nor was it intended to. We are called to speak of the things of God at every turn (Deut 6:4-9) and thus interpret the culture in light of truth. This discernment is what it means to be a Christian in a foreign kingdom. The darkness will make us more obvious.

Some Are Called

Some, however, God has his hand on for a lifetime of ministry as a vocation. If this is you, then please understand that the specifics are not that important at this point. This is not really about a specific call. It's about obedience.

Yet for some God is coming to you, and he is "hedging you in." Like a cowboy on a cutting horse, God is culling you out from the herd. You can't turn to the right or the left. It is just you and God. You know there is a specific call on your life. You want to pretend it is not real, but you are singled out. You can run from lightning, but you can't run from thunder. You can choose not to heed it, but you can't choose not to hear it. Maybe there are a thousand questions in your mind. All those questions have answers, but God is not obligated to answer those before you obey.

The question is not calling; it is obedience.

The Battle of Midway was one of the most fascinating battles in naval history, a strategic battle that protected America from the eastward creep of Japanese forces. It was won on a few tactical decisions—a few decisive moments by the Americans and a few surprisingly indecisive moments by the Japanese.

One of the worst indecisions was the Japanese commander's inability to decide whether to bomb or torpedo. A last-minute decision was made to switch from torpedoes to bombs; the planes were rearmed so quickly that the crewmen left the torpedoes and fuel on the flight deck of the aircraft carrier. When the American dive-bombers descended to bomb the carrier, they were shocked to see all of the bombs, the offensive weapons the enemy was using to attack them, lying in the open. When the American bombs detonated on the carrier, the bombs of the enemy exploded, causing three Japanese carriers to be sunk in moments. The bombs that were offensive weapons became a great tactical advantage for their enemy.

Indecision makes us vulnerable. It allows the enemy the right moment to take our advantages and make them disadvantages. You have heard that an unguarded strength is the greatest weakness. This is because the enemy knows that if we are not seeking after God, we will lose the battle due to overconfidence in our strengths. What we think is our greatest advantage tragically becomes what he will use against us.

Now God is calling you. He is not calling you to do something as explicit as become the prophet for an entire nation. Rather, he is calling you to obey him. This is not about the call; it is about obedience.

Everything God wanted to do with Jeremiah hinged on this one moment of obedience. So it is with you. Obedience is a God-sized risk for a God-sized call. And the opposite is true. Disobedience is a man-sized risk for a man-sized result. The heart of courage is not personality; the heart of courage is faith. So, if God is calling you, believe. Have faith.

Reflect and Discuss

1. How should we understand a call to salvation, a call to holiness, and a call to speak?
2. God's call to Jeremiah was specific. He was to "pluck up and to break down, to destroy and to overthrow, to build and to plant." What are the implications for these four negatives and two positives?
3. What are the three driving verbs related to Jeremiah's call (1:5)?
4. In what way did Jeremiah counter God's initial call (v. 6)?
5. God countered Jeremiah's counter with three responses. What are the three parts of God's counter (vv. 7-10)?
6. What does Jeremiah 1 teach us about the sanctity of human life and the protection of the unborn?
7. What are the similarities between an Old Testament prophet and a New Testament preacher? What are the differences?
8. Every ministry of the church is a ministry of the word. Can you explain?
9. How has God called Christians today to respond to culture, government, values, and entertainment? How should we think and speak to these issues?
10. What is the distinction between a general call to ministry and a specific call to vocational service?

The Anatomy of Divorce

JEREMIAH 2:1–3:5

Main Idea: The God who committed never to leave us is the same God who committed never to leave us in sin.

I. **We Forget What God Has Done for Us (2:5-8).**
II. **We Find Our Satisfaction in Something Else (2:8-37).**
III. **God Files for Divorce (3:8).**
IV. **God Will Not Leave Us Alone (3:1-5).**

There is nothing like young love.

This is one of Jeremiah's early sermons. In the introduction to the sermon, he describes young love in the most poetic way. The love is not between two people but between Judah and God. This metaphor is woven throughout Scripture. The idea is that God is the husband and his people collectively are his bride. This passage describes when the love was new, fresh and exciting.

They are no longer newlyweds, but God remembers when they were. Jeremiah 2:2-3 describes how they felt about each other. When they were newlyweds, the bride was devoted (v. 2). God remembers something specific. He remembers when they were in the wilderness. Things were not perfect. They had their moments. But on the whole God's people remained faithful until Joshua led them out of the wilderness and into the promised land. Those were good days. In fact, God's people were so committed to God that they made an oral covenant with him. Before entering the promised land, they told Joshua, "We will worship the LORD our God and obey him" (Josh 24:24). This was devotion. The generation that entered the promised land had seen Jericho fall; they had seen the tragedy of cheating on God; and still they saw his faithfulness when Ai fell. They had seen the sun stand still so that God could fight for them. No wonder they loved their groom so much.

As for God, he felt the same way. Look at verse 3. "Israel was holy to the LORD, the firstfruits of his harvest. All who ate it found themselves guilty; disaster came on them." Whenever Israel would harvest grain, the first fruit was set apart for God. It was dedicated, consecrated. It was holy. It had no other purpose than for being set aside. It was special. It was so special that if someone came along and ate some of what was to be dedicated to the Lord, he was guilty.

So God says in effect, "All the world is mine; but you, my love, are special. You are the consecrated part of the world. In fact, if anyone touches you, disaster will come upon them." God meant it because he could do it. These were no empty words. God is not posing. He really did wipe out the nations before his people; he really did make a way for them. He really did drive out anyone who came against them. What a husband! He was their husband, and his people were the devoted bride.

That's why it's so shocking that God brings up divorce. Look at 3:8: "I observed that it was because unfaithful Israel had committed adultery that I had sent her away and had given her a certificate of divorce." God is sending her a decree of divorce, and the reason is simple: she was adulterous.

To say the least, this is an odd, even shocking, metaphor. We think of people leaving God; we hardly think of God leaving people. Yet the metaphor is as appropriate as it is shocking. God cannot be blamed for wanting out of a relationship when his bride, Israel, has been serially unfaithful to him. It is also quite predictable. When people part ways with God, it often follows a pattern. This passage shows us the anatomy of divorce.

We Forget What God Has Done for Us
JEREMIAH 2:5-8

God said he remembered the way things used to be (v. 2). But Judah forgot. Look at verses 5-8. The leaders forgot. They stopped asking about the God who delivered them from the oppressive hand of Pharaoh. They forgot about the God who led an entire nation through a wilderness. They forgot about the fertile promised land to which God brought them. In fact, the rulers who were to have this in the forefront of their minds no longer knew God. The shepherds tasked with leading them to God were leading them to false gods.

How did this happen? National leaders did not lead in truth.

When Joshua defeated Jericho and Ai, he took the law and read it to the Israelites (Josh 8:34-35). Joshua was there when God gave this word to Moses, and he knew that God wanted to relate to his people through his covenant law. Yet the law of Moses was forgotten. Josiah, about seven hundred years after Joshua, rediscovered the law and read it to the people. Jeremiah is ministering during the time of Josiah's reforms. He is trying to remind them of the way things were and exhort them not to forget God. If the Word of God is not prominent in people's minds, they forget that God has decided to relate to people through his Word. This is why the indictment of verse 8 is so biting.

> *The priests quit asking, "Where is the LORD?"*
> *The experts in the law no longer knew me,*
> *and the rulers rebelled against me.*

In other words, the leaders who were to lead people to seek God through his law no longer sought God. As the leaders go, so goes the faith. It is no wonder they got into trouble with idolatry. They had forgotten all that God had done for them.

Perhaps the best picture of the ministry of the word in the life of a believer is Psalm 119. Listen to the passionate words of verses 1-8:

> *How happy are those whose way is blameless,*
> *who walk according to the LORD's instruction!*
> *Happy are those who keep his decrees*
> *and seek him with all their heart.*
> *They do nothing wrong;*
> *they walk in his ways.*
> *You have commanded that your precepts*
> *be diligently kept.*
> *If only my ways were committed*
> *to keeping your statutes!*
> *Then I would not be ashamed*
> *when I think about all your commands.*
> *I will praise you with an upright heart*
> *when I learn your righteous judgments.*
> *I will keep your statutes;*
> *never abandon me.*

That passage echoes Psalm 1:1-3:

> *How happy is the one who does not*
> *walk in the advice of the wicked*
> *or stand in the pathway with sinners*
> *or sit in the company of mockers!*

Instead, his delight is in the LORD's instruction,
and he meditates on it day and night.
He is like a tree planted beside flowing streams
that bears its fruit in its season
and whose leaf does not wither.
Whatever he does prospers.

The blessed person is the one who obeys God's instruction! The opposite is also true: the one who forsakes God's instruction is like the chaff the wind blows away. The history of God's people depended on their responsiveness to God's Word. When they believed God in faith, they prospered. When they rejected God's word, they were punished.

The greatest concern in the church may not be that people reject God outright but rather that they neglect his Word. When we preachers refuse to fill our mouths with Scripture, we do not realize how vulnerable we make the people of God. Often a philosophy of preaching is driven by reaction. For example, if we are accused of being dry and irrelevant, we compensate by valuing engagement, relevance, or authenticity. Preaching should be all those things. Yet to suggest that we are helping people if we are not explaining Scripture to them is pretense at best. The Word is the source of life because in the Word we find Jesus, and in Jesus we find the Father (John 5:39; Col 1:15a; Heb 1:3).

It does not matter how strong your historical confession is. If the Word is neglected, the people are vulnerable. So, are you in a position where you hear the Word of God explained regularly?

Neglecting the Word is not the end of the church. It is the beginning of the end. It was for Israel. It was for the early churches of Galatia and Corinth. It was for the churches during the Middle Ages. No church should live in the pretense that their faith will be passed down for generations if it does not teach the Word.

The Word of God stirs the affections for God. If the Word is neglected, the affections are not stirred. This is the trajectory: where there is no communication, separation is soon to follow.

We Find Our Satisfaction in Something Else
JEREMIAH 2:8-37

Once the memory was fuzzy, the heart longed for something else. Which comes first: a heart that drifts from its love or a heart that forgets what love is? It's hard to say. However, if we forget how we have been loved by God, we will certainly look for something else to fill that void. This is exactly what happened to Judah. Forgetting God, they turned to idols. Look at the end of verse 8: "The prophets prophesied by Baal and followed useless idols."

The leaders who forgot God led the people to displace God with other objects of their affection. The leaders were designed to be prophets—spiritual counselors who mediated reform, righted the people's course, and were constantly reconciling the marriage. Instead, they facilitated the separation. Leaders who do not re-present God's Word to God's people are facilitators of ultimate separation between God and his people.

We are getting ahead of ourselves. What caused the separation ultimately was not forgetfulness but idolatry. Idolatry is to forgetfulness what heat is to the sun. The presence of one means the other will follow. No heart can exist in a wasteland of forgetfulness. So when forgetfulness is looming over us, our hearts easily warm to something else. We want something to worship. And when the Word is not revealing the true Son to us, we will find something to worship.

Judah turned to worship false gods and idols. Literally. This is shocking in light of all God, their great husband, had done for them. Forgetfulness makes the greatest love vulnerable. When the word was absent for so long, the people forgot all that God had done. How could they love a God they did not know? So the void of love was filled with an infatuation with other things.

Jeremiah uses several metaphors to paint the picture. Israel is like

- a slave (2:14);
- prey for other nations (2:15);
- a prostitute chasing other lovers (2:20);
- a choice vine that became a wild vine (2:21);
- a donkey in heat (2:24);
- a thief that is shamed when caught (2:26);
- a bride who forgets her wedding dress (2:32).

But perhaps the most telling metaphor is found in 2:13 where God says,

For my people have committed a double evil:
They have abandoned me,
the fountain of living water,
and dug cisterns for themselves—
cracked cisterns that cannot hold water.

This summarizes the whole problem. They have forgotten God, and they have gone after other things. They have abandoned God as the source of life-giving water, and they dug leaky cisterns. A good well could support much life for a long time. However, these broken cisterns were of no value.

Jesus used the metaphor to describe himself. In fact, Jeremiah 2:13 reads like John 4:13-14:

> *Jesus said, "Everyone who drinks from this water will get thirsty again. But whoever drinks from the water that I will give him will never get thirsty again. In fact, the water I will give him will become a well of water springing up in him for eternal life."*

Jesus was talking to a woman who was drinking from the cistern of lost love. She had been married several times and was living with a guy. All this "love," but she was still thirsty. We know intuitively that sex, isolated as a recreational activity, cannot fill the need for love that only God can fill.

Jeremiah is not preaching to individuals but to a group. He is saying that *these people* have rejected God in order to be satisfied with something else. The pattern exists in all of us. If we do not remember all that God has done for us, that is, if we are not exposed to the Word of God, then we will find ourselves dissatisfied. We will want something to fill that void. Yet the question is not an individual one; it is a corporate one. The question we have to ask is about our faith, our people.

This is consistent with how the Bible describes our relationship to Christ. *I* am not the bride of Christ, but *we, the church,* are the bride of Christ (Eph 5; Rev 19). This is corporate. It was the effective, hardworking church at Ephesus that Jesus admonishes for losing their first love. Have *we* lost our first love? Is Jesus enough, or do we need something else to satisfy our thirst?

This pattern can be true of any church. If our leaders do not remind us of all that God has done for us and of how he alone can quench our thirst, we become thirsty for other things. We dig out cisterns that distract us from knowing God. The most dangerous aspect of a broken pot is that it is full for a moment. It is deceptive, giving the appearance of satisfaction. Leaky pots are momentarily full. The slower the leak is, the more real the deception.

God sees dissatisfaction in his people. He files for divorce.

God Files for Divorce
JEREMIAH 3:8

God's people have been faithless for a long time. God wants out.

Would God ever divorce the church for the same reason? Imagine a local church that was worshiping idols. What would that look like? Imagine that its members only had a casual interest in God. The mention of his name stirred no passion. His presence evoked no excitement; they were never aroused by God. Although God had saved them, they had forgotten that. Things like being removed from death and hell, the victory that Christ would promise, and the love for Jesus were forgotten. The reason, as happened with Israel, is that the leaders of the church did not tell people what God said. They did not hold up the Word of God.

As a result, the church members' affections were more stimulated by something else. They got really excited about work, family, vacations, money, and all the things God provided them but not really excited about God. The ironic thing is that they kept all the things about church. They kept coming. And, strangely, they loved the things of church. But to be honest, they loved the music, the friends, the facilities, and all the things about the church as much (or more!) than they loved the God of the church. Imagine that!

If you can imagine that, do you think God would want a divorce?

What if God would say, "Look, I really love you. There is nothing—and I mean nothing—that I would not do for you. I am bound by my character to love you perfectly.

"But it's clear you don't love me. And it's not just about one thing. It's about years and years of you chasing all these other things except knowing me and loving me. I think we want different things: I want you, and you want other lovers. You don't love me. It's obvious you never will.

"I want out. I want a divorce. I want to love you, and you want everything but me. Let's go our separate ways."

God wants a divorce, but even though he wants it, he won't get it.

God Will Not Leave Us Alone
JEREMIAH 3:1-5

Look at 3:1. Even if God wanted a divorce, there is an odd sense in which he cannot divorce. The reason is simple. The law demanded that if you divorce your wife, and she then marries another, you cannot remarry her later. In creating that law, God was trying to protect women from being property to be bartered or borrowed. God loves women, and his Word always protects them. So in an odd sense God cannot divorce Israel because (1) he made a covenant to always be with them, and (2) if he divorced them, he is bound by his own law and could not "remarry" them.

Divorce, then, is not an option for God. What will he do?

This is clear enough from these chapters. He does not want divorce ultimately. But he also does not want this stifled, unrequited love. So, what he will do is allow problems in their lives that will cause them to once again see their need for God. The problems are both at the hand of God and due to the natural consequences of their choices:

> *Your own evil will discipline you;*
> *your own apostasies will reprimand you.*
> *Recognize how evil and bitter it is*
> *for you to abandon the LORD your God*
> *and to have no fear of me.*
> *   This is the declaration of the Lord GOD of Armies.* (2:19)

God knows that, given the right circumstances, they will think straight. Given the right circumstances, they will understand that their cisterns are broken and that they need to seek out ones that will actually hold water.

The judgment is punitive, yes, but like a father, God wants more than to punish them and to cause them suffering. When their only sustenance is God, they will see that he is all they needed to begin with.

They will return to him.

Conclusion

Perhaps you never thought about you and God parting ways. Ending it. Calling it quits. Even so, you did not think that in the Bible God would be the one that would initiate it.

This is because Jesus Christ has made an inseparable bond between us and the Father. In this new covenant arrangement we are actually in Christ. Christ is in the Father, so to be in Christ means that we can never be torn from the Father. The Son ensures our forever bond with the Father.

Jeremiah here is helpful because he reminds us of how deeply God hates sin. It is also a reminder that we are not immune to the same trajectory.

We can forget God. We can have our hearts turned toward other things. What is God's response? He disciplines us. The discipline is not punitive—all of the punishment for sin has been taken on the cross. Rather the discipline is corrective. He is our Father, and no good father abandons discipline (Heb 12:3-11).

God is committed to sustaining the love relationship. He has committed never to divorce us. But think carefully about this: *the same God that committed never to leave us is the same God who committed never to leave us in sin.* God is always pursuing. Whether it's Adam in the garden, Cain outside the garden, Israel in the desert, David before Nathan, the woman at the well, or the one lost sheep, he is always pursuing. He will never leave his people alone. He will never leave his people in sin. The worst form of judgment, therefore, is God leaving someone in their sin (Rom 1:24).

We are different from the nation of Israel, but we are not above them. We can become forgetful. If we forget God, we will look to fill the wasteland of forgetfulness, and we will worship something less than God. When we do, we invite the corrective discipline of a gracious Father. He loves us too much to leave us.

Reflect and Discuss

1. What kind of metaphorical relationship does Jeremiah use to describe the love between Judah and God?
2. When people part ways with God, it often follows a pattern. What is the trajectory of this pattern in 2:5-8?
3. What are the similarities and differences between Jeremiah 2 and Psalm 1?
4. Why is neglecting the Word as dangerous as the rejection of it?
5. What are ways that, today, we forget what God has done for us?
6. Where did Judah look to find her satisfaction (2:8)?
7. What is the relationship between idolatry and forgetfulness in this passage?
8. What are the negative metaphors Jeremiah uses to describe Judah in chapter 2?
9. Ultimately, God did not divorce Judah. What does this passage teach us about God's commitment to his bride and the consequences when she left him?
10. How does a "wasteland of forgetfulness" lead to idolatry?

Repentance 1

JEREMIAH 3:6–4:4

Main Idea: Repentance is God's plan, so plan your repentance.

I.   **God Will Not Always Be Angry (3:12).**
II. **God Expects Repentance (3:11-14).**
III. **Repentance Is a Plan (4:1-4).**
    A.   Remove the idols (4:1).
    B.   Swear to this commitment (4:2).
    C.   Cultivate your heart (4:3).
    D.   Consecrate yourself (4:4).
IV. **Your Repentance Is Part of God's Plan (3:12-18; 4:2,4).**

She sits silently in the counselor's office. She has one question in her mind. Will she ever be forgiven? She was caught cheating on her husband. At some point she knew that he knew. And then she did the unthinkable. She kept doing it. She had multiple affairs over a long period of time and never looked back. Though he was patient, his patience had a limit when he realized that his patience would not result in her returning to him.

We are a part of the bride of Christ. This means sin is now something different from just a mistake or a one-time problem. Sin is an act of infidelity. It is an act of unfaithfulness to the one we love.

This is the context of Jeremiah 3. Israel has been unfaithful to God over a sustained period of time. God decides that he wants a divorce, but as we saw in the previous chapters, his faithfulness to Israel knows no bounds. He is faithful to her even when she is unfaithful. He will stay with her. He will not divorce her. This is good news. While they are technically together, will he stay angry with her forever?

Look at Jeremiah 3:6-11. The southern kingdom, Judah, was being compared unfavorably to the unfaithful northern kingdom. This condemnation had to sting. The people of Judah considered themselves more faithful than the north because of their godly king, Josiah. Yet it is clear that not all of Josiah's reforms were working. The people had so much going for them, but at the core their hearts were still in love with all these idols.

God is going to take them back, but the judgment promised in chapter 2 is real. Will God always condemn them for what they are doing? Will God always be angry? To use the terms of our opening illustration, will this wife live the rest of her days with a husband who will hold this infidelity over her head? That is no way to live, but no one would blame him for being angry forever. No one. With her multiple counts of sexual immorality, even if he held his tongue, surely we could not criticize him for being angry!

This is the question for Judah. It is a corporate question, a question for a group, and that will be the focus of the next chapter. For now, address the personal question. Based on all that I have done, will God always be angry with me?

For some of us, that question is in the foreground of our minds. We went through a period of time when we were so brazen in our sin against God. Now we are thinking that coming fully back to him is not possible because he will always be angry with us. For others maybe it's in the background. We do not worry about this so much, but maybe that's because we have not dealt honestly with sin. When we own up to it, we might ask, "Will God always be angry with me?"

So, will God always be mad at me for all I have done?

God Will Not Always Be Angry
JEREMIAH 3:12

No, as God clearly states in this verse, he will not always be angry with us. However, and this is critical, the reason does not have to do with the nature of our sin. We have sinned in ways that make God's anger justified. No one could blame God for fueling the fire of his anger forever. We deserve it, after all. Yet the reason he gives is his "unfailing" love. This could be translated "faithfulness." The idea is a contrast. Your love failed; God's love is unfailing. You have been unfaithful; God is faithful.

This particular type of unfailing love is unique to God. The Hebrew word here is *chesed*. It refers to love that is kind and faithful. It is a favorite word of the psalmists, used more than 150 times in Psalms and often translated as "faithful love" or "steadfast love." It is used several times in Jeremiah as well.

While we can show a modicum of faithful love, only God's love can be *perfectly* steadfast and faithful. God does not have the capacity *not* to love his people. He will always be faithful to us. It is a faithfulness that is appreciated in light of our unfaithfulness. When we think of all our sin in light of God's goodness, we should rejoice. In every way that I have been wrong to God, he has been right to me. Admitting sinfulness is a way to praise; sin is the opposite of what God has demonstrated to me. The depth of sin reminds me of the height of grace. In the end my depths are all swallowed up in God's heights. His grace towers my guilt.

The psalmist describes it this way in Psalm 57:1-3:

> *Be gracious to me, God, be gracious to me,*
> *for I take refuge in you.*
> *I will seek refuge in the shadow of your wings*
> *until danger passes.*
> *I call to God Most High,*
> *to God who fulfills his purpose for me.*
> *He reaches down from heaven and saves me,*
> *challenging the one who tramples me.* Selah
> *God sends his faithful love and truth.*

God's faithful love is there to save us when we need refuge. God's love even saves us when we need refuge from the anger of God.

He will not be angry with us forever. Look at Psalm 103:8-10 where God's anger is remedied with his faithful love:

> *The Lord is compassionate and gracious,*
> *slow to anger and abounding in faithful love.*
> *He will not always accuse us*
> *or be angry forever.*
> *He has not dealt with us as our sins deserve*
> *or repaid us according to our iniquities.*

Is God angry when you sin? Yes. Sin evokes God's anger. Will God's anger toward those who repent be eternal? No, God will not always be angry. Motivated by his own character, he will forgive. Second Timothy 2:13 encourages us: "If we are faithless, he remains faithful, for he cannot deny himself."

True repentance abates God's anger.

God Expects Repentance
JEREMIAH 3:11-14

This is a shocking request in these verses. The husband who has been cheated on is asking his faithless one to return! Three times in this chapter the cheating wife is asked to return (vv. 12,14,22) (Wright, *Message of Jeremiah*, 81). This invitation is powerful and simple: turn and acknowledge guilt. The expectation is that they love him so much that they will return and acknowledge what has been done. This is the first part of repentance.

The acknowledgment of sin is not the end of repentance; it is the beginning. Over and over we are told to acknowledge our guilt. It is part of the Lord's Prayer (Matt 6:12). It is the foundational part of David's path to repentance: "For I am conscious of my rebellion, and my sin is always before me" (Ps 51:3). It is a part of the fellowship of believers (Jas 5:16). There is no healing without repentance, and there is no repentance without acknowledging sin. Confession of sin is essential to maintaining fellowship with God (1 John 1:9).

Yet admitting sin and changing are not the same thing. Confession is not synonymous with repentance; it is simply the entry point. When people began to publicly confess through the act of baptism, John the Baptist rebuked them and told them to "produce fruit consistent with repentance" (Luke 3:8). Once someone has acknowledged sin, there is heart work to be done. Heart work is always hard work. The heart of true repentance is laid out in 4:1-4, where Jeremiah spells out what repentance looks like.

Repentance Is a Plan
JEREMIAH 4:1-4

The returning was not an emotional reattachment to God as much as it was a plan to demolish the idols and restore the relationship. While the "plan" laid out here is not intended to be exhaustive, it helps us understand some important aspects of the whole.

Remove the Idols (v. 1)

This is simple enough. If Judah is going to restore things with God, they must destroy the other objects of their worship.

This was not a metaphor. God was telling them to literally take a hammer to the idols. Bust them up. Destroy them. The physical act of destruction was showing how much they loved God alone. In the same way, we clean up our lives. What is it that I love more than God? We have to acknowledge what it is, then root it out. Be done with it. Is there an idol we need to remove?

Swear to This Commitment (v. 2)

Then God asks them to commit, to swear, that is, take an oath, a pledge. Oftentimes it had a public component. In ancient times there was no legal or recording system like we would understand it. Still, to swear a verbal oath came with significant legal ramifications. It was binding. God describes his covenant with Abraham as something he swore (Ps 105:4). The idea is verbal, yes, but more than that it is an assertion of the position of the heart.

Now he switches from these direct features to two physical metaphors for repentance.

Cultivate Your Heart (v. 3)

The first metaphor is cultivation of the heart. No field is ready to receive seed unless it is first cultivated. The soil must be broken up. This broken soil is a metaphor for a heart that has the idols rooted out and is now humble before God and ready to receive his word.

The seed is wasted unless the soil is cultivated. The heart as prepared soil was a principal metaphor for Jesus (Matt 13:1-23). Once the idols are removed and we have made our declaration, we now need to keep hearts that are sensitive to the leading of the Holy Spirit. These are hearts that are ready to receive the "implanted word" (Jas 1:21). The word is God's means of communication with us. We will never know what God intended us to know about himself if we do not expose ourselves to the word. Yet that word is kept from us if we do not have hearts to receive it.

The history of Israel turned on how they responded to the word. Abraham, Moses, Joshua, and Saul all faced problems when they did not receive the word. The consequences were devastating. The word in us is our hope. Yet this word is not available to us unless we cultivate our hearts and are receptive to God.

Consecrate Yourself (v. 4)

Circumcision was an external sign of an internal covenant.

In the New Testament, Christian baptism serves as external sign of an internal relationship. The baptism does not save, but the water is a picture of what Christ has done for us in his death and resurrection. The picture is real. The symbol has a reality to it; it is tied to a real historical event and my willingness to publicly identify with the Jesus of the gospel.

Jeremiah's audience had been circumcised. That was not the problem. The problem was that their circumcision was only skin deep. They had the symbol; they did not have the reality. Jeremiah would say to us, "OK, you've been washed in the water. Now baptize your heart."

Zacchaeus was a tax collector who, upon seeing Jesus, repented. He came up with a plan to restore what had been lost. When Jesus heard his plan, he responded, "Today salvation has come to this house" (Luke 19:1-9). It seems that the evidence of the residing salvation was the plan to repent.

There is often confusion about the nature of true repentance. Let's be clear. Repentance is not a feeling. It is not an emotion. It is an action. Repentance is the working out of our salvation. Regret and remorse are merely the runway lights; only repentance can land you safely. If you have a sin you are dealing with, the immediate question and the ultimate question are the same: What's the plan?

As a pastor I would often have someone come to my office to confess a sin and want help. My question, after comforting and encouraging, was simply this: What's the plan? Of course there is more to this. But with the immediacy of the question, I was trying to communicate lovingly that feeling bad about a situation is not enough. It must change. And change will only be worked out over time.

But there is a bigger motivation for repentance. Repentance is not only God's plan for me, but my repentance fits into the plan that God has for all things, including bringing the nations to himself. *Repentance is part of God's plan, so plan your repentance.*

Your Repentance Is Part of God's Plan
JEREMIAH 3:12-18; 4:2,4

Consider the sentence construction here. While repentance is a plan, the purpose of the sentence is not to get the people to follow a plan.

The purpose of the sentence is to get them to see a consequence. Look at 4:2:

> *Then the nations will be blessed by him*
> *and will pride themselves in him.*

The idea is that in their obedience, many nations will be blessed. We will address this theme in the next chapter. Look at 3:17-18:

> *At that time Jerusalem will be called The Lord's Throne, and all the*
> *nations will be gathered to it, to the name of the Lord in Jerusalem.*
> *They will cease to follow the stubbornness of their evil hearts.*

Their repentance was not really about themselves; it was about the nations.

So much hangs on their decision to repent and on ours as well. No sin ever takes place in a void of consequence. Each sin has consequences beyond ourselves. But that is to say it in the negative. The glorious, positive truth is to say that when we repent, when we return, when we come back to Christ, there are effects to this. *Repentance is part of God's plan, so plan your repentance.*

Conclusion

Jeremiah closes this section with a stark warning in 4:4, so let's not play games. In what area of your life do you need to repent? Is it the lingering thought that while you are efficient in every other area of your life you are a spiritual hoarder? You are hanging on to God's money, God's time, or God's forgiveness, unwilling to share any of it with others? If God's goodness, dammed up in your heart, were to be breached, there would be a lot of grace.

Perhaps there is a secret sin of lust. It's imbedded. You feel remorse. And you are partly confusing remorse with repentance. No life was ever changed over a bad feeling. Regret and remorse should lead to repentance. They are not the evidence of it. Remorse is only your friend until it leads you to repentance. After that it is no friend at all.

Repentance is part of God's plan, so plan your repentance.

Reflect and Discuss

1. God showed Judah a particular type of love: *chesed* love. How should we understand love of this type?
2. How does Jeremiah define and describe repentance?
3. How should we understand God's faithfulness in light of our faithlessness?
4. Jeremiah provides a four-part plan to repentance. Can you name his four-part plan (4:1-4)?
5. What was the purpose of repentance, according to Jeremiah? Was this purpose individual or universal?
6. Jeremiah used an agricultural metaphor to describe one of the necessary steps of repentance. Which metaphor did he use, and what are the implications of it (4:3)?
7. What would be the result of Israel's repentance (3:12-18; 4:2,4)?
8. In what way does repentance fit into the plan of God?
9. Is regret and remorse identical to repentance or the forerunner for it?
10. Is acknowledgment the end of repentance or its beginning?

Jeremiah's Journal

JEREMIAH 4:5–6:30

Main Idea: The call of a prophet is a lonely call.

I. **A Prophet Feels like God Is Sending Mixed Signals (4:10).**
II. **A Prophet Despairs (4:19; 6:9-12).**
    A. They are not holy, so they cannot understand the word (6:10b).
    B. God offends them, so they have no pleasure in the word (6:10c).
III. **A Prophet Is Tested (6:27-30).**

The world is a mess. As I write these words, I am grieving the loss of forty-nine people, citizens of my country, who were massacred. The world really is a sick place. Immorality, terrorism, injustice, greed, and hate—they are epidemic. One would think it had reached a boiling point. But the appetite for more of the same has not been satiated. In fact, I'm writing these words confident that greater tragedy awaits the world before this book goes to publication. Perhaps it will even be a friend or family member of mine who is killed.

Jesus is the only answer. Maybe it reads trite, but it is no less true that the only cure is Christ, which brings us to an even tougher problem: The people who have the answer are silent. The gross failure to speak out condemns the church. Those who have the cure, those doctors of truth designated to perform both diagnostics and healing, are silent. It's like the cure is under lock and key. Those charged with giving medicine act like it's too harmful. To put it bluntly, preachers don't explain Scripture. They do not re-present God's Word.

Imagine you went to church and your preacher told the unfiltered truth: If you act like hell, you probably are not a Christian. Abortion is murder. Prosperity preachers are lying. Preachers who do not explain Scripture are culpable to God. The institutional church is so addicted to its own machinery that it does not cry out in desperation to God. We spend more money on dog food than on missions. If your pastor stood in his pulpit and said these things, he would be a lone voice. He would feel ostracized—not by the world but by the church!

Prophets rarely have honor. That much has not changed. Jeremiah 4:5–6:30 is the journal of a lonely prophet who feels isolated in his calling. Let's set the stage.

Context

Judgment is coming. It is absolutely certain that God will not turn a blind eye to all the wickedness of Israel. They have sinned, God has seen it, and now he will use other nations to judge his people. God hates sin, and he will allow the consequences to come on them and to punish them.

Jeremiah warns them of this coming punishment in 4:5-8. The people are warned to flee the "disaster from the north" and to "mourn and wail" the consequences of the Lord's wrath. He further says in verses 23-26 that the punishment will be devastating, virtually reverting the earth back to the chaotic state of "formless and empty." The destruction is certain, and it will be profound, but it will not be total (vv. 27-28).

So the people are wicked, God is responding, yet the prophets, the ones who should be calling the people to repentance, are not helping! This is tragic, and God condemns the prophets. While God says he is bringing destruction, the people reject the word of the coming destruction. They do not want to hear it (5:12). So the prophets, seemingly drunk on man's approval, agree with the people. They suggest that the people are right. In doing so, they become only wind (v. 13). They speak, but there is nothing to it.

These are the cultural dynamics of Jeremiah's life:

- God is bringing destruction.
- The people don't care.
- The other prophets are not saying anything about it.

To speak the truth in this type of environment would be a shock to the system! To speak the truth would make enemies from the people who did not want to hear the message and from the prophets who were not willing to say the same thing. So here is a question: What goes on in the heart of a prophet? When God calls you to speak truth in a world that does not want to hear truth, what happens? Remember, Jeremiah contains the sermons, songs, and journals of the prophet Jeremiah. In this section let's focus on Jeremiah's journal. Yet, as we will see, while this is an individual's journal, it reflects the experience of many.

If you are following Christ, then you will be called to present the message of the kingdom in an environment where the people, and the other prophets of the kingdom, do not agree with you. This is true

culturally. It might be true of your own family. So this might be your journal if you have ever been called to speak truth in a hostile environment.
Jeremiah's journals reveal two feelings and one call.

A Prophet Feels like God Is Sending Mixed Signals
JEREMIAH 4:10

*When we are speaking in a hostile environment, we may feel God is sending
mixed signals.*

In this first entry of Jeremiah's journal, we have the feeling that God
has confused his own people. This is a pretty honest, and pretty harsh,
critique of God's work. Jeremiah complains,

> *I said, "Oh no, Lord GOD, you have certainly deceived this people and
> Jerusalem, by announcing, 'You will have peace,' while a sword is at
> our throats."*

What does he mean by this? The false prophets were suggesting that
none of this destruction is going to happen (6:14; 8:11). After all, there
were visible signs of God's blessing. So Jeremiah concludes that God
is intentionally confusing his various prophets; God is telling the false
prophets one thing, a message of peace, but delivering something else,
a sword. Of course this is not the case, but we cannot blame Jeremiah for
feeling this way. Remember, this is his journal. He feels like even though
God has called him to pluck up, break down, destroy, and overthrow
(1:10), other prophets, false prophets, are promising peace. Why would
God allow this confusion to go on? In other words, why would God allow
the false prophets to exist? The reason may be wrapped up in the mercy
of God, inasmuch as God is being gracious to the false prophets by giving them another opportunity to repent.

What we do know is that it is extremely difficult to speak truth in
a context of confusion. Today is no different. Think of how confusing
these messages are:

- The Scriptures plainly teach that all violations of God's law are
  sin (Rom 3:23).

Yet many preachers suggest we choose what we do because of the condi-
tions of our society.

- The Scriptures teach that sexual sin, like any other sin, incurs
  the wrath of God (Rom 1:18-23).

Yet many preachers preach that God condones sexual sin.

- The Scriptures teach that all who follow Christ will suffer (2 Tim 3:12).

Yet many preachers suggest that all suffering is a result of sin.

- The Scriptures teach that wealth is to be stewarded back into the kingdom (Luke 16:1-13).

Yet many preachers suggest wealth is to be hoarded.

- The Scriptures affirm their own authority (2 Tim 3:16).

Yet many preachers profess that Scriptures are to be interpreted in light of our cultural and political bias.

This is just so confusing. When an open Bible is contrary to a preacher, there is nothing short of confusion.

So perhaps you are confused. Or perhaps you have wondered why God would allow such things to go on. Welcome to the club! You have just joined the rarified air of the prophet Jeremiah whose journals seem to implicate God in the confusion.

But again, God is not the source of confusion. Confusion is the residue of mixing clear truth with lying preachers—preachers who do not re-present God's Word when they preach. It's confusing. The confusion all around us can lead to despair. It did for Jeremiah.

A Prophet Despairs
JEREMIAH 4:19; 6:9-12

When we are speaking in a hostile environment, we might feel despair.

Jeremiah is filled with despair (4:19). He knows that wrath is coming, and he is upset about it. In fact he is so filled with despair that he is about to burst (6:9-12)! Embedded in this journal entry is one of the most concise statements of the problem. Verse 10 provides a twofold description of someone who will not repent.

They Are Not Holy, so They Cannot Understand the Word (6:10b)

He has become tired of preaching because "their ear is uncircumcised." What a provocative metaphor! Circumcision was a sign of the covenant promise. As the only circumcised people in the region, this was their distinctive. It made them different from the Canaanites. It made them set apart, consecrated to God, and holy. They were God's tithe, dedicated to the Lord.

Yet their ear, the means of listening, was not holy. They were filled with the voices of the false prophets, and they could not hear truth—a truth they did not want to hear because their ears were not holy, were not bent toward the things of God. An unholy ear cannot hear and therefore cannot pay attention. Attention to God's word is given when the spiritual ear is receptive to God. They were circumcised in the flesh but not in the heart.

They could never echo the words of Psalm 119:33-35:

> *Teach me, LORD, the meaning of your statutes,*
> *and I will always keep them.*
> *Help me understand your instruction,*
> *and I will obey it and follow it with all my heart.*
> *Help me stay on the path of your commands,*
> *for I take pleasure in it.*

God Offends Them, so They Have No Pleasure in the Word (6:10c)

> *See, the word of the LORD has become contemptible to them—*
> *they find no pleasure in it.*

The Hebrew word translated "contemptible" means they loathe it. Yet the word also is used in the Old Testament to describe resentment, something that is a disgrace and is to be shunned. It is hatred with a hint of sass. It is so tragic that the word that protected them from their enemies, that protected them from themselves, that led them out of slavery, is now rejected.

I love my wife's voice. It is raspy, fun, lively, and a lot of other adjectives. It's not the perfect voice, whatever that is. She will not do voice-overs for animation or be asked to read audiobooks. But that's not what I'm talking about. I love her voice *because I love her.* Her words breathe life into our home. Conversely, the foul odor emanating from Israel is her lost love. She does not love her God; she does not love his voice. What once seemed like a sweet note now sounds off-key; the melody is completely dissonant in their ears.

One cannot help but see in this Jesus's parable of the soils (Matt 13:10-23). The soil does not even receive the word in some hearts because the hearts are so hard. In other soils it takes root, but after some persecution it becomes distasteful. In a third soil it grows, but it is choked out by distractions that are more attractive than the word. In a final soil it takes root and bears fruit.

The people of Israel are like the second soil. They have heard the word. They received the word at one point, but it is simply too demanding. They dislodge it and get rid of it before they choke on his words.

When someone gets an organ transplant, such as a kidney, there is no guarantee that the body will accept the organ. The body can reject it. The body perceives that the organ is a foreign object, and the immune system triggers a "blood transfusion reaction or transplant rejection" ("Transplant Rejection"). In other words, the immune system confuses a friend for an enemy. It rejects the help. This is Israel in Jeremiah's day, but one day God will provide the ultimate organ transplant by removing their old heart and giving them a new heart (Ezek 36:26).

So it's understandable that Jeremiah feels like he is getting mixed signals and that he is in despair. The question is why? The answer is that God is using Jeremiah to test the faithfulness of the people. The one who administers the test is never the favorite person.

A Prophet Is Tested
JEREMIAH 6:27-30

When we are speaking in a hostile environment, we might wonder if God is testing us.

God brought Israel up out of the iron furnace of Egypt (11:4), away from the hot persecution of Pharaoh and, in keeping with his covenant, put them in the promised land. Yet the sick reality is that they did not love God. They wanted him for what they could get from him and not for himself. His blessings were welcome, but his directives were detestable. "God, just leave your favor at the door and kindly walk away, thank you very much."

None of this makes sense in light of what God has done. Yet any honest God follower can relate to wanting God's stuff more than God.

Dropped into this hot house of lost love is the prophet. He is going to be used of God to test the love they have for God. Look at the provocative words in 6:27-30. Jeremiah's responsibility was to be an "assayer." The word refers to one who tests the purity of metals. This was done in a hot environment where a furnace was heated up to a point of smelting. The metal was purified, and the true quality of the metal was shown. However, God's people did not pass the test. So God eventually calls them "rejected silver." They are rubbish. Dross. Refuse. Trash.

This is tragic.

Notice, however, that *God* is not testing them. No, Jeremiah is the tester. So is every prophet of God. When the prophets stood to re-present God's word, when the New Testament preachers stood, when any preachers in church history stood, or when a preacher stands today, they are awaiting an assessment, a response. The difference between teaching and preaching is that preaching calls for an assessment, a response. A prophet of God never speaks where there is no response; one is always demanded. All preachers are children of Jeremiah; they are awaiting a response. To press the metaphor, the pulpit is the furnace, and the words are the fire. The word going forth from the pulpit tests the hearts of men. This is why the prophet of God must faithfully re-present God's Word and be hot in the heart. No man-centered talk ever flamed the coals that would melt a heart toward God. Hard hearts need hot flames.

Back in Jeremiah's journal, we get a sense of what he is going through. As a tester, he has the unenviable position of exposing people to their own impurities. And so do we. Even those of us who are not preachers live holy lives in an unholy world. If we are doing it right, we will be persecuted. Jesus said it would be so (John 15:18-25). If we are doing it right, we will smell sweet to some and stink to others (2 Cor 2:16). If we are doing it right, we will strive to live peaceably with all men. We will live well in this kingdom while we wait for the next. This means we won't be obnoxious jerks. But even the most gracious Christian is a Christian, and as people get close to you, they will inevitably feel the heat. They will sense that you have something they do not have. They might, over time, be drawn to the flame. They may allow the hot fire of God's word to purify them, to save them. However, it is possible that they will fail the test. They will reject God and reject you. Your presence is a test for them.

Conclusion

In one of the most stinging rebukes of God's prophets, God says,

> *They have treated my people's brokenness superficially,*
> *claiming, "Peace, peace," when there is no peace.* (6:14)

Imagine your child has had an accident and is hospitalized with serious wounds. You go into the hospital room to find that the medicine that was provided was not applied. The doctors look you in the eye and tell you that your child didn't like the procedures so they stopped. They quit practicing their profession. They were completely negligent. To say you would be angry would be an understatement. These are medical professionals, professionals you hired to care for your child. They were equipped to heal, but they did not do so.

If you can imagine this, you can get a sense of God's anger. We have, in these false prophets, those who are in charge of the healing of his children. Yet they so fear the approval of the patient that they will not apply the right medicine!

God commissioned Jeremiah to right this wrong. And while the competing voices are confusing, heaven and hell hang in the balance.

Reflect and Discuss

1. What three "cultural dynamics" summarize Jeremiah's life?
2. Jeremiah recorded two feelings and one call in his journal. Name and explain them (4:10; 4:19; 6:9-12).
3. Who performs the test in this passage? Does God or Jeremiah? Why is this significant?
4. What is the twofold description Jeremiah used in 6:10 to explain the person who refuses to repent?
5. What does Jeremiah mean in 6:10 when he says, "Their ear is uncircumcised"?
6. What are the implications of the Hebrew word translated "contemptible" in 6:10?
7. What is the difference between preaching and teaching with regard to "assaying"?
8. What does this passage teach us about how God views false prophets and disingenuous preachers?
9. How should preachers understand giving a biblical invitation in light of this text?
10. What does this passage teach us about the necessity of biblical clarity in preaching and teaching?

The Temple Sermon

JEREMIAH 7:1–8:3

Main Idea: We should fear a fake faith.

Sermon Introduction (7:3-4)
I.   **Make It Right (7:5-7).**
II. **Don't Fool Yourself (7:8-15).**
III. **Obey (7:21-26).**
Sermon Conclusion (7:30–8:3)

Few things are as disheartening as hypocrisy. When we find that someone is not who we thought they were, it is horribly discouraging. Being a minister for a few years, teaching preachers, and knowing a thousand or so of them, I have come to make the acquaintance of a few who were not who they appeared to be. They appeared gracious and kind, even good leaders. Yet in a dark place they were something different. A poseur whose identity was obscured by his giftedness—he was a fake hiding in plain sight. Ministerial hypocrisy is disheartening; the pulpit is often the last place you would expect to find shadows.

Context

Jeremiah is standing in the temple, preaching. This in reality is not a record of the sermon; rather, it is a record of God's telling him what to say. God is telling Jeremiah to preach, telling him what to preach (7:1-15), telling him not to pray because God's anger is already kindled (7:16-20), and finally giving him the outcome of his audience's disobedience and deafness to God—the horrible wrath of God that is coming (7:21–8:3) (Wright, *Message of Jeremiah*, 106–20).

Instead of focusing on the interaction between God and Jeremiah, let's focus on the sermon itself. The sermon essentially has an introduction, three aspects, and a conclusion. The conclusion is a horrific prophecy as to what will happen to them if they do not obey the voice of God.

There are some who like nice, linear sermons with three points and a poem. This is not one of those. Jeremiah makes two bold statements about obedience in 7:5-15; then the rest of the exhortation is for obedience, and it's sprinkled around other aspects of God's judgment. More specifically, it is God's lament that the people have not already obeyed God. Mixed into this we have a record of God's conversation with Jeremiah. Let's work our way through the sermon.

Sermon Introduction
JEREMIAH 7:3-4

Jeremiah begins his sermon with a sermon in a sentence. He essentially gives his listeners the entire sermon right up front: change your ways and stop deceiving yourself. Then he develops the point of getting right in 7:5-7 and the point about not being self-deceived in 7:8-15. The introduction sets up the first point of his sermon, where he tells them to amend their ways.

Make It Right
JEREMIAH 7:5-7

The idea behind this word translated "correct" is not merely "change" but more "make something good or pleasant." If my child does not speak nicely to her sibling, ultimately I am concerned about her heart. Immediately I am concerned that she do the right thing, that she start to encourage her sibling. I would simply say to my child, "Make it right." This is the idea: take your stinky behavior and make it smell better.

He then gets specific. He does address their vertical relationship, "no longer . . . follow other gods," but at this point he is really going after the horizontal relationships with other people. The root of the problem is that they were oppressing other people.

Oppression is real. We do this, even in subtle ways, when we are not meek (Matt 5:8). Meekness is the virtue of taking all our strength, all our energies, and using them in the service of God and others. This was the ultimate beatitude for Jesus. This is the place where he wanted his disciples to be. This virtue is the expression of all the other beatitudes, for meekness ultimately leads to mercy giving (Matt 5:7). The opposite of meekness is to use all our strength and all our resources on ourselves.

So God is telling them to look around and make things right. Stop abusing people. The application to us may be just exactly what the text says: We are oppressing someone financially. We are taking advantage of someone's goodwill toward us. We oppress people by choosing not to forgive them when they hurt us; we have emotional leverage over them and will not extend to them the mercy God showed us. This could be the husband who takes advantage of his wife because she is long-suffering, so he works all the hours he wants, neglecting the family simply because he can get away with it.

Oppression is not just about social justice at large. In its broadest sense it is about not showing others what God showed us: mercy. Our inner monologue argues that they do not deserve that type of mercy. This is when Scripture should get in our heads so we recall that this is why it's called mercy. We give what people do not deserve because God has given us more than we could ever deserve.[1]

God is concerned that his people learn how to make it right with those who had no ability to defend themselves. But that was only half the problem.

Don't Fool Yourself
JEREMIAH 7:8-15

The other major problem was that they honestly believed their allegiance to a place was going to save them. Jeremiah was told to say, "Do not trust deceitful words, chanting, 'This is the temple of the LORD, the temple of the LORD, the temple of the LORD'" (v. 4). The deceitful words were their own. They were the ones lying to themselves by putting false hope in their hearts.

He expands on this theme in verses 8-15. The indictment is provocative. Remember Jeremiah's location: he was told to stand at the gate of the temple (v. 2). He was to say these things as people were entering! "Jeremiah accused the people of repeated violations of the Ten Commandments, specifically mentioning six of them (Eight, Six, Seven, Nine, One, and Two; see Exod 20:1–17; cf. Hos 4:2)."[2]

---

[1] The parable of the unforgiving servant (Matt 18:21-35) is the story of someone who received unlimited mercy but could only give justice. He could not give what he had been given. It could be outlined this way: mercy in, ultimate mercy, justice out, ultimate justice.

[2] "They felt no shame about breaking the moral laws of God and then coming to stand in the temple that bore God's name (i.e., belonged to him; Num 6:27; 1 Kgs 9:3). There they would say, 'We are safe.' They believed that observing the temple rituals freed them to return to their 'detestable things' (a word that often bears sexual overtones) without fear of punishment" (Huey, *Jeremiah, Lamentations*, 106).

It's like the people thought God had provided them a universal insurance policy that covered everything. We tend to lean toward the same presumption when we have a theology of one-liners. These are sayings that are true but become reductionistic and therefore trite. For example, blending "God will supply all my needs" with "God will forgive all my sins" with "once saved, always saved" can produce a faith that suggests, as long as we keep supporting the institutional church, God is obligated to hook me up with the good life. We can act as though God is rich in love and low on demands.

The people of Judah were supporting the religious institution but were not holy. Their sin was terrible, but they did not even know how to blush. This is our problem as well. Supporting an institution can be a blanket that covers a fake faith. In fact, we have no license to sin, even if we think of ourselves as "good people" at heart.

Jeremiah ends this section reminding them what happened at Shiloh (vv. 12-15), the location of the tabernacle after Joshua crossed over into the promised land. Shiloh was eventually destroyed by the Philistines. The logic is, if God would not spare the place where the tabernacle rested, why would he spare the temple?

We tend to think that this angry God is so Old Testament. God did that then, but he would not do that now. He felt that way toward Israel, but he has calmed down quite a bit. He just likes us so much more than he did Israel. As his most recently born children, we are his favorites; he is growing softer and more reflective as he ages.

However, it's not too hard to see examples of our sins in the Old Testament. The history of the church that Jesus established is a history of people who worship auxiliary institutions instead of worshiping Jesus. This worship of the tangential puts us in what we think is an enviable position: We get all the benefits of the kingdom even if our hearts are not fully obedient to the King. But when Jesus established the way of the kingdom (Matt 5–7), it was all about the heart, and it still is. Yes, the church is eternal, but we have no immunity from God's discipline.

God has established the church as an eternal institution. The gates of hell will not prevail against it (Matt 16:18). Yet the expressions of the church in local bodies may experience the favor of God or incur his discipline. We often don't think of the church this way. The church that sins corporately is not immune from God's discipline. All you have to do is look at the earliest expressions of local bodies of believers to whom John writes in Revelation 2 and 3. They were a part of Christ's bride, yet he told them,

> *Remember then how far you have fallen; repent, and do the works you did at first. Otherwise, I will come to you and remove your lampstand from its place, unless you repent.* (Rev 2:5)

> *So repent! Otherwise, I will come to you quickly and fight against them with the sword of my mouth.* (Rev 2:16)

> *Remember, then, what you have received and heard; keep it, and repent. If you are not alert, I will come like a thief, and you have no idea at what hour I will come upon you.* (Rev 3:3)

This sounds like it could come out of the mouth of Jeremiah! Yet these are the hard words of Jesus himself. Jesus loves his bride, and he holds her accountable in the same way God held Israel accountable. Jesus said it most strongly this way: "As many as I love, I rebuke and discipline. So be zealous and repent" (Rev 3:19).

Let's be clear: if you love the institution of the church, you do not have a license to sin. God will discipline both the individual and the church that lives in sin. This is why he ultimately calls us to a heart of obedience.

Obey

JEREMIAH 7:21-26

God wants a heart of obedience. What we are about to read is going to seem tough—remarkably so. Yet remember that where there is warning, there is hope. Judah has the opportunity to get right and get real. They can make it right and stop lying to themselves. That would be a heart of obedience. Without this obedience God's character obligates him to punish them.

In fact, his wrath is so set that he tells Jeremiah not to intercede on their behalf (vv. 16-17). He will punish them. But what have they done that is so egregious? The list is long. They were abusing one another (vv. 5-6), they were worshiping Baal (v. 8), and they were worshiping the queen of heaven (v. 18), but that was not the real issue. The real issue was a heart of disobedience. Simply put, they were not listening to God.

In verses 23-26 God says, "They didn't listen or pay attention. . . . My people wouldn't listen to me or pay attention but became obstinate." Earlier, in verse 13, Jeremiah used similar language: "I have spoken to you time and time again but you wouldn't listen, and I have called to you, but you wouldn't answer." The root of all this sin was that they did not listen to God.

There is more in Scripture about listening than we have time to express here. The first sin was when Adam and Eve listened to someone other than God. The history of Israel is replete with people who knew what to do but did not do it; they did not listen to God. Jesus warned against having the ability to hear but not listening (Matt 13:9). In that same passage in Matthew, he quoted the prophet Isaiah by saying, "You will listen and listen, but never understand; you will look and look, but never perceive. For this people's heart has grown callous; their ears are hard of hearing" (Matt 13:14-15). The problem was not with their *ability* to hear but their *willingness* to hear. Jesus then goes on to tell a story about a soil that was so hard, like a heart that cannot hear, and it therefore rejected the word. This is the archetype of someone who will not hear: hard soil that rejects the word.

When our hearts are hard against God, there is no hope. When we have a soft heart, we listen to his Word, we long for his Word; we love him, and therefore we want to know what he says to us.

This leads Jeremiah to his conclusion: God is going to punish Israel.

Sermon Conclusion
JEREMIAH 7:30–8:3

The consequence of disobedience is God's wrath. God's anger burns against Judah because they have ignored repeated warnings. This is not the child who slips up. This is the child who is openly defiant, does horrible things, but then shows up at church, kisses you on the cheek, and wonders why you have any problem with this at all. Their attitude is, What's wrong with *you?*

God has had enough. So a tragic end is prophesied. The conclusion to his sermon (7:30–8:3) could be summed up in the words of 7:29:

Raise up a dirge on the barren heights, for the LORD has rejected and abandoned the generation under his wrath.

Conclusion

During the time of the judges, we have recorded one of the most famous stories of the Bible, the story of Samson. He had everything a man could want. He was powerful with his personality, he was cunning, and he had seemingly unlimited strength. Every boy growing up in church has fantasized about what he would do with unlimited strength. Samson had it all.

He eventually got the girl he wanted, and it cost him everything. Not everything in the sense that he died the next day. Far worse than that! His enemies bound him, mocked him, tortured him, and enslaved him. His slow, agonizing fall was as unhurried and sluggish as his rise was meteoric. He rose fast; he fell slow.

His death began famously when he told Delilah the secret of his strength. She cut his hair, and the next day the enemy came to take him out. Here some of the most tragic words in the whole Bible are recorded. Samson rose to fight, "But he did not know that the LORD had left him" (Judg 16:20). He had everything but God.

The problem with organizations (movements, institutions, or churches) is when they are effective. When they are well managed and doing fine, it is tempting to perceive that the success lies in their leaders or their resources. When a church—or something created by a church, such as a school—thinks it is the end in itself, the favor of God may depart from it.

You might think this is a scary passage, and you would be right. This was recorded so that we might fear God. No one is exempt from loving Jesus. The potential for us to love organizations and fail to be holy is real. Israel was victim of this idea, the early church was, and we are. No one is immune. Fearing God means fearing a fake faith. So, how is your faith?

Reflect and Discuss

1. Where was this sermon delivered? Why is that significant?
2. How is it possible to have a fake faith?
3. What New Testament passages challenge us to have a real faith?
4. Was Jesus concerned about a true faith?
5. What does Jeremiah call the words of the false prophets (7:4)?
6. What is the significance of Shiloh to Jeremiah's sermon (vv. 12-15)?

7. In its simplest form, what does God really want from his people (v. 13)? If God has not changed, how does that impact decisions we are making right now?
8. What do the letters to the churches in Revelation 2–3 teach us about the consistency of God's feeling toward sin in the body?
9. What are we to think of challenging verses such as Jeremiah 7:29? Is there any application to us today?
10. What does the life of Samson teach us about fearing God and walking in his Spirit?

It's Who You Know

JEREMIAH 8:4–9:26

Main Idea: Our glory is not what we possess but who we know.

I. **Our Glory Is Not What We Have (9:23).**
II. **Our Glory Is Knowing God (9:24).**

When you know someone who knows God more than you, you have two options: you can repent, or you can let them drive you crazy.

It was just after my senior year in college. I had been preaching for a few years, and at some point in the journey, things changed. I'm not sure when. My first sermons were filled with a sense of desperation. I was trying to find my way and begging God to throw light on each step. I wanted his direction. I also wanted him to save me from being bad at my calling; I wanted his strength and power. At the same time I had a deep, genuine love for lost people.

The scaffolding was still there, but it was a structure without residence. My preaching was light with no heat. And I was comfortable with coddling sin as long as I had moderate success in ministry. That's horrible to admit, but I think that's the most concise way to say it.

That Monday morning my façade began to crack. I was invited to speak at a camp. I would do some sessions, and my friend who invited me would do the main, night sessions. We were sitting at breakfast when he told me, quite plainly, that the reason I did not have God's presence was because I was not through with sin. I was seeking God for his presence, his power, and his blessing, but I was not seeking him just to know him. I wanted his blessings; I did not want him. No doubt I had been taught that before, but it was as if I had never heard those words: knowing God. This produced a tension in my heart that I still feel every day: Am I doing what I am doing both because I know God and so that I can know God more? Life is intimacy with God (John 17:3).

It is impossible to overstate the importance of these two verses in Jeremiah. They help us understand what Jesus later unpacks in the Sermon on the Mount. Jeremiah gives us one of the most concise statements in the whole Bible about knowing God.

Context

Jeremiah has completed his sermon from the steps of the temple (7:1–8:3). God is calling people to repent from sin.

This leads to a horrific prophecy of judgment (8:4–9:26). But a flower is growing out of this cemetery; here is one of the most poetic statements of knowing God in all of Scripture.

The passage tells us how to boast.

Our Glory Is Not What We Have
JEREMIAH 9:23

This is what the LORD says:
The wise person should not boast in his wisdom;
the strong should not boast in his strength;
the wealthy should not boast in his wealth.

This is insanely practical. Those are the very things we want to boast in. When we hear the term *boast*, we equate it with bragging. The obnoxious person who wants you to know how wise he is may pepper the conversation with words intended to make him look smarter than he is. The person who wants you to know how strong and powerful he is must attach his name to certain individuals, goals achieved, or specific accomplishments. The person who wants you to know how wealthy he is will always wear his labels on the outside as marketing, not for his brand but for the social strata to which the brand attaches him. These are pretty obvious ways to display wisdom, power, and wealth. But be careful here. Jesus made clear that possession of these things in itself is not sin. Some of the most purehearted people I know have power, wealth, and strength. Jesus makes clear in the Beatitudes that Christianity is below the surface.

Besides, those of us who have been churched for a while have manufactured more subtle ways to brag. For example, I don't want to brag about being smart, but I take a smug satisfaction in thinking I am smarter than other people, even when I'm not. This form of "boasting" is far worse because, in a weird way, we deceive ourselves by thinking we are more spiritual because we keep our thoughts of superiority to ourselves! This is a hypocrite's win-win: we get points for being better than someone else and bonus points for having the humility not to bring it up. The spiritually sensitive person might get tripped up wondering what is the best thing to do in each situation, but that's not the point at all. The point is not what we are to say or not say, do or not do. This type of thinking will create a little idol carved from our own insecurities. Jesus sees the heart. He knows when I am sincere. This is the real point. We want a heart that longs for his presence.

Our Glory Is Knowing God
JEREMIAH 9:24

This is our true boasting:

> But the one who boasts should boast in this:
> that he understands and knows me—
> that I am the Lord, showing faithful love,
> justice, and righteousness on the earth,
> for I delight in these things.
> This is the Lord's declaration.

Our true boasting is that we know God. If the antidote to idolatry is intimacy, what exactly does it mean to know God? Well, there is something specific in mind. First, *that God shows faithful love*. This is God's kind faithfulness that is specifically directed toward those with whom he has a covenant relationship.

Second, *that he is a God of justice*. What is perfectly clear from the context is that they did not know God was a God of justice. They were living in presumptuous sin (Prov 19:13), assuming that God was never going to notice that their hearts had turned away from him, even while they were religious practitioners. They were in the temple, but the temple was not in them.

Finally, they should boast to know that *he is a God of righteousness*. The implication is that those who follow him should also be righteous. This triad of character is interrelated. God's love motivates his justice and expresses itself in righteousness.

The idea behind boasting is not what we would consider bragging. Bragging is rooted in insecurity. The words of a braggart are flimsy stilts propping up a fragile ego. The braggart's words are thin.

Boasting in the Lord is more akin to glorying in something. Like when I see my college alma mater, it makes me proud that I graduated from there. The idea of boasting has a trajectory throughout Scripture. Paul quotes this passage in 1 Corinthians 1:28-31 when he writes,

> *God has chosen what is insignificant and despised in the world—*
> *what is viewed as nothing—to bring to nothing what is viewed as*
> *something, so that no one may boast in his presence. It is from him*
> *that you are in Christ Jesus, who became wisdom from God for us—our*
> *righteousness, sanctification, and redemption—in order that, as it is*
> *written: Let the one who boasts, boast in the Lord.*

This is the New Testament equivalent of the same idea. We boast in the Lord because we have to. When he brings something significant out of something that was insignificant, all the glory goes to him. Those who boast in the Lord are not more intellectual than others, but they are wiser. They understand that absolutely nothing comes from ourselves. It all comes from God.

Again in Galatians 6:14 Paul writes,

> *But as for me, I will never boast about anything except the cross of*
> *our Lord Jesus Christ. The world has been crucified to me through the*
> *cross, and I to the world.*

In the context of Galatians 6 the boasting took place because of the ritual of circumcision. The Jews were boasting that they were pure because of the condition of the flesh. It was their national identity. Yet Paul says he will not glory in his national identity; he will only glory in the cross of Christ. His nationality and his religious heritage, as rich and pronounced as they were, were nothing compared to the glory of Christ.

Echoing the words of Jeremiah, James encourages us not to boast in wealth:

> *Let the brother of humble circumstances boast in his exaltation, but*
> *let the rich boast in his humiliation because he will pass away like a*
> *flower of the field. For the sun rises and, together with the scorching*
> *wind, dries up the grass; its flower falls off, and its beautiful*
> *appearance perishes. In the same way, the rich person will wither away*
> *while pursuing his activities.* (Jas 1:9-11)

So the idea behind boasting is what you project, what you want people to perceive about you. This is your boast. Someone who has been close to God has a sense of perspective. They know exactly how small they are compared to God. No one brags in God's presence. And if you know him—not know *about* him but really *know* him—then you have nothing to brag about but him. The sheer weight and majesty of God thwarts our sense of pride; it stunts our sense of greatness; it inhibits boasting. Yet the mind that senses his presence is shocked when his significance thrusts itself through our insignificance. Like a filthy broken window, the greatest thing about it is what comes through it. A filthy, unbroken window is useless. A filthy window, when broken, can exude the glorious light that makes life on our planet happen. The source of all light is magnified in the souls so porous in their brokenness that, instead of bragging, they dim their own light and let the real glory shine through them. The brokenness becomes a way to see the real light.

Again, the person who sees this is not smarter but does know more. If you know God, you have everything he wants you to know as well as the means to find all he wants you to have. Jesus said that this was eternal life! In John 17:3 he says,

> *This is eternal life: that they may know you, the only true God, and the one you have sent—Jesus Christ.*

And then, in the same chapter, he goes on to make the shocking confession,

> *I have glorified you on the earth by completing the work you gave me to do. Now, Father, glorify me in your presence with that glory I had with you before the world existed.* (vv. 4-5)

Jesus, although he was God, pushed pause on receiving all that was rightfully his. In his incarnation he demonstrated what had always been true: that his goal was to give glory to the Father. Why did Jesus, God's Son, give all the glory to the Father? Why did he boast in the Father? The reason is because he knew the Father more than any other, and to know God is to exalt him, because to know God is to know more than other people. Those who know God are not daydreaming idealists; they are the biggest realists. They know that this life is dissipating and being subsumed in the kingdom. They know this. So they glory in the eternal, not the temporal—like mere wealth, power, or human wisdom.

And then those idols.

The following chapters are God's take on the worship of idols. In the West we generally do not cast statues of metal and bow down to them. For those of us who go to church, the distance between us and pagan idol worshipers is even greater. But going to church does not displace idols and can even trap us into thinking that presence equals piety. We should of course be faithful to our local church, but the purpose of our presence in church is to lead us into God's presence. It is interesting that the best way to understand how God wants us to relate to him is discovered in the ancient prophet Jeremiah. God is not satisfied with us until we are satisfied with his presence. God's greatest desire for us is for him to be our greatest desire. He wants intimacy and nothing less.

We do too. We want something to be our object of affection, be it family, sports, a friendship, a work or academic goal, a social status, or a material thing. All of these things, ideals, and ambitions can hold a place in our hearts. Yet the great thing about them is that they ask little in return. I don't have to be vulnerable with a new car. I can idolize it, then trade it in. I will only give it part of my heart. This is different from our relationship with God. To make him the object of my worship means I am all in. There is no middle ground to all of this. There is no halfway. Being "sort of intimate" is oxymoronic. We are either intimate or we are not.

This is important. In Jeremiah's treatise the opposite of idolatry is intimacy. The cure for worshiping false gods is to know the one true God.

Conclusion

So there I was at camp, laid bare before God, knowing all of my faults, secrets, and insecurities. I was at a crossroads. That week I threw all of my sermons away. Trust me, even though it was difficult at the time, it was no loss for the kingdom. I was starting over. For the first time in my life, I was seeking God not for fame or blessing or prosperity or favor. I was seeking God just to know him. This was the defining moment of my life. It was a more emotional experience than even my salvation. I had a true sense of sin, and for the first time the way out was not an out. It was a he. A person. Jesus was not just my way maker; he was my way. It was out of darkness and into presence.

The ambient culture tells you to idolize fame. Idolize self. Idolize family. Idolize accomplishment. Idolize religion. Idolize ability. These are the shadows we chase. We are the child who, with the light directly behind him, keeps chasing the shadow that can never be held. This is because fame, glory, success, achievement, and love are all shadows of the great light. God is not calling you to reject them but to find the source of light that gives them meaning. Turn around and step into his presence. Glory is knowing him.

Reflect and Discuss

1. What is the connection between this passage and Jeremiah's temple sermon? How should we understand the two texts in light of each other?

2. How does Jeremiah view boasting? Is all boasting unbiblical? Is there a type of boasting Christians should engage in?

3. What does this passage teach us about "boasting" as Christians?

4. The text teaches us that true boasting is that we know God. What are the three truths provided in this passage that assure us of this intimate kind of boasting?

5. Is biblical boasting the same thing as bragging? If not, how can we distinguish the difference between the two?

6. The idea of boasting has a trajectory throughout Scripture. Discuss what Scripture says about boasting from 1 Corinthians 1:28-31; Galatians 6:14; and James 1:9.

7. How did Jesus demonstrate humility in the incarnation?

8. What does Jeremiah say about the worship of false idols?

9. What was the opposite of idolatry for Jeremiah?

10. What was Jeremiah's cure for worshiping false gods?

Idolatry

JEREMIAH 10:1-16

Main Idea: God is nothing like idols.

I. **Idols Are Worthless (10:1-5).**
II. **Idols Are Nothing like God (10:6-16).**

As the crowds began to gather around the mountain, any observer would be struck by the massive diversity. The bad were there—those people who had abused others, abused themselves, and abused the system. Yet the religious were there, the long robes with ornamental decorations speaking to the nature of their gravitas. They were important. Their presence made this event important. But the vast majority who gathered on that hill in first-century Palestine were commoners. These were the people who had given their time and energies to the act of living. They worked; they took care of their families and depended on one another to make it from one generation to the next. Their presence, the presence of the everyman, made this event so shocking.

At the crest of the hill was a man who was one of them and none of them. He looked like any of the other men in their early thirties. You would have a hard time picking him out of the crowd. Yet this man claimed to have the most distinguished bloodline of anyone who ever breathed this planet's air. He claimed to be the Son of God. More specifically, he claimed to be the Jewish Messiah. No one would care that this commoner made audacious claims; it would simply be gossip to run in the background of their otherwise boring lives, except for the miracles. He was healing the sick and walking on water and doing things that aroused suspicion that this local boy had actually emigrated from an otherworldly place.

He had no enemies, but he was the enemy of those with religious authority. The reason is simple: he was there to tear down one of the most revered national treasures—the religious system.

You see, at the close of the Old Testament and before the coming of Jesus in the New Testament, a group arose called the Pharisees. What distinguished them is that they took the law that was given to Moses and they added to it. They modified it in some extreme ways. The result was that the faith of their fathers was only accessible to those who had means. Only the wealthy had the leisure to study the law, know the law, and therefore keep the law. Religion had become elitist. But it's worse than that. Religion had become their idol.

So on this day Jesus preaches the most famous sermon ever preached, the Sermon on the Mount. During this sermon he pits his new ways against this religious system. In this new kingdom Jesus is after one thing: the heart. This was encouraging because those who were broken over their sin, those who were pure in heart, were now qualified for the kingdom. Those who mourned were comforted, and the meek inherited the earth. This was the new way. It was good news for all, except for those who made religion their idol.

Jesus has always been, and always will be, tearing down idols. In the Sermon on the Mount, he tore down many idols.

Those who worshiped their own nationality, he warned that the salt might lose its savor and be useless (Matt 5:13). Those whose idol was money, he encouraged to lay up treasure in heaven (Matt 6:19-21). Those whose idol was their spiritual reputation, he warned not to pray and give just to be seen (Matt 6:1-6). Those whose idol was comfort, Jesus encouraged not to worry; God would take care of them. Before Jesus made a whip and cleaned the temple, he verbally assaulted the idols of their hearts, and of mine.

Jesus is after anything that steals my affection, anything that I hold as precious. Whether it is a reputation, a status, a friendship, or an approval, anything we think we can't live without, that is the thing God is most interested in showing me that I can. Once we realize God is all we have, we learn he is all we need. Perhaps it's trite, but nothing is more true than the reality that God is still allowing things in our lives that cause our idols to seem, well, idolatrous. We praise him for that. Not only is he doing that years after he came to earth; he was doing that years before.

God was very concerned with the idols that existed during the time of Jeremiah. Jeremiah makes two profound statements about idolatry in this passage, and his discussion raises two preliminary questions: What exactly are idols, and why are idols so attractive?

What Is an Idol?

An idol is an image. But it's not just any image. It's an image to which deity is attributed. It is considered worthy of worship. So when we think of idolatry, we immediately think of people in pagan, maybe ancient cultures, who bow down to a god. The idol is made of wood, metal, or stone, but they worship it as if it is worthy of all their worship and adoration. It is a material thing, but it is treated as if it were much more.

This is where Christianity comes in and explodes the idea of idols. All material things were created by Jesus, they were created through Jesus, and they were created for the glory of Jesus. All material things were given to us for our enjoyment. In that enjoyment we are to redirect our worship to the one who created them. This is the purpose of material things. When those things garner the kind of affection that is to be given only to God, those things, knowingly or unknowingly, become idols. Any good thing can become a bad thing when we give it affection that God alone deserves. The material world is not inherently bad. Rather, we taint the material world when we demand that it bear the weight of our affections. It was not designed to do this. Eventually it fails. We rightly enjoy creation by enjoying its Creator. This is the created order and the only way life is right.

The problem is not the created things; it's what we make of them. The heart of the problem is the heart.

Why Are Idols So Attractive?

Jeremiah is addressing actual idols. They were physical, material objects created by men to be worshiped by men.

The issue was international peer pressure (Ryken, *Jeremiah and Lamentations*, 185). All of the other nations were worshiping idols (v. 2). How could Israel be the lone monotheistic culture? This seems strange to us, yet think of the pressure we are under: to achieve, to own, to consume. We may not bow the knee to a pagan idol, but we bow our hearts before the gods of sports, leisure, food, clothes, achievement, and consumerism.

Perhaps a way to understand this is to imagine its opposite. Imagine you have friends who are very sharp. They decide that they will stop consuming things and live simply. Their clothes, their food, their material possessions all start to reflect that they are not living for this world but for the world to come. How would that make you feel? The truth is, it would make us feel a little uncomfortable. Their actions would expose the fact that this world is not all that it should be. It would also expose the fact that it is much easier to go with the flow of this life than live for the next. The temptation to give our hearts to something else is very real.

Jeremiah's words are penetrating. There are two things we need to know about idols. First, idols are vain.

Idols Are Worthless
JEREMIAH 10:1-5

The Oklahoman inside me wants to say, "They ain't real!" because, well, they ain't. Idols are vanity; they are meaningless. This is shocking because they look so good. Jeremiah describes them in verses 3-5.

They are attractive. They were, in their ancient context, quite dazzling. We think of them as monochromatic and predictable. The ancients idols represented the most dazzling creation using the highest technology available to them. Idols were stunning. And stunningly stupid.

Jeremiah describes them as scarecrows (v. 5). They had no propensity for evil or for good for the very reason that they had no power. They did not exist as we would like to imagine them. They were at once beautiful and hollow. People might as well have been worshiping the air. They were just that empty.

It's been said that an addiction is anything we cannot live without that is smaller than us. In the same way, an idol is anything that receives affections that belong to God alone. This is tricky because we are created to love. All things that we have been given can deserve some affection. However, that thing is a conduit. The affection goes through that object and back to God. This potential is what gives meaning to life, things, and relationships.

The hollowness of idols is not a foreign concept. It's not difficult for us to imagine the adolescent girl who is crushed by the weight of unrequited love; the relationship was an idol. We can relate to the young man who made his boss's approval his idol when, all the while, his boss had no integrity and was using him. We can imagine the young man whose torn ACL tore apart his dreams of playing professional sports. Sports were everything so now life is nothing.

Again, this is tricky because relationships, work, and athletics are all gifts of God. Yet the gifts have a design: they are nothing without the designer. Everything God gives us has value because of God. I really enjoy my family. At the end of the day, I see that the reason they have so much goodness is because God placed that goodness within them. When I engage them, I should bow down and worship God. If I did not know that God is the giver of sports, work, food, and relationships, then I would have nothing to which to direct my affections but the object itself. Ironically, when I worship something it loses its meaning. It's like cotton candy. When we touch cotton candy, it disappears. This is why people are increasingly disenchanted with the American dream. The blessings are not the end, but rather they lead us to our end: to worship God.

The psalmist echoes the same contrast in Psalm 115:3-8 when he writes,

> Our God is in heaven
> and does whatever he pleases.
> Their idols are silver and gold,
> made by human hands.
> They have mouths but cannot speak,
> eyes, but cannot see.
> They have ears but cannot hear,
> noses, but cannot smell.
> They have hands but cannot feel,
> feet, but cannot walk.
> They cannot make a sound with their throats.
> Those who make them are just like them,
> as are all who trust in them.

Notice that phrase, "Those who make them are just like them." Nothing subtle about that. Those who make idols out of scarecrows become like scarecrows. The deafness of the idols is transposed on the heart of the person who deifies them.

The idol has no value, and as such it is nothing like God.

Idols Are Nothing like God
JEREMIAH 10:6-16

Here we have the main idea of the chapter. It's found in verse 6. Simply stated, God is nothing like these false idols.

Derek Kidner describes this chapter as a polemic and a psalm (*Message of Jeremiah*, 56; Ryken, *Jeremiah and Lamentations*, 183). A polemic is a strong verbal rant against a wrong. A psalm is, of course, a song. Jeremiah has just dealt a blistering blow against the false idols, calling them out for what they are. The next section compares these idols against the living God.

The song is majestic (vv. 6-10). Unlike the weak idols, God is great, he is wise, he is the true God, and in his wrath the nations quake. The idols are beautiful and powerless; God is invisible and all-powerful.

This is the irony. The God who made all beautiful things is himself invisible. God created all beauty (Gen 1–2), yet God commands us not to create beautiful things to worship (Exod 20:4-6). The beautiful things he created are to be a stimulus for worshiping him (Ps 104). Idolatry is twisted ignorance inasmuch as the creation becomes the object of worship. Idolatry aborts the natural flow of worship through things to God. The material world is then a stimulus for worship.

Perhaps the best way to understand this is by reading Psalm 104. The psalmist praises nature for its glory, but the praise is in transit. It is praise that is moving up to where it belongs, to the Creator. This is how a God-fearing person relates to the universe.

Yet God has done something more profound. It is more profound than his material creation and sets him far apart from the false gods: he created his own people. Jeremiah writes,

> *Jacob's Portion is not like these*
> *because he is the one who formed all things.*
> *Israel is the tribe of his inheritance;*
> *the Lord of Armies is his name.* (10:16)

The phrase *Jacob's Portion* is a title for God that is only used here and in 51:19. "Jacob" was a synonym for the nation of Israel. So while nations had land and monarchies, the real portion, the real inheritance of Israel was God himself. Similarly the psalmist writes,

> *Lord, you are my portion and my cup of blessing;*
> *you hold my future.*
> *The boundary lines have fallen for me in pleasant places;*
> *indeed, I have a beautiful inheritance.* (Ps 16:5-6)

This reminds us of what Jesus said in Matthew 5:5: the humble will inherit the earth. Jesus's words do not tell us from whom the humble will inherit the earth, but it is implied of course. God is the one who gives everything to those who humbly trust him. When the Lord is our portion, we really need nothing else. We especially do not need scarecrow idols that look nice but have no power.

Conclusion

Remember the scarecrow in *The Wizard of Oz*? He was perplexed because he did not have a brain. Oh, what he would do if he only had a brain!

In the end the scarecrow and his friends go to Oz. Of course they find that the wizard is an imposter. In the book he gives the scarecrow a brain, which proves to be fake. As the tale unfolds, the scarecrow finds that he already had all the brains he needed. He really did not need more brains. Rather, he needed confidence in what he already had. This then is another irony in the story. All the brains he needed were within him. The scarecrow becomes a metaphor for personal empowerment.

What we need cannot be given to us by the false gods of this world. What we need cannot be given to us by ourselves if we are only personally empowered to receive it. No, what we need can only be given to us by God. A God who is not distant but personal, a God who is not contrived but real, a God who is not pretense but authentic, a God who is not hiding but is actually granted to us—he is our portion. The things we idolize will continue to take from us until we realize how empty they really are. They are especially empty compared to the God who is our portion.

If Jeremiah could say God is our portion, how much more can we say he is ours, since "the Word became flesh and dwelt among us," calling us to abide in him and he in us (John 1:14)? He is our Portion. He lives in us, and we live in him. Therefore, every idol of my heart should be consumed in the white-hot heat of my love for him.

I stand with a heart on fire for him and hold all things as conduits to his praise, knowing always that these things do not have the power to hold me.

Reflect and Discuss

1. What does Jesus's Sermon on the Mount teach us about how he views idolatry?
2. How does Jeremiah define idolatry? How should we define idolatry today?
3. How do idols steal our affections?
4. Jeremiah made two profound statements about idolatry in this passage. What were they?
5. What are some contemporary manifestations of idols, and why are they so attractive?
6. According to Jeremiah 10, what attracted Israel to her idols?
7. How is Jeremiah 10 a polemic and a psalm?
8. How should we understand the idolatry in Jeremiah 10 in light of Genesis 1-2; Exodus 20:4-6; and Psalm 104?
9. How are idols nothing like God?
10. How are idols meaningless?

Covenant and Conspiracy

JEREMIAH 11

Main Idea: We fight conspiracy by listening to the covenant.

I.   **Listen to Your God (11:1-5).**
II. **Look to Your Past (11:6-8).**
III. **Fear Your Future (11:9-23).**

If you want to lose a few hours of your life, google "conspiracy theories." There is an endless rabbit hole of conspiracies involving everything from Elvis and who shot JFK to government cover-up of alien visitors in Roswell, New Mexico. The idea behind these theories is that an evil-intentioned outside force, let's say the US government, creates a distraction and obscures or covers up the truth. It seems that we have an appetite for things that do not appear as they are. We are suspicious that there has to be a story behind the story.

If you have ever talked to someone convinced of such a theory, you, again, can lose several hours of your life. Some people are obsessed with them. However, there is one thing worse than someone believing there is a conspiracy when there is not, and that is not believing there is a conspiracy when there is. This is the difference between asking, "Is Elvis still alive?" and "Was a crime committed at Watergate?" In the first scenario the conspiracy is, by all credible accounts, unfounded. In the second scenario the conspiracy was real. Someone actually did conspire to do wrong. To ignore the first theory and not to ignore the second are both rational acts.

So each of us is a living conspiracy. I want to find the truth and live by it. I really do. However, something is conspiring against my spiritual success: it is myself. Part of me, my flesh, with bad intentions distracts me and obscures the truth. To suggest otherwise is simply to ignore the facts and the plain witness of Scripture. Why are we told to put on armor and engage in invisible warfare (Eph 6:10-20) if there is not a real enemy conspiring against me? And why would Paul be so conflicted in Romans 7 about doing what he did not want to do if the enemy was not internal as well as external?

So what do you do when you are conspiring against yourself? What is the strategy for this type of warfare?

Listen to Your God
JEREMIAH 11:1-5

This is a provocative passage. First God tells them to listen to the covenant. Listen. This reinforces the idea that the covenant was originally given orally, from the mouth of God to the ears of Abraham (Gen 12). The covenant was enforced again from the mouth of God to the ears of Moses (Exod 20). And the covenant was explicit from the mouth of God to the ears of David (2 Sam 7). It was a spoken covenant from a speaking God. God speaks, and every time God speaks, he demands a response.

This notion of "listening" to the covenant brings to mind a spiritual law that Israel had forgotten: God's word stands. Dozens of years had passed since God first gave his covenant. Yet, when God speaks, he speaks so clearly, with ultimate authority, that his words hang suspended with everlasting clout. Once God has spoken, it reflects his presence. Responding to the spoken word is responding to God. And, for those of us who live so long removed from the oral tradition and from God's original written revelation, responding to the written Word is responding to God.

This is a difficult sell in the modern culture. It really is. Science textbooks are often out-of-date by the time they are printed. New information is surfacing on a daily basis. It is difficult for us to believe, really believe, that Psalm 119:96 is true:

> I have seen a limit to all perfection,
> but your command is without limit.

It is hard to imagine that all things are out-of-date, except the Word of God. It will be an increasing problem for modern people of faith to communicate our absolute confidence in the Word of God. Yet it is not a new problem.

God tells Jeremiah to listen to the covenant, and then he gives specific instructions for Jeremiah to tell Israel to obey the covenant (vv. 2-5). A curse was to rest on those who did not listen to and obey the covenant. Listening was important to God because God is a God of communication. He has always been speaking. From the garden to the burning bush, to the baptism of Christ, it is shocking how many times God willfully, overtly, plainly speaks to those whom he created.

God's ultimate form of speech was the incarnation of Jesus Christ, the living Word.

We evaluate communication by how well it represents the original. We say that a photograph "does not do that person justice." By this we mean it is not a good representation of reality. Or we may say that an artist "really captured that person." We determine that a speaker is "good" if she takes something difficult and makes it clear. Communication is good or bad based on how well it represents the original.

This is why Jesus is perfect communication. Everything the Father wanted him to say, he said. Everything the Father wanted him to do, he did. He perfectly represented the Father. He is the exact expression (Heb 1:3). He is the exact image of the Father (Col 1:15). We know the Father because Jesus communicates him perfectly. This is why, when Jesus was being transfigured, the Father said, "*Listen* to him" (Matt 17:5; emphasis added).

For this reason ignoring Christ is terrible. Christ is still communicating to us through his Word. We are accountable to God for what we know about his Word. God is here and he is not silent. Not to read the Word is to ignore God.

In this case God wanted to "establish the oath." He wanted to re-up the covenant he had made with *his* people. Jeremiah says, "Amen." In other words, let it be so.

Look to Your Past
JEREMIAH 11:6-8

From listening to God, God then calls them to look to their past. God's warnings begin with the exit from Egypt. God began to prepare them for a new covenant relationship. They entered Egypt a small family and left a huge nation. In order to protect his nation, God set up boundaries— instructions and rules meant to protect his people and reflect his character. His love was so profound that his warnings were intended to protect them. See, for example, the whole book of Deuteronomy. However, it does not stop there. The warnings are given throughout their history (2 Chr 36:15; Jer 7:13,25; 25:3; 26:5; 29:19; 32:33; 35:14-15; 44:4).

What they failed to see, what we fail to see, is that warnings are an act of love. Concern for safety posts a speed limit sign; out of love I warn my children not to touch the hot stove. Warnings are not motivated by hate but by love.

On January 10, 1962, the residents of the Peruvian villages of Ranrahirca and Huarascucho heard a loud crack coming from the extinct volcano, Mount Huascaran. It was a giant block of ice cracking from the mountain. This was a fair warning. Usually when they heard this sound, they had about thirty minutes to evacuate before the ice came down the mountain. This time, however, the block of ice was massive, weighing some six million tons.

It travelled down the 9.5 miles in only seven minutes. Four thousand people died ("Avalanche Kills Thousands").

They heard the warning but did not heed it. They underestimated the power of the danger and assumed there was more time. This is Israel. For hundreds of years God has been so patient. But now they are about to enter into an exile that will make them think Egypt was not so bad. Yet, mercifully, God is giving them chance after chance to repent. Even in this darkest of warnings, he rings the note of hope (12:15-17). No one could be more patient than God in this moment. He is warning of impending danger because it is real.

When I first began to preach, a guy about my age asked me plaintively, "Are you one of those preachers who try to make you feel guilty?" I can't recall my reaction, but I thought about it long enough to come up with an answer in the event it came up again, which it has. The answer to the question, "Are you going to make me feel guilty?" should be, "Only if you are." Guilt is to the soul what pain is to the body. If you have a painful stress fracture in your leg, you should stop running on it. You can cause permanent damage. If you tear your rotator cuff, you need it repaired. You cannot use it without causing more damage.

One of the more controversial medical treatments in sports was Novocain or ethyl chloride spray. The spray numbs the pain of an injured player so the player can keep playing. Good so far. However, it is often hard to tell the difference between a sprain and a torn ligament. When the pain is treated but not the injury, there are consequences. The warning is heard but not heeded. The mentality of "spray 'em and play 'em" became the cause of life-altering injuries for many football players (Johnson, "Spray 'Em, Play 'Em").

So when a preacher preaches, he should clearly indicate the problem. The preacher who makes people feel good when God has an entirely different opinion is liable. He is indifferent to the real needs of people. We can't ignore the warnings.

If you will not listen to God or look to your past, then you must fear your future.

Fear Your Future
JEREMIAH 11:9-23

It is not clear what exactly this conspiracy is (v. 9), but perhaps some are planning to return to false gods after this renewal under Josiah has faded.

This is tragic. Josiah has done just about everything an earthly king could do. However, he is only able to move the needle so far. The reason? You cannot legislate the heart. You can call for reform, plan reform, encourage reform, and even institute reform. Yet if the heart is still away from God, there is no hope. God is still after their hearts. Verses 10-13 and on into chapter 12 explain God's response when his people do not share his heart.

It is so bad that God even discourages Jeremiah from praying to fix the problem (vv. 14-16). God's mind is made up. His judgment is clear in verses 21-23: those who threatened Jeremiah would be exterminated. For Jeremiah this was a working out of his call. He had been told that if he were afraid of his audience, God would make him cower in front of them, but if he fulfilled his call, he would be invincible (1:17-19). His call was to keep preaching. He knew the fight was coming. What he may not have intended is that this war would be personal.

Tucked away in this passage about God's judgment on a people whose heart was not his is a response from Jeremiah. There is a back-and-forth dialogue. In 11:17-20 Jeremiah responds to God's impending judgment. What had evidently escaped Jeremiah is that there was a plot against his own life. This seems like a strong punishment for a prophet who is simply saying what God says! Yet this conspiracy against him is really a metaphor for the state of the nation of Israel. They were conspiring against Jeremiah because they were conspiring against God. And the leaders, instead of rooting out this conspiracy, perpetuated it, causing it to fester and grow and ultimately incite God's judgment.

Application

If you do not listen to God and you do not look to your past, then you should fear your future. This applies to us on two levels.

For a Believer

As a church we are, in a way, like Israel, God's chosen people. We have not replaced God's covenant promise with Israel, but rather we are grafted into God's covenant promise (Rom 11). Yet, like Israel, we tend to harden our hearts, and what is going on in the heart is a conspiracy. It is in my heart and in all of our hearts. It affects me as an individual and in the collective minds of a church. Sin that is not rooted out completely from our hearts lies in wait. It will be at some moment always there waiting to take me out. There is a conspiracy inside of me.

This is Paul's point in Romans 7. There are things he wants to do, but he does not. There are things he does not want to do, but he does. This leaves him to throw his hands up and say, "What a wretched man I am!" (Rom 7:24). Paul is in a horrible state. He is internally conflicted. He wants to do one thing, but he consistently does another thing. It's as if this is driving him mad! Yet, oddly, he is as spiritually and psychologically healthy as he can be.

Paul is spiritually healthy because he is awakened to the reality that he has two natures inside of him. He has the Holy Spirit, who is compelling him to do what is right. Yet the works of the flesh are also present with him because he is still in the flesh (Gal 5). This was true for Paul. It's true for me. His spiritual health was determined by the fact that he realized this. He knew what was going on inside of him. He knew that inside of him was a conspiracy. His own flesh was conspiring against his own soul to take him out and leave him completely empty. It is a war fought every day. And since a war is going on, it's good to know about it! Christians who are not aware of the war are naïve; they cannot fight the conspiracy that is brewing inside them.

Paul is, if we could venture there for a moment, psychologically healthy as well. As a layman to the field of psychology, I could at least observe that one's psychological health can be observed by how self-aware one is. If you believe you are Abraham Lincoln, then you are not mentally healthy. There is a disconnect between your self-perception and reality.

The healthiest Christians have a little angst to them. They are tempered; they are broken; they are conflicted. Some of us preachers, music worship leaders, and church leaders posture that this is a wrong approach because Jesus wants you to be happy. The idea that Jesus wants you to be happy has everything going for it except the witness of Scripture. The great figures of the early church struggled with suffering;

they, to put a fine point on it, struggled with their own autonomy. They wanted, like we all want, independence from God. Yet God wants us dependent. He is the vine; we are the branches (John 15).

This is why the rules in the new kingdom are clear. Our brokenness, in this case our sinful nature and the acts of sin we commit, should drive us to mourning, and that desperation over sin should drive us to meekness. From this bottoming out we are now useful. This is the trajectory of the beatitudes—the beatitudes being the new value system of the new kingdom.

So the believer who understands that his greatest enemy is within him understands reality. The breezy faith of the uninitiated believer, floating from one positive religious experience to the next with no suffering and no battle scars, is not as spiritually healthy. He has the outward signs of health but not the inward signs. Spiritual health does not come from acting healthy. Spiritual health comes when we realize that our sin nature produces death inside of us; we then realize that our sin was crucified with Christ and we are reborn in his new life. Christ does not promise a wispy Christianity. He promises that his new life implanted within ours stands ready to do battle with our flesh. A war rages. And the sin and death will ultimately be overcome by the resurrection and life. Grace over guilt.

For an Unbeliever

Perhaps you come to this passage and you have not yet entered the fight. You think neutrality is the way to go. "I will not enter the war, and therefore I will not get hurt." You are firmly committed to taking no position on Jesus, no position on his church, no position on his death and resurrection. Could I say with all humility that those who do not take a position on Jesus have in fact taken a hard position? Those who are of the notion that to have any certainty is wrongheaded have the least grasp of reality. If there was a first-century Jewish peasant who claimed to be God (and there was), if he did rise from the dead validating his claims (which he did), and if he did begin the most historically significant movement ever (which he did), then to be neutral is, if I may say it, willful rejection of Christ. We might wrangle with that language. "I am not willfully rejecting Christ!" Yet the alternative is not good. If this is not willful rejection, it is the psychologically unhealthy position of not perceiving the obvious! So this is not to suggest that all people who are not Christians are psychologically unhealthy, but just to suggest that *neutrality on the person of Christ is not a logically tenable position.* Jesus's presence calls for love or hate, clarity or confusion, life or death, and a thousand other ways we could express the choices he presents, but neutrality on who he is is not an option. To say it bluntly, if you are not aware of the conspiracy, then you are part of it.

So, what do we do? We listen to the covenant, we remember our past, and we fear a future of disobedience. In other words, we fight the conspiracy with the covenant. God's promises are not weak, but often they are not claimed. Fight the conspiracy with the covenant.

Reflect and Discuss

1. What does it mean to conspire against yourself?
2. What does Jeremiah mean by listening to the covenant?
3. Is there a relationship between listening to the covenant and listening to the Word of God?
4. What was behind the conspiracy against Jeremiah?
5. How do God's warnings demonstrate his love for us?
6. What are the evidences that God wants to communicate with us?
7. What does it mean to "harden your heart"?
8. What are specific ways we can know if our hearts are hard?
9. Is it possible to be neutral about Jesus Christ?
10. What does this chapter have to do with the idolatry mentioned in chapter 10?

Unliked

JEREMIAH 12

Main Idea: We can respond to God when we feel forgotten.

I. **Jeremiah Has an Honest Complaint (12:1-4).**
II. **God Has an Honest Response (12:5-17).**
   A. Personal response (12:5-6)
   B. Corporate response (12:7-13)
   C. Future response (12:14-17)

As of this writing, the most widely used social media platform is (still) Facebook. One of the early pioneers of the platform was Justin Rosenstein. Rosenstein, now in his early thirties, has the distinction of being the engineer who created the "like" button. This seemingly innocuous creation is now a source of joy for many addicted to the app and to the devices that facilitate it.

This is why Rosenstein does not have the app on his phone. He purchased a new phone and told his assistant to apply settings that keep him from downloading apps. The problem was that he found his own invention too alluring, too distracting, too addictive. He told the guardian, "It is very common for humans to develop things with the best of intentions and for them to have unintended, negative consequences" (Lewis, "Our Minds Can Be Hijacked"). It seems that one of the people who helped create a potentially addictive tech is weaning himself off his own product. The "unintended consequence" is that it's too distracting. Fixating on it can distract you from reality.

Jeremiah is distracted. Perhaps Jeremiah has forgotten the overall plan. He has forgotten that this is what God set him on this course to do. Jeremiah's attention was so diverted by his present problems that he has forgotten that, embedded in his call, he would uproot and tear down, destroy, and demolish (1:10). Not a position for those who need "likes."

Jeremiah has forgotten his purpose and become distracted from his mission. Interestingly, this is what he is accusing God of doing. God,

Jeremiah concludes, must have a short attention span. God has already forgotten him. He is ignoring him. And God's amnesia is wearing thin on Jeremiah. How long will God go on like this (12:4)? Jeremiah is losing patience with God's inaction.

Is Complaining to God Ever Justified?

Is complaining justified? Well, God did not exclude complaints from Scripture. The book of Jeremiah is filled with them, and Jeremiah wrote a whole songbook of complaints in Lamentations! One third of the psalms are songs of complaint. God knows where we are, and he allowed the human authors of Scripture to identify with their human readers in this way.

Jeremiah's complaint reminds us of Psalm 13:1-2, where David wrote,

> How long, LORD? Will you forget me forever?
> How long will you hide your face from me?
> How long will I store up anxious concerns within me,
> agony in my mind every day?
> How long will my enemy dominate me?

The question is one of time. How long will God go on ignoring the wrong and those who do it? The answer, as David saw and as Jeremiah will see, is that God is far more concerned with the ultimate than the immediate. God has activated an entire plan by which he will use Judah to bring the Messiah. The Messiah will be rejected and killed but then raised and ascended. Followers of the Messiah will take the message to the whole earth. And in the end the Messiah will come back and be exalted in a new heaven and a new earth.

For me it's easy to get so distracted with today that I forget that. My hard season is a drop in the great fountain of mercy that God is pouring on the earth. We are free to complain, after which we should run to Scripture so that all things can be put in perspective.

This chapter lays out Jeremiah's honest complaint in verses 1-4 and God's honest response in verses 5-17. The honest confession gets an honest answer. Let's look at his complaint and God's threefold response: a personal response to Jeremiah, a corporate response to Judah, and a future response to both Judah and their persecutors.

Jeremiah Has an Honest Complaint
JEREMIAH 12:1-4

Jeremiah begins by framing the complaint in the correct way. He acknowledges that God is sovereign over all things. He wants God to know that he knows God is the source of all that is right. In this way his complaint is justified. After all, God is the only one who can do anything about it.

His complaint is simply this: the wicked are prospering. His complaints sound similar to the psalmist's in Psalm 94:1-7.

> LORD, God of vengeance—
> God of vengeance, shine!
> Rise up, Judge of the earth;
> repay the proud what they deserve.
> LORD, how long will the wicked—
> how long will the wicked celebrate?
>
> They pour out arrogant words;
> all the evildoers boast.
> LORD, they crush your people;
> they oppress your heritage.
> They kill the widow and the resident alien
> and murder the fatherless.
> They say, "The LORD doesn't see it.
> The God of Jacob doesn't pay attention."

Jeremiah's description of the wicked is similarly accusatory toward God (v. 2). "You planted them." This is an interesting choice for a metaphor, and it has a trajectory all over Scripture. Notably, Jesus used the metaphor to describe the true believer. They were the ones who, unlike the rejecting soil, were receptive of the word, bore fruit, and remained (Matt 13:17-23). In the same chapter true believers were described as wheat in the field (Matt 13:36-43), and in John 4:34-38 potential believers were described as a ready harvest. The receptive soil was a metaphor for both God's favor and for those who were truly in him.

Most telling is Jeremiah 2:2-3.

> "Go and announce directly to Jerusalem that this is what the LORD
>   says:
> I remember the loyalty of your youth,

your love as a bride—
how you followed me in the wilderness,
in a land not sown.
Israel was holy to the LORD,
the firstfruits of his harvest.
All who ate of it found themselves guilty;
disaster came on them."
        This is the LORD's declaration.

Is Jeremiah reflecting back on this passage? If so, what a strong condemnation: "Why, God, are you treating them like you should be treating us? Why are you blessing them when we, Judah, are your choice vine? So, you are planting *them*?!"

The question of the prosperity of the wicked always troubles believers. As we wonder about the prosperity of the wicked in our time, we can take comfort in the angst Jeremiah felt when he saw others prosper. This is why we are warned repeatedly not to envy evil people (Prov 23:17). We are further reminded that a fool does not understand that God raises up the wicked, but only for the day of destruction:

A stupid person does not know,
a fool does not understand this:
though the wicked sprout like grass
and all evildoers flourish,
they will be eternally destroyed.
But you, LORD, are exalted forever.
For indeed, LORD, your enemies—
indeed, your enemies will perish;
all evildoers will be scattered. (Ps 92:6-9)

Then Jeremiah gives God a directive: slaughter them (12:3). What Jeremiah cannot understand is that God's unwillingness to annihilate them does not have anything to do with God's ignorance of the situation. Neither does it have anything to do with his ability. God is not ignorant; he knows everything. God is not impotent; he can do anything.

The issue is God's plan and God's timing. This is fascinating. God did not surprise Jeremiah with this assignment. From the start he promised it would be a hard road. I do not at all blame Jeremiah, but his statements are a little cringeworthy, like those of a child who yells at his own parents. How can he talk to someone like that? How can he talk to

God like that? Yet God is not fazed, even when Jeremiah accuses him of treating the pagan nations better than Judah. He knows what Jeremiah is thinking and does not chastise him for verbalizing it.

In fact, God, in his remarkable patience, gives an honest response to the honest complaint. There is a practical lesson here in being honest with God: to receive an honest answer we need to pray honest prayers.

God Has an Honest Response
JEREMIAH 12:5-17

Personal Response (12:5-6)

God begins by challenging Jeremiah. What a great metaphor! Jeremiah, if you can't keep up with mere men, how will you compete against horses? In other words, God is saying, "Jeremiah, if you can't handle the persecution that is on you now, how will you handle the persecution that is coming?" In a way, this is an encouraging word. It's good to know God has confidence in Jeremiah. It's good to be told every once in a while to right yourself.

Jeremiah is facing persecution, but it's at least a footrace, not a horse race. He has at least a chance of success. It's a race that is small compared to what is coming. And that's where the metaphor is negative. This is God's way of saying, "Well, OK, but this is just the beginning of the persecution that is to come." How are you going to run with horses?

He is calling for personal resolve and personal endurance. In 1914 Earnest Shackleton attempted to cross Antarctica from sea to sea. This had never been done. Before he and his men could reach the starting point for the trek, their ship, *Endurance*, was trapped in pack ice. While the crew disembarked, this was the end of the attempt, as the ice eventually crushed the ship and it foundered. In what is now known as one of the most heroic rescues in naval history, Shackleton set out in a small lifeboat to seek help, leaving the majority of his men on the small Elephant Island. He traveled 720 miles in an open boat to find help. After reaching help he went back and rescued each man (Lansing, *Endurance*). God is calling for this type of endurance. Jeremiah needs to run with the horses later, so he must learn to run with men now.

Following his personal response, God now gives a corporate response.

Corporate Response (12:7-13)

God's response to Judah is that they have abandoned him. He describes it in vivid terms using word pictures.

God counters that he has abandoned his people, his "inheritance." This is a significant word and a favorite one of God's to describe his people. They are his heritage, his portion. They are what he treasures. Yet his love for them is met with disdain. He explains this disdain with vivid word pictures.

God's people as a nation have been like a lion roaring at God. His inheritance has been like a hyena howling at him. They have been like birds of prey swooping down toward him (vv. 8-9).

He then, in a passage reminiscent of Ezekiel 34, describes his shepherds, his leaders, as those who have trampled the vineyard. Remember that the nation is God's choice vine (2:1-2). This mixed metaphor is provocative. The shepherds charged with keeping the sheep have trampled God's vine. The outcome is tragic (12:10-12). As a result, they have stimulated the anger of God (v. 13).

After a personal response to Jeremiah and a corporate response to Judah, God then gives a future response to both Judah and the nations.

Future Response (12:14-17)

God promises to uproot those who had gone against his people (v. 14). Perhaps God is picking up on the metaphor first used by Jeremiah. "Oh, you thought I was planting your enemies? Well, I am actually promising to uproot them!"

He says that Judah will be plucked up as well. However, the implication is that they will be plucked from the foreign land and placed where they belong in their own land. The first plucking is negative, and the second is positive. Or, in a way, they are both positive. One will be extracted as a way of punishment; the other will be extracted to fulfill God's covenant promise to bring his people back to himself.

However, this restoration was contingent on obedience. And there is a strange twist to the end of the story. God promises to offer hope to the nations that persecuted his people! However, this is only if they will repent and turn to him (vv. 16-17). In this way God is not only restoring Judah; he is offering hope to a nation that is against him. He is so compassionate! Even though Jeremiah can't feel it at the moment, God's logic is airtight and his compassion is clear. He is restoring Judah and even offering hope to the nations that persecuted Judah. You can't fault a God like that.

Conclusion

In summary, Jeremiah's honest complaint is met with an honest response: a personal response for Jeremiah to endure, a corporate response to Judah's explaining his own people's revulsion of him, and a future warning to the nations that while God was going to uproot them, there was still hope.

Jeremiah, an Early Pharisee

In the messianic prophecy of Isaiah 49:6, Isaiah prophesied that it would be too small a thing for the Messiah to redeem Judah back to God. What God really wanted was for the Messiah to be a light to the Gentiles. The significance of this passage is huge. When Mary and Joseph took Jesus to be dedicated in the temple, Simeon quoted this passage of Scripture. Clearly he believed Jesus was to be that light to the Gentiles. Later, in Acts 13:47, Paul quoted this passage to explain why he was taking the gospel to the Gentiles. It seems that this had a dual fulfillment. Christ was not just for Judah but for the nations. Paul was not just to go to his fellow Jews, but he was also to bring the light to the nations.

Now we understand how Jesus was more than peeved at the Pharisees. Their chief criticism of Jesus was that he was a friend of sinners. But, hello, that was the point! No shocker. This was the prophecy and point from the beginning. The path of the Messiah has a trajectory toward Judah and beyond Judah. Their myopic vision of a one-nation God was too small. It would still include Judah, of course, but it would also fulfill the promises of the gospel—namely, that Christ would be slain for sin (Isa 53:5), bear the sins of many (Isa 53:12), and eventually conquer (Isa 53:12). This Messiah King is our King and is the Lord of all. The message of his death and resurrection is the message of the gospel.

This has everything to do with Jeremiah's complaint. God's plan was always to take those who were far away from him and bring them close. Jeremiah needed to endure because this plan was unfolding. His impatience with the wicked was in reality his impatience with God's unfolding his plan.

Jeremiah thought God had *forgotten* him. God had not. In fact, God's actions reflect how much God *remembered* Jeremiah. God said that he was going to uproot and destroy (12:17). This was exactly the call on

Jeremiah's life (1:10). God is carrying out what he said he would do, and Jeremiah, as predicted, is all caught up in this. The challenge, the struggle of Jeremiah, seems to be *how* God is doing this. He was using the pagan nations to accomplish his ultimate plans. In the meantime, God was calling him to endure as God worked out the plan—to learn how to run with the horses.

The metaphor of running with horses is distressing. It signaled that more persecution was coming. Yet it's encouraging, and I need to hear it from time to time. When I experience discomfort, being treated unfairly, or any number of forgettable offenses, this is God's way of saying, "Look, if you want to run with the horses, you have to at least run with men first."

Reflect and Discuss

1. Is it possible for God to be distracted and forget us? Explain your answer.
2. Is it wrong to complain against God? Why or why not?
3. What did God mean that Jeremiah could not run with the horses (12:5)?
4. What did God mean that he had abandoned his house (v. 7)?
5. Why is Israel referred to as God's inheritance (v. 7)?
6. Who are the shepherds who destroyed the vineyard (v. 10)?
7. Notice all the agricultural metaphors. What does that say about God's desire to communicate with us?
8. When we complain honestly to God, what should we expect in response?
9. Is there a connection between God's actions (v. 17) and Jeremiah's call (1:10)? Explain.
10. Could we speculate that Jeremiah's emotions are related to a forgetfulness of his call?

Pride

Main Idea: Pride before God leads us to exile from God.

I. **Two Word Pictures (13:1-14)**
   A. Sin spoils (13:1-11).
   B. Sin destroys (13:12-14).
II. **Two Warnings (13:15-27)**
   A. We are warned against pride (13:15-17).
   B. Pride brings exile (13:18-27).

Throughout the teaching of Augustine, humility is put forth as the chief Christian virtue. This is no frivolous superlative. He was right. Think about the liability involved in the presence of pride and the absence of humility.

- Only the humble can have God's leadership (Prov 3:5-8).
- Only the humble can forgive (Matt 18:21-35).
- Only the humble can rejoice when people come to Christ (Luke 15:25-32).
- Only the humble can be saved (Matt 5:3)!
- In fact, the humble are the greatest in the kingdom (Matt 18:4).

By way of contrast, pride is sometimes referred to as the mother of all sins. This is not a reach. We talk about stumbling into sin. The metaphor is a little misleading. Every sin is a choice. It is willful. And it is willing against what God has willed for us. Sin is suggesting that God's way for us is not as profitable for us as our own way. Perhaps this is why Proverbs 5–7, the most direct warning to young men on the danger of sexual sin, is woven with discussions on seeking wisdom. The antidote to sexual sin includes self-restraint, but it does not end there. The ultimate antidotes to sexual sin are seeking God's wisdom on the subject and acknowledging that his way is the best way. The root of sexual sin is pride. It is saying that what we want is better than what God wants for us. His will is deficient in some way. We simply don't trust him. This is a heart filled with pride.

A prideful heart cannot be led by God because it cannot hear from God. Prayers become about us and not about God (Luke 18:9-14). Pride keeps us from seeing the future clearly (Jas 4:13-16). Pride can ultimately damn our souls (Matt 27:23-44).

Relationships are strained because of pride, and this is why the opposite of a prideful heart is the heart of Christ. Unlike those of us who focus on the offenses of others and will not let them go, the humility of Christ deferred to others. Christ lived as if our need for salvation was more important than his comfort. Therefore, he willingly laid down his life for us; then he was exalted like no other man. He humbled himself like no other man; therefore, God will exalt him like no other (Phil 2:1-11).

Jeremiah's sermons have had many sins in the crosshairs. However, now he deals with the mother of all sins: pride.

God gives Jeremiah two powerful word pictures: the loincloth and the wine jars. This leads to a discussion of pride and the most explicit warning about exile thus far. The remainder of the chapter shows the fruit of the root of pride: iniquity, forgetting God and trusting in lies, and spiritual adultery.

Pride is intuitive to the way we live; humility is counterintuitive. In fact, pride is so natural to our fallen flesh that we may think God is fine with it. It's an acceptable attitude—just white noise in the background of our lives. Yet that's not the way God sees it. God reacts strongly against pride.

Two Word Pictures
JEREMIAH 13:1-14

How does God react to pride? Before God gives his specific response to the sin of pride, he gives Jeremiah two provocative word pictures that illustrate how God feels about Judah's sin generally.

Sin Spoils (13:1-11)

God gives Jeremiah an odd assignment. The "linen undergarment" was the loincloth, the fine linen garment that was worn under the robe as the most intimate article of clothing. Jeremiah was commanded to buy the garment, wear it, and then go to the Euphrates and stuff it into a crevice. This was a long journey for Jeremiah, which would have had a profound impact on his audience.

Of course, after he hides it in the rock and then retrieves it a long time later, it is ruined. It was a perfectly useful garment, but now it cannot offer intimate protection from the elements as it was designed to do. The symbolism is explained in verse 8. The loincloth is Judah. The kingdom was filled with pride. They were intended to be close to God, so close that they would be God's people for his "fame, praise, and glory" (v. 11). However, they would not obey. In fact, they refused to listen to God, were stubborn, and followed other gods (v. 10). For this reason God was going to ruin them. The reality is that they effectively rejected the intimacy that God wanted with them. They no longer wanted to make God's name known. Now the de facto separation became formalized. They didn't want God to use them, and now God is obliging: they will be useless.

In this metaphor the elements of nature—the wind, rain, etc.—decay something that had been perfectly good. It was exposed. In the same way, a relationship with God that is exposed to the elements of sin and not protected will eventually be ruined.

Our temptation is to think we can sustain a moderate position toward God: not aggressively going forward yet not walking away from him. Like a car that is not in drive or reverse, it is just in neutral. However, this metaphor assumes we are on level ground. A car in neutral is a dangerous thing if it is parked uphill! In that case neutral is not neutral; it is backwards. The most ordinary mental behavior of a Christian is to underestimate how steep the ground is we are facing—to underestimate our potential for failure and the power of our enemy. Exposed to the elements of our natural environment, the elements of sin, our relationship with God is destroyed.

In Judah's case, they could not see that the pride of neglect had destroyed their relationship with him. Here it is again: they would not listen (v. 11). The refusal to listen carried the other consequence of not hearing the warning about the destruction that was coming. God reacts to pride. Sin spoils, but sin also destroys.

Sin Destroys (13:12-14)

Here we notice a shift. The first metaphor warns about the passivity of sin. The second warning warns of what God will do when he is neglected.

This includes an odd saying: "Every jar should be filled with wine." Some have suggested, "The saying may have originated as a raucous cry at a drunken feast, but it probably had become a confident expression that God would continue to prosper the people" (Huey, *Jeremiah, Lamentations*, 145). However, Jeremiah turns this into a statement of judgment, as if this cup of wine were the cup of wrath. Jeremiah specifically uses the idea of the judgment of God as a cup of wrath in 25:15-29. This brings to mind the wrath of treading the grapes from Isaiah 63:2-4. God is trampling his enemies, as one would tread the winepress. So in the metaphor, now Israel is the enemy.

God was going to cause them to be as if they were drunk. In other words, the blessing of the wine was now going to be a curse. The provision of wine now made them as vulnerable as if they were drunk. Then in confusion they would turn against one another and eventually be crushed against one another. Empty jars are easily smashed. A nation whose leaders were drunk on God's wrath would not be able to stand. They would fall into confusion.

Here there is a twist on the old axiom that an unguarded strength is the greatest weakness: A blessing that we abuse becomes a curse. They were blessed with prosperity; their jars were always filled with wine. In their pride they assumed that this would always be the case, even if they rejected God. Like Saul they committed presumptuous sin, assuming God would bless them despite their sin. Tragically, their great blessing became their curse, making them vulnerable.

This is true over and over in Scripture. Saul's victories, David's courage, and Peter's boldness—all these great blessings would become great liabilities. When we act in pride, God is not afraid to curse our blessing. This leads us to the big warning of this passage: their pride would lead them into exile.

Two Warnings
JEREMIAH 13:15-27

After the two word pictures come two warnings: against pride and of exile.

We Are Warned against Pride (13:15-17)

Verse 15 is an imperative. "Do not be proud, for the LORD has spoken." In other words, don't stiffen your neck and reject the Lord. Instead, give glory to God before it's too late. This brings to mind Proverbs 29:1:

> *One who becomes stiff-necked, after many reprimands*
> *will be shattered instantly—beyond recovery.*

From the general warning against pride now comes the specific warning of exile.

Pride Brings Exile (13:18-27)

Verses 18-20 are a specific encouragement to humble oneself because exile awaits those who reject God. For this reason Judah should consider themselves warned about the future.

A hard heart will ultimately be destroyed. In fact, this hard-hearted pride is similar to that in the strong warnings of the book of Hebrews. Those who live in pride and do not respond to the Word will experience spiritual drift (Heb 2:1-4). Eventually, a hard heart will attract God's judgment (Heb 3:8-15; 4:7). This is Israel's pattern. It cost them protection in the wilderness, forced forty years of wandering, and eventually brought a divided kingdom. The tragedy here is the inability to learn past lessons. Even though the tapestry of their past is woven with the threads of pride, they can't see it. Since they were already drunk with their own sense of invincibility, God now makes them as vulnerable as a drunken person. This leads to the painful result of pride: captivity.

If there is one driving thought to this passage, it is that pride leads to exile. Make no mistake, this is a specific warning to a specific people at a specific time. Based on a life of pride as expressed in a rejection of God's Word, they would be in exile. It would be hard for them to imagine, while they were experiencing the blessing during the reign of Josiah, that they would, ultimately, be in exile. But it was true. It happened. Its seeming inconceivability did not alter the reality. Pride brings exile.

While this is a specific promise for a specific people at a specific time, it is a perfect metaphor for what pride does to us. Pride isolates us from God. In fact, this is more than a metaphor for us to examine. James expresses this as a promise in James 4:6:

> But he gives greater grace. Therefore he says:
> God resists the proud, but gives grace to the humble.

This promise, also quoted by Peter in 1 Peter 5:5, comes from Proverbs 3:34:

> He mocks those who mock,
> but gives grace to the humble.

What does it mean that God resists the proud? Well, the word hardly needs elaboration. Simply put, he is against you. He is not ambivalent or undecided; God is decidedly against the proud. Bill Elliff uses the metaphor of playing football in the NFL. You are on the line, and across from you is a lineman who weighs over three hundred pounds. He is not ambivalent about your presence. No, he is against you. He resists you. The force that resists the proud is God himself.

Pride is a form of spiritual plagiarism. It is taking credit for what God and others have done in our lives. God knows that this is not right, and he rejects us. The same God that exiled Israel due to their pride is the God who exiles us. The person who is full of himself will, in the end, only have himself. He is exiled to do life on his own with his own resources. God not only resists the proud; he isolates the proud—exiled to their own powers, abilities, and desires.

God resists the proud. God exiles the proud. Pride is synonymous with loneliness. When we think of ourselves in terms of singular goodness, we are left with just ourselves. A day would come when the children of Israel would weep when they thought of their glory days.

We are given other reasons for why God is so angry with them. They have incurred general guilt (v. 22), they have forgotten God and trusted in lies (v. 25), and they have committed the spiritual equivalents of adultery and depraved prostitution (v. 27). The enemy from the north is coming. Israel will be exiled. But like a leopard that cannot change its spots, the nation cannot repent from its sin.

Again, pride is the mother of all sins. The taproot of all these sins is the sin of pride.

Conclusion

Rather than a taproot and a tree, perhaps a better metaphor would be a centrifuge—an instrument used in laboratories. The centrifuge spins at a high rate of speed. Denser particles are pushed to the outside, and less dense particles are borne toward the center. Thus, the centrifuge gives researchers the ability to understand which particles are denser by spinning them off to the sides.

Unlike a vortex that draws things to its center, a centrifuge repels them. So this grocery list of sins is actually created with the singular centrifugal force of pride. That's all. When pride is actively rotating in our hearts, multiple sins spin off from it. A life of sin is the symptom of pride spinning in the heart. It is the force that pushes the heavy seeds of sin to fully mature action.

This tough passage ends with an appeal in verse 27: How long will you be unclean? What is the specific length of time you will stay proud and dirty? Good question. Hopeful question. It implies that we prideful people are not destined for pride.

In other words, the centrifuge can be turned off. If we want to stop spinning out sin into our marriages, our parenting, and our work and schooling, then we need to be purified by the Word that crushes all pride. And this is the good news: since all sin is rooted in pride, if we attack pride, we turn off the source that is spinning sin out into our lives. Pride leads to exile, but the exile from God is not predetermined. We can crush it under the weight of the Word, then we can repent and be made clean.

This is because Jesus Christ, our Savior, modeled the ultimate form of humility. He humbled himself to the point of death (Phil 2:5-11). In his ultimate trajectory of humility, we are able to have true salvation.

This passage is a warning against pride. Yet the strange irony is that the prideful cannot repent. They cannot turn because they cannot hear the Word. Pride keeps us from God's Word, and God's Word keeps us from pride. Pride exiles us. Yet your exile is not your destiny.

The cause is not hopeless. Every warning is a hope. Grace overcomes hopelessness. Repent and be clean.

Reflect and Discuss

1. What is the one driving thought of this passage?
2. In what way is pride the mother of all sins? Was Augustine correct when he called humility the chief Christian virtue?
3. What are the two powerful word pictures God gives Jeremiah (13:1-7,12-14), and how do these word pictures relate to pride?
4. What are the "fruits of pride" Jeremiah discusses in this passage?
5. How does the sin of pride spoil and destroy?
6. How do abused blessings become a curse? Explain.
7. What do Hebrews 2–3 and James 4 say about pride?
8. What does it mean for God to resist the proud?
9. In what way is pride a form of spiritual plagiarism?
10. What was the specific warning of exile in this passage? How does Jeremiah relate the exile of Israel to their incessant pride?

Sunset Repentance

JEREMIAH 14:1–15:9

Main Idea: It can be too late to repent.

I. **A Confusing Confession: God Responds to Pretense in Prayer (14:7-12).**
   A. Plea (14:7-9)
   B. Refusal (14:10-12)
II. **A Confusing Message: God Condemns Lying Preachers (14:13-18).**
III. **A Confusing Confession: God Responds to Procrastination in Repentance (14:19–15:9).**
   A. Plea (14:19-22)
   B. Refusal (15:1-9)

Sitting across from my desk is a guilty student. He has been caught breaking the ethical code of conduct at our college. The offense warrants expulsion. He is facing calling his parents and letting them know he has been kicked out of school. My responsibility, in this moment, is to adjudicate the right way to move forward. We must uphold the integrity of the campus by respecting the code of conduct, yet I want to be redemptive. So I listen closely.

As the conversation continues, something becomes clear to me. This student is indeed sorry, but I'm not sure why. I do not know if this is regret leading to remorse or repentance leading to change. It's just unclear. My fogginess is a result of the student's attitude. He seems to think that while his action was wrong, he can bounce back. In fact the real problem, if he could put a fine point on it, is me. He can do this. He just needs a second chance. If I will do what I am supposed to do, he can get on in life. It would be a shame if I held him back from his goals because I would not extend a little grace.

While he may get a second chance, a second chance is almost always lost on those who think they deserve one. Rather, those who anguish over the consequences of their choices actually have the opportunity to change them—to repent. The bite and sting of sin's consequences are the fuel of genuine repentance and change.

This is the position in which Judah finds itself in Jeremiah 14. They've had so many chances to repent, to change. They have neglected so many prophets—so many warnings unheeded, so much sin, so much rebellion, so much rejection of the God who loves them. We often think change takes a long time, and it does. To move our lives from one position to the next tier of virtue, the next level of discipline, or the next goal takes time. We don't like the inconvenient truth that the opposite is true, yet at a faster rate. When we neglect God, there is a moment-by-moment hardening of our hearts—baked-on sin that is not easily removed. This is the sense of this difficult passage.

It has grown so dark that God finally says he is done. They have squandered their one-hundredth second chance. Finally, it seems, God has had enough. In this passage he makes strong statements such as, "Do not pray for the well-being of these people. . . . I will not accept [their offerings]" (14:11-12).

There is no doubt that this is a strong word in a book of strong words. God could not be more clear. He is done. There will not be another chance.

The structure of the passage—a dialogue between God and his people—is telling. Twice they plead to God for help, and twice God refuses.

- Plea   14:7-9
- Refusal   14:10-12
- Plea   14:19-22
- Refusal   15:1-9

This dialogue, along with the context (14:1-6) and the condemnation of lying prophets (14:13-16), gives a sense of the structure of the passage.

This leads us to a question: If we rebel for so long, does God finally give up? Is there a point of no return?

Context: Drought (14:1-6)

The setting of the conversation is drought. Though the impact of this is lost on many in the West, drought can ravage a country. The description here is awful. The people are crying for help (v. 2) because they come to the wells, but there is no water (v. 3). The farmers cannot produce crops (v. 4), the doe cannot feed her young (v. 5), and the donkey pants in the air with no water to drink and no vegetation to eat (v. 6). This is a horribly desperate situation.

One immediately thinks of the cracked cisterns of 2:13. The drought is in its own way a metaphor for the soul of Judah. They are stricken with the consequences of their choice to quench their thirst with something that can never satisfy. They have been swimming in the muddy, salty water of depravity, lust, and rejection of their God, and they come up thirsty for the fresh living water. This is the story of the woman at the well of John 4. She drank and drank but was still thirsty. Jesus then offers her living water that causes a cessation of thirst. The desperate longing for refreshment ceases because the individual is perfectly satisfied.

However, to be clear, this drought is not just a metaphor. This is real. Crops are wilting, livestock are dying, and the people of Judah fear for their own future and the immediate future of their children. Imagine the Dust Bowl of the 1930s. People were not just thirsty, but they also could not grow crops and the livestock were dying. The dry was killing them.

In Judah's darkest moment they cry out to God.

A Confusing Confession: God Responds to Pretense in Prayer
JEREMIAH 14:7-12

Plea (14:7-9)

The drought seems to have created a thirst for God. They call on God to act on their behalf while they confess their rebellion to God (v. 7). Also at this time Judah begins to confess that God is their hope (v. 8). Now this is interesting.

Physical desperation produces a spiritual desperation. Pressure helps us understand our spiritual state. Perhaps this is why Jesus constantly warned the rich. For example, in Matthew 6:24 he warned,

> *No one can serve two masters, since either he will hate one and love the other, or he will be devoted to one and despise the other. You cannot serve both God and money.*

The problem with money is never money. That is the presenting problem. Yet in counseling, as in all of life, rarely is the presenting problem the real problem. The problem, Jesus said, with a focus on possessions is that as our wealth grows it produces grappling hooks in our heart. And, to the point of this passage, they produce a false sense of security.

This is why the poor are blessed and the rich are warned (Luke 6:20,24; 16:14-31). The poor get it. Their physical desperation mirrors their spiritual desperation. The wealthy have the same spiritual desperation, but they don't know it. The wealth has provided a cover of comfort that masks real need. So in this way the wealthy are dumber than the poor, or at least less insightful. The mental liquid of wealth seeps into the part of the brain that assesses spiritual need, and they assume, quite understandably, that their spiritual needs are met by material wealth. Everything seems all right—like Novocain for the soul.

In the kingdom, therefore, poverty is a blessing because it actually corresponds with poverty of spirit. And here in Jeremiah an entire nation is broken by desperation. The drought is a metaphor for spiritual drought, but again, this is not just a metaphor. Their crops and livestock are dying. Life is changing. Aspirations for a clear and comfortable future are evaporating like the morning fog.

Their prayer, while authentic, also seems disingenuous. They pray and confess their sins in verse 7, and they acknowledge that God is among them, but something odd is sitting in these two bookends. They accuse God of being like a traveler who will only stay for a night, just passing through (v. 8). Further, they accuse him of being like a weak warrior (v. 9). Sure he is a warrior, but they say he is passive; he can't help.

While this is a confession, it's certainly a confused one. In fact, God has been present with them for a long time and has pursued them! He is anything but a transient traveler or a weak warrior! This is a twisted take on reality. Imagine Lewis Carroll, the author of *Alice in Wonderland*, is rewriting the story of the prodigal son. In this version the prodigal son wakes up in the pigpen and wonders why the dad won't come visit him. Why is the dad so passive? Why is the dad so weak? It's laughable, but Judah has been so sinful for so long, they can't even think straight. So God responds.

Refusal (14:10-12)

Notice the Hebrew parallelism of verse 10. The line that God speaks is reinforced and strengthened by its parallel. This makes for a provocative condemnation and is a synopsis of the whole chapter in one verse. The force of the poetry is, "It's not just that they wander, but they never put their feet up to rest from all their wandering." God's response is, "It's not only that I do not accept them, but I am remembering the guilt and punishing the sin." Judah was not just sinning; they were tirelessly sinning. God is not just ignoring them; he is actively punishing them. Neither party is passive. God will be as active in his punishment as they are in their sin. It's so bad that God tells Jeremiah not even to pray for them. God is done. Prayer won't have any effect.

So, after reading this, how do we reconcile this with the earlier idea that when God gives a warning it implies that there is hope? There seems to be absolutely no hope! Let's address that question at the end of the next plea and response.

There is another plea and response, but interjected between these two pairs is a specific problem God wants to address, namely, the lying prophets. So we will look at the second plea, but first let's read about this specific prayer request Jeremiah brings to God.

A Confusing Message: God Condemns Lying Preachers
JEREMIAH 14:13-18

The problem, Jeremiah asserts, about God's condemnation of Judah is that the prophets who are supposedly speaking for God are deceptive (v. 13). God is threatening punishment while they are promising peace. Jeremiah sees this as an inconsistent, confusing message.

God responds to Jeremiah (vv. 14-16). The prophets will meet the same end that they are predicting will never happen. They are, unwittingly, prophets of irony. They will die by the judgment they do not believe exists. You get the sense that they treat God as an impersonal force. However, God is real. He can really be offended, and he can enforce judgment on those who disobey him.

God is not just creating an irony; he is responding to one. The real irony here of course is not that God is going to give them what they do not think exists but that they are representatives of God who do not represent God. They were to be ambassadors, yet they went out—unsent, without any authority, without permission or commission—and spoke for God. An ambassador has no authority when he speaks on his own. By definition an ambassador represents another person. So God responds (vv. 17-18).

And here again we see the stupidity of sin. The confusing message comes from prophets who go to a "land they do not know." This is perhaps a reference to exile, or, perhaps more likely, it is a telling indictment of their stupidity. They are leaders who do not know where they are going. An old T-shirt said, "I'm their leader. Which way did they go?" This might be laughable on a shirt, but it was tragically true in this case. The prophets were really pawns at the hands of sin. The people chose the life they wanted to live and then affirmed and encouraged the prophets that told them what they already wanted to know.

A Confusing Confession: God Responds to Procrastination in Repentance
JEREMIAH 14:19–15:9

Plea (14:19-22)

Here is another confusing confession. The confession here seems authentic on the surface. The people cry out to God. They acknowledge their sin and express their concern that the heavens are silent (vv. 19-20). Then they do something good but, in this context, too late. They invoke the name of God (v. 21).

God's name was sacred. It was only spoken in the most serious ways. So they say that their motivation for confession is the name of God. They then acknowledge that only Yahweh, their covenant God, has the power to allow drought or bring rain (v. 22).

Refusal (15:1-9)

Confession is the right prayer, God's name is the right motivation, and that only God can do it is the right hope. It's all correct, accurate. The problem is that it is just too late. God responds in 15:1-9. Judah will experience "four kinds of judgment."

There is not much else to say. Reading this leaves one breathless. Even if the two leading intercessor-prophets of a bygone era, Moses and Samuel, would plead on their behalf, it would be fruitless. Their end is destruction, and God will not change his course.

This challenges a notion we mentioned back in the first chapter, namely, that each warning was a mercy. A warning, by definition, is a means of hope, of escape from pending judgment, yet here it seems that there is no escape. So, how is this merciful in any way? Well, in its immediate context, it's not. Perhaps you have heard someone use the patently obvious phrase, *It is what it is.* Yet in this case, it applies perfectly. The judgment of God is the judgment of God. But here it is important to remember that preexilic Judah is not the only audience.

Judah, like Israel, would go into exile. The Babylonians would take them into captivity. The Babylonians would be taken over by the Assyrians and then eventually by the Persians. Then comes the Persian King Darius who would decide, providentially prompted, that the people should return to their land (2 Chr 36:22-23). When they did return to their land, they were led by Ezra the scribe, who would skillfully study the law (Ezra 7:10) and then faithfully declare it (Neh 8:1-8). It is logical to assume that a newly returning people, reenergized in their love for God, would read Jeremiah's words. So the words of Jeremiah were written to those coming out of exile as well as those going into exile. For those going in there was no hope. For those coming out this was a great warning. They did not want to face the wrath of God in a similar way.

Conclusion

Jeremiah 14:1–15:9 was written for the moment and for later. Right now is later. Meaning, if you will, there have been at least three intended audiences for this text: the preexilic nation, the postexilic nation, and us. You. Me. So what does this passage teach us? What is the meaning in front of the text?

God Takes Sin Seriously

What we know about the seriousness of sin is explored by what God has revealed about himself since the time of Jeremiah:

- God will punish sin, and some will be given over to their sin (Rom 1:16-32). So to the question of our introduction, yes, there is a point of no return. There can be a time when God says that he has had enough. When is that time? The answer is simply, do not tempt God. If you do not know him, then repent now. Change. Turn and ask him to save you today (Heb 3:7-19).
- When a believer sins, God, like a loving Father, will discipline the believer (Heb 12:2-17).
- The ultimate expression of God's hatred toward sin is what Christ experienced on the cross for our sin (John 19).

God Rejects Lying Preachers

Read Ezekiel 34 and you will see how God feels about shepherds who do not act like shepherds. He rejects them because he loves his sheep.

Read John 10 to discover how Jesus is the opposite of a lying preacher. He is the *good* Shepherd.

Judgment on Others Is a Warning for Us

A smart person learns from his mistakes, but a wise person learns from the mistakes of others. This is not just a truism; it is a foundational principle for interpreting the Old Testament. We read a history of a people because we want to learn how we ourselves should be warned. The book of Hebrews is written using the nation of Israel as a warning to us individually as believers. As Paul would say explicitly in 1 Corinthians 10:11, "These things happened to them as examples, and they were written for our instruction, on whom the ends of the ages have come."

God hates sin. God punishes every sin that has ever been committed. Either the punishment for our sin is taken upon us, or it is redirected from God toward Christ on the cross, where he absorbed the weight of God's wrath for the sins of the world. The cross is at once hope and warning. Yes, the cross is Christ reaching up to heaven and down to us. But the stretched arms of Jesus are a warning. Jesus's arms are held up to warn us to stay back, not to enter into the hell of God's wrath from which there is no return—from which no one at all, in heaven or on earth, can save us. So read and be warned.

Reflect and Discuss

1. What do Jeremiah 14 and 15 teach us about the timing and promptness of repentance? Can we, as believers, repent too late? What are the consequences of repenting in a sluggish manner?
2. What were the two confusing confessions and the one confusing message of 14:1–15:9?
3. Did God refuse the pleas of Israel in this passage? If so, why?
4. If we rebel for so long, does God finally give up? Is there a point of no return?
5. Is the drought metaphor in 14:2-6 a physical or spiritual drought?
6. In what way does physical desperation lead to spiritual desperation? How does God use the physical circumstances in our lives to produce a spiritual thirst for him?
7. Who are the three audiences of Jeremiah 14:1–15:9? Was the text written for then, now, or later?

8. How do we know from this passage that God takes sin seriously? What do Romans 1:16-32; Hebrews 12:2-17; and John 19 teach us about how God views sin?
9. What does Jeremiah teach us about lying preachers? How does God view lying preachers? Panning out in Scripture, what do Ezekiel 34 and John 10 teach us about lying preachers?
10. How are we, as Christians, to understand God's judgment on others? What lessons of warning can we ascertain from God's judgment on others?

The Disillusioned Believer

JEREMIAH 15:10-21

Main Idea: When disillusionment descends into self-pity, repentance is paramount.

I. Complaining Can Lead to Disillusionment (15:10-14).
II. Complaining Can Lead to Bitterness and Resentment (15:15-17).
III. Complaining Can Lead to Self-Pity (15:18).
IV. How Does God Respond to Self-Pity (15:19-21)?
    A. A condition (15:19)
    B. A promise (15:20-21)

I still remember the gnarly grass of our makeshift football practice field—small patches of crabgrass amid the dirt. It was not designed for long sits. The youth pastor at our church was to give a challenging devotional to the guys before practice that day and, though he shared it years ago, I remember his testimony. He was mentored by someone who had a severe physical handicap but never complained. This was his life lesson for us: never complain. It was a great reminder during two-a-days in August. Playing a sport was a recreational privilege—a privilege that demanded hard work. Never. Never. Complain.

When I would take mission trips with students, I established complaining as a cardinal sin—one that would get you a trip home. Complaining reveals a self-orientation. Complaining suggests that the circumstances of life do not meet the expectations I have set for everyone and everything else in my life, so, no matter how it affects someone else, I am going to verbalize my dissent with life. It is the responsibility of the loving parent, caring friend, or committed family member to keep others' complaining in check. While accountability is uncomfortable, complaining left unchecked leads to another place—to self-pity.

This is where we find Jeremiah. His complaints are leading him to self-pity. This issue leads us to questions, some more relevant than others.

First, *Is complaining ever warranted?* The answer is of course in the eye of the beholder. We joke about "first-world problems" of poor Wi-Fi connections and slow smartphones. These are hardly justifiable complaints when painted on the canvas of the world's ubiquitous suffering. So complaining seems ill advised.

This raises the second question: *What does this say about the nature of Scripture?* As noted before, Scripture includes many complaints. This helps us understand the perfection of Scripture. Scripture freely records complaints without passing judgment on the complainants. So, what does God do when we complain?

Context

We would certainly be sympathetic with Jeremiah's complaint. He is sent on a difficult errand to preach, to re-present God's words to a people who do not love God or want to hear what he says. The frequent references to the false prophets throughout the book testify that the people have chosen to displace true prophets with ones who say what they want to hear. Jeremiah has competition. In fact, when God called him, he called him "to uproot and tear down, to destroy and demolish, to build and plant." There are twice as many negatives here as positives. Few, if any, wanted to hear this message.

God is going to hear the complaint of Jeremiah and respond.

Christopher Wright identifies three sources of his complaining: disillusionment, bitterness and resentment, and self-pity (*Message of Jeremiah*, 176–82).

Complaining Can Lead to Disillusionment
JEREMIAH 15:10-14

Jeremiah's general complaint is that he is the source of "dispute and conflict" (v. 10). This is intensified by the fact that he did not do anything wrong. He has not personally wronged anyone, yet they curse him. In fact, he rues the day of his birth. This is interesting because he was called in his mother's womb:

> *The word of the LORD came to me:*
> *I chose you before I formed you in the womb;*
> *I set you apart before you were born.*
> *I appointed you a prophet to the nations.* (1:4-5)

Is 15:10 Jeremiah's backhanded way of rejecting his call? He is not just complaining about his immediate situation but the *source* of his situation: his call to this difficult ministry. He's not just complaining; the feeling of the text is that he wants to walk away—to trade a calling for a job.

The life of ministry is not for the faint of heart. There are many things that a preacher *can* do that he never *will* do because of his call.

God graciously responds to Jeremiah's complaint in two ways. First, he affirms his protection for Jeremiah (v. 11). God will take care of him, though his enemies are strong and numerous.

Second, God affirms Jeremiah's call by affirming the inevitability of the coming events (vv. 12-14). Judah *would* be taken into captivity by Babylon. The events were so sure it was as strong as "iron from the north."

However, Jeremiah has more than disillusionment with his call. His unchecked disillusionment is leading to bitterness and resentment.

Complaining Can Lead to Bitterness and Resentment
JEREMIAH 15:15-17

Jeremiah identifies the source of his problem: God (v. 15). Jeremiah is suffering disgrace, and he is doing it for God—for the sake of the call. His bitterness is now compounded because he clearly doesn't deserve such trouble. This is why he is so upset. His expectations are unmet. This type of thing should not happen to this type of man. It's not reasonable.

First, Jeremiah loved the word of God (v. 16a). Second, Jeremiah was called by God (v. 16b). Third, Jeremiah did not associate with those who hated God (v. 17). In fact, he was filled with godly indignation against that type of people. It just did not seem justifiable that such bad things should happen to such an obedient person. So with all of that, why would God treat him this way? In this passage Jeremiah says he is like the man of Psalm 1:1-3. He loves the word of God and does not associate with sinners. The man of Psalm 1 is the blessed man, but Jeremiah feels like the cursed man. Why is this happening?

Typically a blessing is indeed attached to obedience. This is clear enough from Scripture. However, a blessing is not a right or mandate. A blessing is just that: a blessing. It is given at the dictate and will of the divine Blesser. Since those he blesses do not have his perfect wisdom, it stands to reason that they will not always understand why he gives and takes away. This is a mercy, of course, but it is also a mystery.

The mystery of missing blessing is leading Jeremiah down the road of bitterness. Tragically, perhaps, this bitterness is leading to self-pity.

Complaining Can Lead to Self-Pity
JEREMIAH 15:18

Jeremiah asks, *Why am I in this situation that will never go away?* It is like a wound that will not heal. The thought of relief cannot be conceived.

Then he uses a telling metaphor for God: God is like a mirage. A mirage is a problem because it appears real, but a mirage never quenched any thirsts. A mirage never refreshes. A mirage never heals. The mind is playing tricks on the body. This is how we feel in the low point of self-pity: we cannot be healed, and it is God's fault.

Remember, self-pity is self-induced and therefore is self-oriented. It is not required or demanded. It is something we bring on ourselves.

So how does God respond to complaining that leads to disillusionment, bitterness, and self-pity? Jeremiah is told to repent.

How Does God Respond to Self-Pity?
JEREMIAH 15:19-21

Jeremiah had gone too far. In resenting his call, developing bitterness against others, and manifesting self-pity, he had sinned. The call was a privilege but a hard privilege. God never promised that it would be easy or filled with affirmation. "By accusing God of deceiving him and of failing him when he needed him, Jeremiah had overstepped the bounds of what a servant of God can say" (Huey, *Jeremiah, Lamentations,* 163).

God then rebukes him (v. 19a). It is a simple and clear call to change his heart and to seek God and his call on his life. Yet, while the call is clear, it is also conditional. God expects things. The expectations God gives here serve as a model for ministry.

A Condition (15:19)

God was going to restore him. That was clear enough. However, the restoration was conditioned on a fresh commitment to God's word. This may be the most concise statement on the call in Scripture: the choice to speak noble words and not worthless words. This is the antithesis of the prophets who were running when not sent and speaking before they had heard from God.

A Promise (15:20-21)

Once Jeremiah decides that he will speak God's words and not his own words, God makes some specific promises. First, God will make him impenetrable (v. 20). This clearly does not mean a life free from attack. Rather, while he will be beaten, he will not be broken. As Paul would later say, "We are afflicted in every way but not crushed; we are perplexed but not in despair; we are persecuted but not abandoned; we are struck down but not destroyed" (2 Cor 4:8-9).

Second is a promise of deliverance (v. 21). Even though he will be attacked, he will not be broken, and even though he will be faced with powerful and evil people, he will not be under their control. Is there anything else one could ask for in ministry? We could of course ask to never face any hard people, but that is not ministry in any meaningful sense. Hardened people are in need of ministry. This is a good thing because ministering to hard people develops "hide" on the minister who is called to speak to them. This is Christian ministry: the ability to listen to God in the still quiet moments and then to take those insights where people do not respond. Soft heart, thick skin.

Perhaps this is why in Titus 1:8-9 Paul told Titus to find men to pastor churches who would hold "to the faithful message as taught, so that he will be able both to encourage with sound teaching and to refute those who contradict it." A true pastor is both a lover and a fighter. Or more accurately, he fights because he loves. He loves God's Word, so he is a steward of the Word, but he loves God's people, so he is a shepherd of the sheep.

Conclusion

The existence of a disillusioned pastor may be more common than we know. Or perhaps it is not common enough. Jeremiah descended into self-pity because he was obedient. Don't miss this. Jeremiah's depression is not the hangover brought by the guilt of last night's sin. He is not waking up to find that he has played fast and loose with the prompting of the Holy Spirit to his own demise. This is the residue of righteousness, what remains when someone has a long obedience in the same direction, as Eugene Peterson terms it. This is the ten-year pin of faithful service. He is suffering because his message was so contrary to the direction of the culture that he was understandably maligned, mistreated, abused, and eventually threatened with death. Perhaps we are not more disillusioned because our message of hope, peace, and prosperity can, in some synchronistic way, share the same vocabulary with a world that does not want suffering at any price—a world whose god is comfort and guilt-free sin. We are not discouraged by how the world treats us because we feigned niceties in order to be accepted by them. So, while we never want to be disillusioned, we should want the same obedience Jeremiah had.

Perhaps we struggle with disillusionment but for all the wrong reasons. We have expectations that God is obligated to provide a certain comfort in life, a certain set of circumstances, a certain gravitas in our career and grace to our life. Yet the life promised to the follower of Jesus Christ is no greater than the life of Christ. Jesus promised a discipling equity: If they hated Jesus, they will hate us. We are the mediator between a God who demands holiness and a world that demands its right to be unholy. How can we, under any circumstance, avoid that tension?

So, in a strange way, there is a disillusionment that would be natural for a believer. This cannot be avoided. What can be avoided is the descent of disillusionment into bitterness and self-pity. Disillusionment is unavoidable, while self-pity is a choice—a choice of which we can repent.

Reflect and Discuss

1. How does God initially respond to Jeremiah's disillusionment (v. 15)?
2. Compare verse 15 with Psalm 51:10-12.
3. What is the difference between David's restoration in Psalm 51 and Jeremiah's restoration in Jeremiah 15?
4. What other Scriptures speak of God's responding to us in similar ways?
5. How was God like a mirage to Jeremiah (v. 18)?
6. Can you relate to the word picture of God's being a mirage?
7. Can you think of other biblical characters who had what they thought were genuine complaints against God?
8. Why is Jeremiah in an emotional tailspin?
9. Distinguish between being distraught because of sin and being distraught because of obedience and faithfulness.
10. What do we do if we find ourselves disillusioned?

Prominence

JEREMIAH 16

Main Idea: When we mentally replace God's prominence, we will practically doubt God's dominance.

I.   **The Warning: Don't Challenge God's Prominence (16:1-13).**
II. **The Promise: God Will Restore His People (16:14-18).**
III. **The Warning: Don't Question God's Prominence (16:19-21).**

Introduction: The Waiting

As I was a single man for a long time, someone once gave me this piece of advice: "Don't worry about getting married because the only thing worse than being single is wishing you were." Many people have entered a relationship with someone only to later regret the decision. They wanted the spouse they didn't have, and now they don't want the spouse they do have. Patience is necessary if we are going to have God's best in marriage. The issue is not marriage but the wisdom to wait on the Lord and receive what he has as the best for us. As someone said, God's delays are not always his denials. Sometimes God, always wanting the best for us, forces us to wait for that best until a later time.

Has God ever told you to wait for something? Waiting on God is rarely easy. My father often says, "God is never late, but he is rarely early." That phrase expresses the sentiment that it is difficult to understand God's timing, much less sync with it. God is gracious to us, and his mercies are new every morning. This means we have mercy for each morning. It does not mean we will have the clarity we want every morning. I've noticed that I have grace for each thing I face, but rarely do I have the grace before I need it. This is the walk of faith. This is what it means to wait on God. Waiting on God is not passive; it's aggressive. Here is a good definition of waiting on God: *Doing everything I can do until God comes and does what I can't do.* Meaning, I am acting as a good steward of the current situation in which God has me, until he provides clarity for what is next. I am doing what I already know to do until he intervenes. The point is that stewardship of current situations precedes further revelation. What's now, then what's next.

Waiting is not idleness. Waiting is the difficult work of quietly and doggedly positioning ourselves for what God will bring later.

The beautiful prayer of Psalm 5:3 encourages us. David writes,

In the morning, LORD, you hear my voice;
in the morning I plead my case to you and watch expectantly.

What a remarkable position! This prayer expresses trust. All the pressure is on God to come though in this situation. This prayer expresses confidence in God's ability to act: God, I am waiting on your reply because I can't fix this myself. A person who is forced to trust in God is not in a bad position. This is why pressure is often positive. Pressure is the splint that protects broken thinking from becoming "set." It allows us to know the joy of dependence on God.

This was God's call to Jeremiah: Do not get married and start a family with the people in this land. God was not trying to punish Jeremiah; he was trying to protect him. The people of the land were about to be punished. Why would it make sense for Jeremiah to begin a relationship with these people and, by extension, bring wrath on himself? So God keeps from him something he might want in order to protect him from something he knows he does not want. When God does this, it might seem like God is being difficult. Why doesn't God just give us what we want? However, this warning is not the hardest part of Jeremiah 16. This chapter calls for Jeremiah to create a strong distance between himself and the people in profound ways.

The Warning: Don't Challenge God's Prominence
JEREMIAH 16:1-13

God was calling Jeremiah not to get involved in order to protect him from the wrath that was coming. God gives him several commands.

Don't Marry into the Families (16:2)

Again, the reason for the warning is that God is protecting him from penalty by association. He would be hurt with his proximity to the punished people. Yet the next warning is stronger than personal protection.

Don't Mourn for Them (16:5-9)

Jeremiah was not even to participate in the mourning process when they were killed and punished by God.

Why was he to create this actual physical and seemingly emotional distance from them? The answer is that God was protecting Jeremiah. Why fall in love with someone and entangle yourself with a family that will soon be destroyed? Why give your passions to something that will be so short-lived? God is not trying to punish Jeremiah; he is trying to parent Jeremiah. He is trying to protect him from the coming disaster.

Imagine a father who denied his daughter a trip on the maiden voyage of the *Titanic*. The daughter would have been heartbroken at first but grateful later. Aren't we all glad we don't get what we ask for when we ask for it? God is too loving to give us what we think we need. He is too kind to play those games. Something much bigger is going on.

The Promise: God Will Restore His People
JEREMIAH 16:14-18

Consistent with so much of Jeremiah, here is another desert rose, a beautifully refreshing breath of fresh air in the godforsaken smog of sin and judgment. God promises that he will return them to the promised land (vv. 14-15). What a promise! He will restore them. But he will do it after severe discipline (vv. 16-18).

So that is what is going to happen. How it plays out in the future has an interesting connection back to Jeremiah 16. God again will promise a time of restoration, a time of a future, and a hope. This comes to pass after verses 16-18 are fulfilled. Under the ugly reign of Zedekiah, the last vestiges of Judah's pride are torn down, and the nation is officially decimated and demolished. This is itself a warning to us. God is not unwilling to tear down what he has built if those who built it commit these two egregious sins: they have idolatry in their hearts (vv. 11-13), and they do not acknowledge God's strength (v. 21). These twin sins will ultimately bring Judah low, and apparently they are the sins motivating this verdict.

After the nation had been in captivity for a long time, Ezra the scribe realizes that the seventy years of exile are complete, and he senses that he is seeing the fulfillment of the promise given to Jeremiah. In Ezra 1:1-4 he writes,

> *In the first year of King Cyrus of Persia, in order to fulfill the word of the LORD spoken through Jeremiah, the LORD roused the spirit of King Cyrus to issue a proclamation throughout his entire kingdom and to put it in writing:*

> *This is what King Cyrus of Persia says:* "*The* LORD, *the God of the heavens, has given me all the kingdoms of the earth and has appointed me to build him a house at Jerusalem in Judah.*
> *Any of his people among you, may his God be with him, and may he go to Jerusalem in Judah and build the house of the* LORD, *the God of Israel, the God who is in Jerusalem.*
> *Let every survivor, wherever he resides, be assisted by the men of that region with silver, gold, goods, and livestock, along with a freewill offering for the house of God in Jerusalem.*"

So now it's on. The judgment is lifted, and the people begin the return. Except that this attempt, and another one under Zerubbabel, are both ineffectual. Enter Nehemiah. When Nehemiah comes on the scene, we find that he is brokenhearted, presumably because he does not see God fulfilling his promise to Jeremiah.

God uses Nehemiah to bring the people back, and almost as if in a direct reaction to Jeremiah 16, Nehemiah repents of the sins of the past (Neh 1:6-7) and attributes his success to the good hand of God that was on him (Neh 2:8,18). While Jeremiah pictures God as a God who is bringing judgment along with his faithful love, Nehemiah paints God as a God of strength.

In a sense Nehemiah is blessed because he is repenting of idolatry and attributing all the strength to God. In his humble obedience he fulfills Jeremiah 16. After seventy-plus years God's people know he is a God of strength. They know, they really know, he is the Lord.

The Warning: Don't Question God's Prominence
JEREMIAH 16:19-21

The last two verses of the chapter are powerful. In these verses we have the great twin sins of Judah.

The first great sin is idolatry. They illustrated that they forsook God by going after false gods and serving them (vv. 11-13). This is tragic. Jeremiah describes them as gods that are "not gods" (v. 20). The logic of Jeremiah is simple: "If gods are really gods, can they be created?" However, this logic is lost on the nation, as they are hell-bent on following after the gods and chasing them. The result is that they will be cast into the land of the false gods that they embraced (v. 13).

God is so frustratedly angry with them because they fail to recognize God's power in the calamities they are experiencing. This is the second great sin that is always tied to the first: not recognizing God's power. It is an insult to his name. Thus, God says he will "make them know" (v. 21). In other words, what seems to have been forgotten he will put right in front of them in a way so undeniable that they will have to relent and acknowledge his power.

The first sin is believing there was something to the false gods and worshiping them. The second great sin is either the result of or a consequence of the first: It is attributing a power to the god that it does not really have and thus not recognizing God's supreme power. This is the situation in which they find themselves. First, they had displaced God as their object of worship, and second, they had failed to recognize his power.

One always follows the other. When we replace God's prominence, we will doubt God's dominance. If we doubt that he is worthy of the centrality of our worship, our affection, our emotion, our love, and our devotion, then ultimately we must question whether he is strong enough to be Lord. This is the main idea of the passage. It comes as a warning: when we replace God's prominence, we will doubt God's dominance.

God drives home the point by referring to himself as "Lord." This is Yahweh. He cannot be displaced, and he cannot be replaced. He will not be marginalized, sidelined, shelved, demoted, excluded, downgraded, or dismissed. He can't be. His name is "the Lord." Nothing is so big it can eclipse him, and nothing is so powerful it can threaten him. People who think otherwise are lying to themselves. They, for whatever reason, are believing what they want to believe, not the truth.

And this is the truth: when we mentally replace God's prominence, we will practically doubt God's dominance. God's response in Jeremiah's day is simple. He wants them to know this so that he can prove that he is dominant over all things. Therefore he says that he will show them that he is the Lord.

Conclusion/Application

So here's the question: Have you begun to mentally make God less prominent? We know that we could never make God less prominent (he will always be the center of all things). We also know we cannot change his dominance (he will always be all-powerful). Yet this is the problem with idolatry: it always plays in the realm of fantasy. Idolatry is always posing. Idolatry pretends it is reality when in fact it is fantasy.

This is why God makes so clear that Christ is supreme over all things. Four New Testament passages stand like giant beacons pointing to Christ: John 1; Philippians 2; Colossians 1; and Hebrews 1. These are often called the four major Christological passages in the New Testament. The whole New Testament points to Christ, but these are monoliths. They clarify for us who Christ is and what he has done. One thing they are clear about is the superiority of Christ. And the word *superior* requires no adjectives such as "great" or "ultimate." It is singular, needing no superlative ending. Christ is superior. Full stop.

Therefore, all idols are inferior.

So, what are the idols in my life? Have we made an idol of our bodies—worshiping and pampering them? Have we made an idol of our time—guarding it from one thing, even a kingdom thing, that would threaten it? Have we made an idol of our reputations—keeping people at arm's length so as not to make ourselves vulnerable? Have we made an idol of our egos—where people are unable to navigate around us socially without offending us? Have we made an idol of our money—hoarding it instead of unleashing it for kingdom advance? The list is endless. The point is to remember this remarkable truth: When we mentally replace God's prominence, we will practically doubt God's dominance. These are twin sins. Wherever one is, the other is right there along with it. If there is something in my life that wants my attention, affection, or emotion, and I relent and allow it to have that place in my life, then I concede affection that should belong only to God. This is a sad reality, but it is a reality nonetheless.

When we mentally replace God's prominence, we will practically doubt God's dominance.

Reflect and Discuss

1. Why was Jeremiah told not to marry?
2. What were considered challenges to God's prominence (vv. 2-9)?
3. What does this chapter have to do with Ezra 1:1-4?
4. How does this chapter relate to the work of Nehemiah?
5. What does Colossians 1:15-18 say about the prominence and centrality of Christ?
6. What are the two great sins of Judah (vv. 20-21)?
7. What is the significance of the name of "the LORD" in verse 21?
8. How is that both a comfort and a challenge?
9. What are idols we might be holding on to?
10. Why are those idols inferior to Christ?

The Anatomy of Hope

JEREMIAH 17

Main Idea: The trusting life is the blessed life.

I.   Trusting Self Is the Cursed Life (17:5-6).
II. Trusting God Is the Blessed Life (17:7-8).
III. God Knows Us More Than We Know Ourselves (17:9-11).
IV. Our Trust Is in the Lord (17:12-18).

So there you are in the middle of a crisis. Pressure is mounting on you, and you must make a decision. Gratefully you have already concluded that your immediate instinct in the moment was not correct. God, in that way, has saved you from yourself. Now to reflect and make the wisest choice. As you think about this, two options become apparent: you can trust in what you think is best, or you can trust in what God says is best.

As a pastor I counseled people countless times who made choices contrary to Scripture. They trusted in themselves, ignored Scripture, and then lived with the consequences of that choice. At times, perhaps most times, the person acted in what he thought was the wisest way because he did not know Scripture speaks to the issue. Some acted out of ignorance. However, and this is important, this is willful ignorance. If we do not know how God would lead us, it's often because we do not know his Word. But ignorance is a choice. God's Word brings life (Ps 119:40). To refuse to learn the Word is to refuse to learn to live. We can hurt ourselves and the ones we love by proactive neglect of the Word as much as by reactive rejection.

So, to speak plainly, we have to decide whom we will trust. Will we trust our own wishes and desires, or will we trust God? The problem you might be facing is not really the problem. The real dilemma is whether you will trust God.

The problem you are facing is simply the crucible in which you will exercise your freedom (the choice to do what you want) with true liberty (the freedom to do what is right). The result? Blessing or cursing. The blessed life is the trusting life.

In this way the road to the blessed life is counterintuitive. We are not trusting in ourselves; we are trusting in God. The trusting life is the blessed life.

So, in the midst of crises, whom do we trust?

Context (17:1-4)

Judah's sin is profound; this has been established. However, in this chapter God, in the same spirit as chapter 13, says there is no hope. Sin has left a permanent stain that cannot be removed; it is written on something more permanent than paper. The language is powerful (v. 1). The sin God has in mind is the specific sin of idolatry (vv. 2-3), and it comes with the price of losing the inheritance God wanted to give them (v. 4). Instead of living in the promised land, they will be serving in someone else's land—a land they do not even know.

Once again this is the ignorance brought on by sin. When they do not want to know God through his word, they will now wander in a land they do not know. All this ignorance is cultivated by a desire to know anything but God—to put something in the place of God as an object of worship. What they did with statues of wood and metal, we do more creatively.

Another specific sin God has in mind in the end of the chapter is the sin of breaking the Sabbath (vv. 19-27). While this may seem like a small sin compared to the sin of idolatry, the Sabbath-day ordinances were designed to make Israel unique. It was a sign of the covenant. To reject Sabbath observance was to refuse to honor God, who rested from his work on the seventh day.

The following verses reflect a shift in tone. Verses 5-11 are a collection of wisdom sayings, the kind of literature typical of Proverbs. As with Proverbs, the collected sayings are not necessarily clustered into groups by topic. However, there seems to be a theme here. While there is a curse for disobedience (vv. 5-6) and blessing for righteousness (vv. 7-8), we cannot even know our own hearts (vv. 9-10)! Our hope then is not in ourselves. Our hope is in God who sits on his throne (vv. 12-13). This is why Jeremiah can have hope in God as his refuge from trouble (vv. 14-18).

But we are getting ahead of ourselves. The best way to understand this text is to meditate on each of its individual components. So, where is our confidence? Whom do we trust?

Trusting Self Is the Cursed Life
JEREMIAH 17:5-6

The person who calls his own strength his greatest strength is the one who is cursed. This reminds us of Jeremiah 9:23-24.

> This is what the LORD says:
> The wise person should not boast in his wisdom;
> the strong should not boast in his strength;
> the wealthy should not boast in his wealth.
> But the one who boasts should boast in this:
> that he understands and knows me—
> that I am the LORD, showing faithful love,
> justice, and righteousness on the earth,
> for I delight in these things.
>   This is the LORD's declaration.

Notice the juxtaposition in 17:5-6. If a man calls himself his strength, he turns away from the Lord. The two ideas are tied together. To trust in your own strength is to turn from the Lord. The result is that he will be like a dry bush in the desert—parched and alone. This is what makes self-consultation so dangerous. We depend on our own knowledge and not on the wisdom of God. In the end we are solitary and withered.

We are not cacti that can exist and thrive on little water. We need the water of the Word to refresh us and bring life to us. So when someone trusts in himself, the result is that he is alone in that determination.

Trusting God Is the Blessed Life
JEREMIAH 17:7-8

Contrary to the cursed life is the blessed life. Look at the description. Blessed people have their confidence in the Lord. In other words, their moral, spiritual, and emotional compass understands that a relationship with God is the true north. Following him is where life is. When God's presence with us is our ambition, we have true direction, true wisdom, a true path.

The passage immediately brings to mind Psalm 1. The blessed man is like a tree that is "planted beside flowing streams." In other words, the blessed man is fruitful and productive. He prospers in what he does. The living tree does not fear when the pressure of heat is on. It is not worried about drought. It will not cease to produce fruit. Why would it not be worried about drought? The reason is not because it is immune to drought. The reason it has no fear is because of its location. It need not relocate to avoid the drought. The tree is located near the water. The drought will come, but the tree has a sustainable source of moisture in the water. God's Word, according to Jesus, is living water. The secret to the tree is not its strength but its source. Fear is quelled by its location.

This is a picture of the believer who has a right relationship with God through his Word. It's not that he will not go through the fire of persecution but that he will be sustained through the Word.

This is an important point. Our faith is in *God*, not in *our faith*. If our confidence is in our ability to live out our faith, this is simply a religious way of trusting in ourselves. I have seen in my own heart the temptation to have confidence in my own environment, my own way of thinking, my own Christian subculture. I find that the heart is just as likely to make an idol of good works as it is of material things. God knows our hearts.

God Knows Us More Than We Know Ourselves
JEREMIAH 17:9-11

We might say that we know our own hearts, but God thinks otherwise. God asserts that we do not have the wisdom to assess the deceitfulness of our own hearts (v. 9). This is a shocking thought. My own mind is a poor EKG for my heart. The results are always skewed with the optimism of my own perceived goodness. I really can't know my own heart. But God does (v. 10). So the Word functions like a mirror. It exposes us to ourselves.

This is because the Word exposes us to the presence of God. When we are exposed to his presence, then our own sickness is properly diagnosed. Like Isaiah, who saw a vision of the Lord and, when seeing God clearly, thought he was doomed (Isa 6). His assessment was that he was "ruined." Through. He was a man with a wicked mouth who came from a wicked people, and he was in the fearsome presence of the holy God.

Jeremiah follows this observation with an example of someone who has been self-deceived (v. 11). This proverb asserts that those who make money in unjust ways are like a bird that sits on another bird's eggs. However, in the end, what is "hatched" will fly away.

So our confidence is not in our own flesh because there is a curse there. Instead, we are experiencing the blessing of trusting in the Word of God. Yet we cannot trust in our perception of our walk with God. So where do we put our confidence? Here is a wonderful picture.

Our Trust Is in the Lord
JEREMIAH 17:12-18

A throne in heaven awaits those who trust in God (v. 12). This takes the mind to Revelation 4–5, where John paints the vivid and timeless picture of a throne in heaven. The throne is surrounded with creatures, elders, saints, and all living things who bow down and acknowledge that God is Lord of all things. In the next chapter of Revelation, John sees the identical scene with the exception that joining God at the throne is the Lamb of God. All of the praise centers on God on the throne and the Lamb. So, to be clear, this really exists. There is a place in heaven we will see one day where the glory of God sits.

As a result of this reality,

> LORD, the hope of Israel,
> all who abandon you will be put to shame.
> All who turn away from me will be written in the dirt,
> for they have abandoned the LORD,
> the fountain of living water. (Jer 17:13)

Notice the contrast between the writing here and the writing of verse 1. There the sins were permanent and would be remembered. And here, in a sad irony, the remembered sins lead to forgotten people. Their names and lives will dissipate as quickly as a name written in the dust. Why? They have abandoned the source of living water. This again brings to mind Jeremiah 2:13. They have traded off living water for stagnant cisterns that can hold no water.

This is the theological reality. Our trust is in God and his Word because our hearts are fixed on the coming reality of seeing the throne of the God who judges all.

Now the proverbs are over. Jeremiah is facing a personal dilemma. With all the trouble around him, he simply asks that God would be his refuge, his hiding place for protection during this time (vv. 14-18).

Conclusion

Imagine going to a doctor. He asks you how you feel. You explain your symptoms and talk for a while. Then, with no test, without examining you, he diagnoses you. That would be horrible! No doctor would ask how we feel then write a script based on our own self-perception.

Spiritually we don't make a prognosis based on self-diagnosis. There is a sense in which self-confidence is natural. In order to function in society, we must believe we have some such capacity. Yet there is a difference between a God-honoring confidence and self-reliance. The former comes from knowing who we are in Christ, the latter from an overinflated sense of our ability to lead ourselves.

Rather than trusting ourselves, we should trust God, who knows us better than ourselves. The trusting life is the blessed life.

Reflect and Discuss

1. What is the particular sin Judah is indicted for in 17:2-3?
2. Judah is guilty of another sin in 17:19-27. Name it.
3. What is the connection between Psalm 1 and Jeremiah 17:7-8?
4. Why is there a shift in tone in 17:5-11?
5. Jeremiah discusses the ignorance of the human heart in 17:9-10. Why is the adage "Listen to your heart" poor advice? What does Scripture say about the condition of the heart and man's ability to discern it?
6. Is it possible to trust in your own strength and trust God at the same time? Are these two behaviors mutually exclusive?
7. What is faith, and why is it absolutely necessary for the Christian life?
8. Discuss the irony of this passage. How is it that Judah's permanent sins would lead to a forgettable future?
9. Is there a difference between God-honoring confidence and self-reliance? If so, explain.
10. In what way does this passage undercut the mundane patterns of religiosity that permeate our hearts?

Brokenness

JEREMIAH 18–19

Main Idea: God will not break the broken.

I. **God Will Not Break the Broken (18:1-11).**
II. **We Can Remain Unbroken (18:12-17).**
III. **God Ultimately Breaks the Unbroken (19).**

When we sin—and we all sin—God desires brokenness. What is brokenness? Brokenness is a state of awareness of our sinfulness and inability in light of God's presence. This, again, helps us understand the first beatitude: "Blessed are the poor in spirit, for the kingdom of heaven is theirs." The poor are not those who are financially poor; they are those who see their sin deeply. Now think about the irony of this. People who see their sin deeply are "blessed." Exactly how are they blessed? The answer is to translate the word *blessed* as "congratulated." The person who is broken should be congratulated. Why? Because he gets it. He understands the right relationship. If I play one-on-one with Kevin Durant and don't take any coaching, if I post up and trash talk, that doesn't make me great; it just makes me self-deceived. People who understand their limitations are to be congratulated. They understand reality. They get what is real.

It may be helpful to say what brokenness is not: pride. The opposite of brokenness is not wholeness; the opposite of brokenness is a perceived wholeness. Prideful people are not aware of their need for God. Perhaps this is why, when God came into the brokenness of the world, he was constantly fighting pride in the form of self-righteousness. The self-righteous person has not been in the presence of God.

Think about this from a macro level. God offers himself to all people in the form of the Holy Spirit. The Holy Spirit, through the Word of God, leads us to Jesus, who leads us to the Father. So our relationship is culminated with us prostrate before the throne of God. The best picture we have of this is Revelation 4–5. Literally, all creation is praising God. There is no strutting there, no pretense, no jockeying for position or status. All are humbled. All are bowing. All, upon seeing the throne, acknowledge what has always been true: that he is holy and above all things. That is where all this is going.

The way into the throne room is the person of Jesus Christ who, when he allowed his glory to be shown, was as blinding as the throne room of God (John 18:6). So when we know the means to the throne, the person of Jesus, we find him as glorious and awe-inspiring as the throne of God. The Holy Spirit, the means to Jesus, is just as glorious. Meaning, when we expose ourselves to the Word of God, we expose ourselves to the Spirit of God, and God the Spirit has the same effect as being in the throne room of God. The Holy Spirit of God brings a brokenness of life, a hatred of the sin of pride.

Since this brokenness is the natural response in those who love and know God, God expects this of all people.

Here is something we may not have thought of: Everything in me reacts against brokenness. I do not want to expose my mistakes; rather, I want to hide them. Therefore, I use the caulk of my words to fill the gaps in my character. I want to be Kevlar when people critique my spirituality.

Here is one of the most telling passages on brokenness in all of Jeremiah. However, the point of the passage is not about our brokenness but about God's response. This passage motivates brokenness. The motivation is that it gets God's attention. God, in his sovereignty, responds to our brokenness.

The context of the passage is that God is still pursuing Judah. He stills wants them to respond. So he carefully explains how he responds to our brokenness.

God Will Not Break the Broken
JEREMIAH 18:1-11

The story begins with the familiar metaphor of the potter and the clay (vv. 1-4). Then God explains how he responds to those who respond to him (vv. 5-10).

This remarkable passage explains the unexplainable: how God responds to people who follow him. Just like the clay in the potter's hand, so is Israel. Israel is at God's disposal. God might announce that he is going to "uproot, tear down, and destroy," a phrase that harks back to Jeremiah's call. In other words, God may say this to Jeremiah. However, God's plan allows for the potential of obedience. If the nation will repent, God will "relent" of the disaster. Conversely, if God decides he will "build and plant"—again a nod to Jeremiah's call—and that nation does evil, he will relent of the good. In other words, God's plan for prosperity allows for the potential of disobedience. Christopher Wright imagines the Creator's relationship with the pot this way:

- Plan A: "I intend to make this clay into a wine jar."
- Response: Something in the clay runs counter to the plan.
- Plan B: "I've changed my mind; I will make it into a soup bowl."

- Plan A: "I intend to act in judgment against you."
- Response: "Repent and change—you can counteract Plan A if you choose to."
- Implied Plan B: "I can change the plan and suspend the judgment. You don't *have to* suffer Plan A, if only you will respond in repentance."

That last line is not spoken here, but it is clearly implied by the logic of verses 7-10, and it had already been expressly urged upon Israel from the beginning of Jeremiah's ministry, most powerfully in 3:12–4:4, and in the temple sermon of 7:3-7 (where the language is similar to 18:11). In other words, the prime message from the divine Potter is, "Work with me here; respond to what I say. Change your ways, and I will change my plans" (Wright, *Message of Jeremiah*, 213–24; emphasis original).

God's word of judgment may be modified due to a broken heart. God's word of blessing may be modified due to a prideful heart.

We Can Remain Unbroken
JEREMIAH 18:12-17

So God posits that not all final things are final. There actually is some hope if they will return. Yet the response is tragic.

After this explanation and appeal, the reply comes back from Israel:

> But they will say, "It's hopeless. We will continue to follow our plans,
> and each of us will continue to act according to the stubbornness of his
> evil heart" (18:12).

So, even though God has offered them this opportunity to respond, even though God is willing to suspend judgment, even though another opportunity for them to repent may await, they will not do it. They will assert themselves in a downward spiral of sin against God.

God's response is fascinating (vv. 13-15). Rejection of his will is unnatural. Mountaintops are always snow covered, and cold water always flows from a distance, but these natural processes are not mirrored in the way Judah shows affection for God.

God has no other choice. After many opportunities, and after an explicit offer for them to repent one more time, they refuse. God will not hold back on his judgment (v. 17).

The application for those of us in the New Testament era is clear. For those who have constantly rejected Christ, there is still time. Yet, if someone goes to his grave rejecting Christ, the opportunity expires, there is no hope, and he will face the wrath of God. This is clear enough.

Yet the passage applies to believers as well. We are told not to grieve the Holy Spirit but to be responsive to him (Eph 4:30). Does God lose his patience with believers? The answer to this question draws us back again to this fundamental theological truth: God does not punish believers; he disciplines them. While this may seem like a theological technicality, it is important. All the punishment for my sin was taken by Christ on the cross. He absorbed all the wrath of God when he died for our sins. Yet when we sin, it strains our relationship with God. Therefore, we must continue to pray for the filling of the Spirit, and we must fear the discipline of God that he extends to everyone who walks away from him. He is too good of a Father not to discipline us.

When bad things happen, this question comes to our minds: Is God punishing me, or is this something that is just "happening"? This is a question we may not be able to answer, and that is fine. The discipline of the Lord, broadly speaking, is anything that draws us into relationship with him. Therefore, the constant advice in the Proverbs is to look all around us for wisdom (Prov 8). In the broadest way of conceiving of this, we are to use every opportunity to submit to God. When we refuse, he disciplines us. Therefore, we are to take on a spirit of brokenness, to willingly submit at every turn in order to avoid the chastisement of the Lord, a discipline that is very real.

God Ultimately Breaks the Unbroken
JEREMIAH 19

For those who remain unbroken, God—well—he breaks them!

Jeremiah is commanded to go and buy a pot. After describing how God feels about Israel's sin, he breaks the pot in their presence. Now this is brokenness. The sense here is the finality of it all. The broken pot cannot be restored. It is broken beyond repair.

This is our motivation for being broken before God. The first application is, if someone is rejecting God, God can bring a judgment from which there is no recovery. This is eternal separation from God in hell.

There is an application for believers as well. For many reasons the culture we produce as Christians in our books, music, and literature is a swelling tide of conversations on the grace of God. This is understandably so. Is there a more remarkable topic? God's grace can engulf any past mistake and make us whole. Yet there is an important condition for this conversation: the grace of God is only remarkable within the presence of the law. Grace is remarkable because we have violated God's law.

The grace of God is so profound that my sin cannot stand against its power. This means grace is greater than sin. It does not mean my sin in itself has little effect. Nothing could be further from the truth. My sin is not ineffective to hurt me; rather, it is only ineffective in the presence of God's grace. The point is that we can make mistakes that will have long-term consequences. Long after we have been forgiven, Christians who ignore the prompting of God will need to live with the consequences of their sin. Therefore, be broken.

Conclusion

Nancy Demoss's classic contrast of proud people versus broken people is clarifying and convicting:

> Proud people focus on the failures of others.
> *Broken people are overwhelmed with a sense of their own spiritual need.*
> Proud people have a critical, fault-finding spirit; they look at everyone else's faults with a microscope but their own with a telescope.
> *Broken people are compassionate; they can forgive much because they know how much they have been forgiven.*
> Proud people are self-righteous; they look down on others.
> *Broken people esteem all others better than themselves.*
> Proud people have an independent, self-sufficient spirit.
> *Broken people have a dependent spirit; they recognize their need for others.*
> Proud people have to prove that they are right.

Broken people are willing to yield the right to be right.
Proud people claim rights; they have a demanding spirit.
Broken people yield their rights; they have a meek spirit.
Proud people are self-protective of their time, their rights, and
    their reputation.
Broken people are self-denying.
Proud people desire to be served.
Broken people are motivated to serve others.
Proud people desire to be a success.
Broken people are motivated to be faithful and to make others a
    success.
Proud people desire self-advancement.
Broken people desire to promote others.
Proud people have a drive to be recognized and appreciated.
Broken people have a sense of their own unworthiness; they are thrilled
    that God would use them at all.
Proud people are wounded when others are promoted and
    they are overlooked.
Broken people are eager for others to get the credit; they rejoice when
    others are lifted up.
Proud people have a subconscious feeling, "This ministry/
    church is privileged to have me and my gifts"; they think
    of what they can do for God.
Broken people's heart attitude is, "I don't deserve to have a part in any
    ministry"; they know that they have nothing to offer God except
    the life of Jesus flowing through their broken lives.
Proud people feel confident in how much they know.
Broken people are humbled by how very much they have to learn.
Proud people are self-conscious.
Broken people are not concerned with self at all.
Proud people keep others at arms' length.
Broken people are willing to risk getting close to others and to take risks
    of loving intimately.
Proud people are quick to blame others.
Broken people accept personal responsibility and can see where they are
    wrong in a situation.
Proud people are unapproachable or defensive when
    criticized.
Broken people receive criticism with a humble, open spirit.

Proud people are concerned with being respectable, with what others think; they work to protect their own image and reputation.

Broken people are concerned with being real; what matters to them is not what others think but what God knows; they are willing to die to their own reputation.

Proud people find it difficult to share their spiritual need with others.

Broken people are willing to be open and transparent with others as God directs.

Proud people want to be sure that no one finds out when they have sinned; their instinct is to cover up.

Broken people, once broken, don't care who knows or who finds out; they are willing to be exposed because they have nothing to lose.

Proud people have a hard time saying, "I was wrong; will you please forgive me?"

Broken people are quick to admit failure and to seek forgiveness when necessary.

Proud people tend to deal in generalities when confessing sin.

Broken people are able to acknowledge specifics when confessing their sin.

Proud people are concerned about the consequences of their sin.

Broken people are grieved over the cause, the root of their sin.

Proud people are remorseful over their sin, sorry that they got found out or caught.

Broken people are truly, genuinely repentant over their sin, evidenced in the fact that they forsake that sin.

Proud people wait for the other to come and ask forgiveness when there is a misunderstanding or conflict in a relationship.

Broken people take the initiative to be reconciled when there is misunderstanding or conflict in relationships; they race to the cross; they see if they can get there first, no matter how wrong the other may have been.

Proud people compare themselves with others and feel worthy of honor.

Broken people compare themselves to the holiness of God and feel a desperate need for his mercy.

Proud people are blind to their true heart condition.
Broken people walk in the light.
Proud people don't think they have anything to repent of.
Broken people realize they have need of a continual heart attitude of
    repentance.
Proud people don't think they need revival, but they are sure
    that everyone else does.
Broken people continually sense their need for a fresh encounter with
    God and for a fresh filling of his Holy Spirit. (Demoss, "Proud
    People vs. Broken People")

There is something remarkably refreshing about the idea of brokenness. God does not crush the vulnerable and broken; rather, he uses
them. This was true for Abraham, for Moses, and for Peter. God takes
those who are broken, and he uses them.

Even the idea of brokenness is suggestive. God likes those who
are broken because they have an accurate sense of their relationship
with God. Against the backdrop of God's goodness, glory, and magnifi-
cence, we are ruined and broken people. We have nothing to offer God.
Broken people are not better than others, but they are more self-aware.
They understand reality, and are blessed.

Reflect and Discuss

1. What is the main idea of this passage?
2. What is brokenness? How should we understand brokenness in
   light of the Beatitudes (Matt 5)?
3. You've thought about what brokenness is. Now describe what it is
   not.
4. How does brokenness differ from self-righteous pride?
5. Is brokenness a natural response in those who love and know God?
6. What is our motivation for brokenness?
7. Reflect on these statements: God's word of judgment may be modified due to a broken heart. God's word of blessing may be modified
   due to a prideful heart.
8. What does this passage teach us about the results of disobeying God?
9. How should Christians respond to brokenness?
10. List several passages in Scripture that discuss the call to repentance
    and brokenness.

Fire in My Bones

JEREMIAH 20:7-13

Main Idea: There is strength in honesty.

I. **God Is Our Strength When We've Lost Confidence in Our Call (20:7).**

II. **God Is Our Strength When People Attack Us and Our Message (20:8,10).**

III. **God Is Our Strength When Our Call Won't Leave Us (20:9).**

IV. **God Is Our Warrior (20:11-13)!**

Sometimes brilliance manifests itself in a matter of minutes. Other times it takes a lifetime. Think of Picasso. He burst onto the art scene in his twenties and made a significant contribution, forever changing the landscape of modern art. On the other hand, consider Cézanne. He also was a brilliant artist making no less of a contribution to the world of cubist art, yet it took him a lifetime. Among his best-known works are actually some unfinished drafts. He was always working. It was never quite right. One of his subjects was asked to come back to sit a hundred times!

They were both creative. They were both effective and brilliant, but the brilliance came at a different pace. Sociologists refer to these two types of creativity as conceptual creativity and experimental creativity. Conceptual songwriters pen songs as they come to them in a few minutes. Experimental songwriters pore over multiple drafts to get it right. Often experimental creatives are tortured by the process. They know there is a song there, but it is going to take them multiple drafts to get it right. Leonard Cohen, the Canadian author of the hit song "Hallelujah," is said to have worked on the song for years and penned around seventy verses before the final version! He could not leave the song, and the song would not leave him.[3]

---

[3] "Hallelujah" from Revisionist History Podcast. Malcolm Gladwell. Released Wednesday, July 27, 2016.

Of course, Jeremiah is not a creative. He is a prophet. Jeremiah is not trying to come up with what to say. He is expressing, out loud, the message God has given him. Still, the message will not leave him, and he will not leave the message. Or, to be exact, God will not leave him alone. In this way he is more like the experimental creative than the conceptual one. He does not have one great message that he gets off his chest and then moves on. That's not Jeremiah. Jeremiah has internalized this message, and he has to keep working it out. It won't leave him. It tortures him. He is the epitome of the tortured prophet.

We are not always sympathetic to the tortured prophet. First of all, they are no more popular today than they were in Jeremiah's day. When people have a message God has driven deep in their hearts and they are called to work out what God has worked in, they become annoying. Often they can't handle it themselves. If they have poor social skills, the problem is compounded. These are the prophets that do not have a sermon; rather, they have a life message. They will spend the rest of their ministry working out what God has worked in them.

Maybe you can relate to this. Maybe as a preacher you have wanted to do something else in some other way, but God has you running in your lane, doing the one thing it seems that no one else is called to do. This passage, for you, will be a friend, a mirror, and maybe a word of encouragement.

While we won't examine every time Jeremiah is working out his angst with his call, this is a classic example to examine. Jeremiah wants to quit his call, but his call will not quit him. He is stuck with the message. In this passage Jeremiah explains four reasons to be discouraged and one reason to be encouraged. And then there is the really messy ending.

So, why do we get discouraged with our call?

God Is Our Strength When We've Lost Confidence in Our Call
JEREMIAH 20:7

Jeremiah is brokenhearted. It's not that there is a hint of desperation here; it is utter desperation. It's not that there is a small note of exaggeration but full-bore exaggeration: God has become his enemy, and everyone is ridiculing him. We could recoil at his self-pity. After all, self-pity has at its core "self."

On the cross Jesus wondered aloud why God had forsaken him (Matt 27:46-47). This in itself is remarkable. What is even more remarkable is that Jesus is quoting Psalm 22, what we might call a "psalm of complaint." Since Jesus was without sin, we can conclude that there is a difference between the sin of self-pity and a genuine self-awareness of the situation.

Those of us who have been in the ministry are probably hesitant to criticize Jeremiah because we understand the feeling. I remember, at one particular low point, a friend asking how I was. I replied that the ministry was struggling, people were coming against me, I didn't feel well, but other than that everything was great.

While we all struggle, Jeremiah crosses a line that few are willing to cross when he suggests that God deceived him and was his enemy. He will change his tune below, but for now he feels as if God tricked him into this ministry. The implication is that no person of sound mind would follow such a call. In order to get him to obey the call, God pulled a bait and switch: he promised him one thing but delivered another. Yet, as noted, God had promised him a life full of challenges (Jer 1). He was promised ultimate victory preceded by immediate suffering, yet he is drawing the bitter water of disappointment from the well of emotion.

Jeremiah has lost confidence in his call, and now he tells us why.

God Is Our Strength When People Attack Us and Our Message
JEREMIAH 20:8,10

Here again is full-on exaggeration. It could be paraphrased this way:

> Every time I speak, I call for complete destruction of the nation because God's word, through me, brings me to disgrace!
>
> Look, everyone is saying, "His message is so negative about all the terror. Really, he is a verbal terrorist! Someone needs to call him in. We have to find a way to take him out."

Before we ridicule his penchant for exaggeration, we must appreciate his dilemma. Jeremiah's calling is to call a people back to God, a people who have demonstrated they will never repent. There is no conceivable way the people will repent. What's more, there is no way God will alter the demands of his holiness. He can be nothing less than the perfectly loving Father. So what is Jeremiah to do? Well, he is to obey and keep preaching. But why? Because Jeremiah's voice is a verbal life preserver. Imagine someone drowning. A flotation device is right beside her; she just needs to grab it. However, she is carrying a suitcase full of bricks. Her last bit of stamina allows her the opportunity to consider her fate. She can drop the weight and grab the life preserver. Even though she chooses not to, the life preserver stands witness against her. She would only have to let go of one, grab the other, and be saved.

Ultimately, waves of judgment will cover God's people. Nations will conquer and plunder them. As the rising tide takes them under, Jeremiah's voice just floats there like an unwanted life preserver—an unused monument to mercy. God is not silent. He is never passive. He is reaching out to his people, calling them to repent.

This is why the call is so difficult. Jeremiah is the mediator between two parties who will not compromise.

It's also difficult because he cannot do anything else.

God Is Our Strength When Our Call Won't Leave Us
JEREMIAH 20:9

Jeremiah considers keeping his mouth closed. His logic is, while I can't keep God from speaking to me, I don't have to speak for him. It doesn't work. Impression without expression leads to depression. The message of God, once inside the prophet, is so potent it eats away at him until and unless he works out what God has worked in. He can't suppress it. He's like a trumpet without a mute. There is no mortal governor capable of keeping the message down; it just bellows out. It's like a fire in his bones.

Jeremiah is stuck. He is a prophet. By definition he has an unpopular message. You've heard the phrase *popular preacher* or *well-loved pastor*, but we don't usually use the phrase *popular prophet*. Even if there is such a thing, the words sound discordant. God raises a prophet up because there is a problem to address. The call is not popular, and it is equally unshakable. Jeremiah can no more cease to be a prophet than he can change his age. It's in his DNA. Literally. Remember, in 1:5 God called Jeremiah with the words,

> *I chose you before I formed you in the womb;*
> *I set you apart before you were born.*
> *I appointed you a prophet to the nations.*

As the sinew was coalescing on Jeremiah's bones, God knew that those fingers would point down to man and up to God, that the feet would take him to stand where few were willing to stand, and that the vocal cords would arrest the attention of the nations. God made him for this reason. And for this reason he cannot escape.

So Jeremiah feels that God has deceived him, that his message will never be received, and that he was trapped with no way of escape. An unpopular prophet, an unwanted message, and an unalterable call: he is called and stuck.

Yet there is some good news. There is a reason we should be encouraged: God fights for us.

God Is Our Warrior!
JEREMIAH 20:11-13

This is not the fourth point of the sermon. It does not fit with the other three. This is the contrast. We have an unpopular prophet with an unwanted message and an unalterable call, but we have an unstoppable Warrior who fights for us. How glorious!

Jeremiah says all this in one breath: "Well, I feel like God tricked me, I hate what I am doing, and I don't even want to do it, but in the midst of that, God is going to scare my enemies out of their minds! He is a dread warrior." He knows he is unpopular, he knows he does not want to do it, he knows he is hated, but he knows God is going to defend him. What a wonderful concept! Look at the imagery here:

- The Lord is with me as a terrifying warrior.
- My persecutors
  o   will fall,
  o   can't overcome me,
  o   will be ashamed,
  o   will not succeed, and
  o   will have eternal dishonor.

Then he prays that God's vengeance will be on them because—get this—he has committed his cause to God.

What an emotional ride! The mental picture evokes Jeremiah on a windswept hillside cliff with his fists toward heaven. He is telling God that he does not want to do this. Jeremiah is so unpopular, but he is trapped and must be a prophet. As he talks to God, he counsels himself. He realizes the irrationality of telling God off. So two massive things happen: he acknowledges that God is the ultimate Judge, so he asks this Judge not only to try his case but to defend him as well. He goes from resenting God to trusting God in one breath.

Life as a preacher has its ups and downs. It's good to know that one of the seminal prophets in history—someone God tapped to speak the truth and someone God hardwired in the womb for prophetic ministry—could, in one breath, resent God and trust him. What's more, the God we serve chose to allow this to be in the pages of Scripture. Nothing glossed over there.

By the way, there is an important lesson here: God is the opposite of passive-aggressive. He's always in your face!

- When Adam sinned, *God sought* Adam (Gen 3).
- When Ahaz used passive-aggressive excuses for ignoring God, Isaiah prophesied that the God whom Ahaz ignored would be Immanuel, God with us (Isa 7:14).
- Jesus seeks the lost like a shepherd would a sheep, like a woman would a coin, and like a father would a son (Luke 15).

God is always active. God is never passive. It's just all out there.

If Jeremiah were to journal this privately then tear it out and throw it away, something would be lost. This passage is not whispered, it is screamed. With the same voice that called for repentance, the custom-made prophet yells out to God. In the end he was not just complaining; he was counseling himself. He would have made a horrible counseling client if he did not tell the truth. So he did. His angst led him to the truth that God was going to take care of everything.

When we discuss our unwanted call, we have an unstoppable warrior. There is strength in honesty. But the strength is not ours, it is his. He is on the other side of honesty. The question is, Are we willing enough to follow him there? It's as scary as it is real.

Pastor Ronn Dunn would often use the illustration of God unplugging us. What he meant is that we have all these valued sources of life, like an electric wall outlet overloaded with a dozen different plugs. When we are overloaded with idols, idols from which we think we are drawing strength, God has a tendency to unplug them. One by one. When he unplugs one, you at first freak out, then you realize you can live without it.

Life is the process of God's getting more of me. From God's perspective, he is yanking all the other things out so I can see that he is all I need. What a glorious God we serve! Jeremiah is totally unplugged. He tells God as much. And in doing so, he acknowledges God and is now free. He commits it to the dread warrior.

Conclusion

One would think that after such a compelling message, the prophet would tie this up in a neat bow and move on. After all, this passage follows the up-down trajectory we all want: situation, rising tension, and release of tension. He has a problem, he knows God is the solution, so the problem is solved. But then again, this is Jeremiah. So the end is not the end—he adds a somber lament—and that's perfectly fine.

Those of us who believe the gospel see it everywhere. We see the death, burial, and resurrection of Jesus in the child who expresses faith in Christ. From that young life, God gives new life. We see the gospel in the horrid souls tortured by the consequences of sin who, when giving their lives to Christ, find new life. Death followed by resurrection. So it's somewhat natural, I suppose, that we would want to see that everywhere, even when it does not ultimately exist. This is what theologians call an "overrealized eschatology," meaning that, while all the promises of the gospel are given to us, the ultimate expression of the gospel, God's victory over sin and the devil, will not come until some time later. Revelation 19 is as real as if it were right now, but it's not real right now. Jesus is the warrior Messiah, but the execution of his enemies is stayed at the moment. They have more time to be saved; we have more time to live in a lost world. The one entails the other.

All that to say, the messiness of Jeremiah is, in this way, comforting. He has this full-blown expression of trust and confidence in God, yet he is confident that it's not over.

The messy ending is encouraging, but that's not its function. Jeremiah is not thinking of how to encourage us thousands of years later. This is not a greeting card; it's a journal entry. He is not pretending authenticity so he can relate to us; it's simply that raw. And in his honesty he really is encouraging. Even in the midst of difficulty, God is our dread warrior. He fights for us.

Reflect and Discuss

1. In what way is God our warrior? How does he fight for us?
2. Is it true that we must work out what God is working in us?
3. Have you ever wanted to quit your calling but God wouldn't call it quits on you?
4. Jeremiah explains four reasons to be discouraged and one reason to be encouraged. Name them.
5. What type of resistance should Christians expect from those outside the body of Christ?
6. Why were the Old Testament prophets unpopular? Why did people reject their message?
7. How does Jeremiah go from resenting God to trusting God?
8. Does God exercise active love or passive aggression toward believers?
9. What does this passage teach about the incessant need to trust in God generally and trust in our calling specifically?
10. In what way is there strength in honesty?

Rescue

JEREMIAH 21:1–22:10

Main Idea: God reacts to us when we respond to others.

I. **God's Heart: Do Justice for the Defenseless (22:1-3).**
II. **God's Promise: God Reacts to Our Response (22:4-10).**

In whatever ways we might describe the heart of God, at its core it is a love for those who are marginalized. There is not enough time to list all the Scriptures that speak to this, but think of the trajectory: God went after Adam when he was not worthy to be sought (Gen 3). Jesus did not come for the well but for the sick—for the least of these.

When I was standing at the altar, I remember looking up into his eyes. The evangelist who was speaking at our church called people to repentance. I had to respond. Neither can I forget what he said that day, even if I wanted to—which I don't. He said,

> Imagine that you are taking an elevator down into your soul.
> You go down and down all the way to your heart. You get out
> and you look around. And there you see all that God sees.
> You see the areas you have blocked from God. Some rooms
> say, "Keep Out!" God is not allowed to see what's in there. You
> see the things you pray no one else sees. Down in the locked
> closets and deep crevices of your heart, you see everything
> God sees. Do you see it? Now that you see what God sees, will
> you repent?

As these words form on the page, I can imagine that those not raised in my tradition of altar calls and invitations will cringe at a rhetorical strategy intended to probe the heart deeply. I get that. But it's no matter. God used the evangelist that day. And if no one else needed it, I deeply needed the challenge. Sitting here years later, I remember the metaphor like it was yesterday. Sinking down, down to the place where no one sees but God. Wow! Even now it is convicting. The metaphor helps me visualize the dark crevices, closets I have closed off to God and to spiritual introspection. It's really scary what lay down there, down where there is no spiritual oxygen. If I were a miner, my canary would be dead. It's hard to imagine a place in my life, even in moments of hot spiritual fervor, where there was not some area I was wrestling with, some locale I did not want to think about, some region I did not want to expose to the light of God's Word.

To read Scripture is to reverse the metaphor. Reading Scripture is to go as deep into the heart of God as we can. And as we go deeper, what we find is this deep and abiding love for lost people. The deeper you go into God's heart, the more you find extravagant, deepening love.

Perhaps the most revealing words from God on this are from Deuteronomy 15:15 where he reminded his people, "Remember that you were a slave in the land of Egypt and the Lord your God redeemed you." In other words, Israel was to show mercy to those who were marginalized because *they themselves* were marginalized. They were the outsiders. They were the slaves. Therefore they should extend to others the grace that God extended to them.

Context: A Faithful Word from a Persecuted Prophet (21:1-14)

Jeremiah has been sought out before. He has been sought out as the subject of scorn and the subject of abject persecution. He is in the stocks awaiting further persecution and humiliation. The one who was the object of scorn is now the one sought out for good. In this fascinating passage the prophet is being asked to function like a priest, a mediator between the will of God and the will of man.

However, there is something powerfully presumptuous in this request. First, even though Jeremiah has been beaten by Pashhur, he is still sought out for wisdom. While they did not like what Jeremiah was saying, there was at least a measure of confidence in that he was hearing from the Lord.

The prophet is asked to be a fixer.

What they wanted was clear enough. They wanted the mercy of providence without the pain of repentance. They had rejected God as Lord but wanted him as protector. But God is not a civil magistrate bound by oath to protect those who reject him.

Throughout the book of Jeremiah, God had used the language of love to describe himself. There is a remarkable beauty to the first verse of this passage: "This is the word that came to Jeremiah from the Lord." Even though the prophet is in a terrible position, the word was still coming. God was still delivering. And, ironically perhaps, the same strong word that has him locked up in the first place will come straight from the mouth of the prophet.

There is a practical lesson here. Depression and lament are not the same as cowardice. Jeremiah is beaten down but unwavering in his commitment to his call, the call simply to say what God says. What a wonderful attribute!

It puts us in mind of Paul's words from 2 Corinthians 4:8-12:

> We are afflicted in every way but not crushed; we are perplexed but not in despair; we are persecuted but not abandoned; we are struck down but not destroyed. We always carry the death of Jesus in our body, so that the life of Jesus may also be displayed in our body. For we who live are always being given over to death for Jesus's sake, so that Jesus's life may also be displayed in our mortal flesh. So then, death is at work in us, but life in you.

The motivation for Paul's words is that his crushing circumstances were in imitation of Christ who was crushed for us.

This Christ would be crucified outside of the walls of Jerusalem—walls that were about to be destroyed in Jeremiah's time and later rebuilt. This picture of a prophet, in stocks but still hearing from God, is wonderfully instructive and a prototype of New Testament ministry and all future ministry. The collective ministries of the Old Testament prophets, New Testament apostles, and all who came after are ministries of hearing and speaking for God amid great persecution. So now the prophet faithfully speaks the word of the Lord.

Jeremiah prophesies that the mission will implode and that Jerusalem will be taken. This prophecy of a city that is destroyed and people who are taken into exile is tragically fulfilled (ch. 39). The people who would not put their necks under the yoke of the king of Babylon (Jer 27:12) were taken into exile there. Jeremiah 21 stands as eternal witness against them and an eternal warning to those who resist God.

Why is God so angry with them? The chief charge God levels against his people in this chapter is idolatry. That is, they have displaced a relationship with God and substituted a love for something else. God has been edged out. The charge addresses their relationship with God, but Jeremiah 22 addresses their relationship with others. However, the vertical and the horizontal are related. When you don't love God, you don't love what God loves. When your idol becomes a god, then your emotions will follow. God is critiquing Judah because they no longer love what God loves. It is not important to them. Their attention was warped away from God, so now their love is warped away from others. Attention always follows affection.

The text answers two questions: How does God want us to respond to the underprivileged? This is the question of God's heart. The second question is, How does God react when we do or do not respond to the needs of the underprivileged? This is the question of God's promise.

So, how does God feel about the underprivileged?

God's Heart: Do Justice for the Defenseless
JEREMIAH 22:1-3

Jeremiah is told to go and speak to the king. Perhaps there is an intentional reason for him to address the king. The king would be in the best position to set the spiritual temperature for the nation. God wants the king to respond to this. But perhaps there is more. The use of the phrase *throne of David* is telling. It was David who, though a mighty warrior, was over and over again challenged to show mercy—for example, to Nabal (1 Sam 25) and later to Mephibosheth (2 Sam 9). David is an example of a tenacious warrior with a tender heart. In other words, while it was not in David's nature to be compassionate, it was in God's nature. And, since David was a man after God's own heart, he loved those God loved, even when it was inconstant with his personality or his nature. This is God's concern: that they share his heart for those in need.

In verse 3 Jeremiah is commanded to tell the king to "administer justice and righteousness." This sentiment echoes 21:12-14. The command is simple. The implication is that not all people will have access to justice. God is concerned with those who cannot defend themselves. He gives specific examples: those who have been robbed and those who have been oppressed, that is, the financially oppressed. Further, the king and his people are not to exploit the stranger who, by his status as a resident alien, will have no defense in the community. This is the same with those who have no father or with the widow. Of course they are not to take the life of the innocent.

What all of these cases have in common is that there is no structure in place to care for them. There is no social system. If someone does not intervene in their cases, they will be doomed. So God is going far beyond the culturally accepted standard. He has commanded them to be proactive and to defend those who have no defense.

Again, this has a massive trajectory across Scripture.

James explicitly tells us that when meeting the needs of others, our actions are to match our words, when in James 2:14-17 he writes,

> *What good is it, my brothers and sisters, if someone claims to have faith but does not have works? Can such faith save him?*
>
> *If a brother or sister is without clothes and lacks daily food and one of you says to them, "Go in peace, stay warm, and be well fed," but you don't give them what the body needs, what good is it? In the same way faith, if it doesn't have works, is dead by itself.*

James, the half brother of Jesus, was perhaps reflecting on his own interaction with Jesus. How could anyone not have noticed the amazing way Jesus dealt with those who were marginalized? Whether it was the woman at the well (John 4:1-38), the woman caught in adultery (John 8:1-11), or the sinner who washed Jesus's feet (Luke 7:36-50), Jesus is overtly demonstrating his love for the marginalized. This attribute of Christ is not lost on the Gospel writers. A quick search reveals that around thirty times the word *sinner* is used. Jesus is not just bumping into them; he is around them. He is healing them. He is with them. What was the number-one criticism leveled against him? That he was a friend of sinners. Indeed, not only did he not mind being seen with them; he sought them out.

Extending justice in our culture may seem difficult for several reasons. First, let's be honest: for those of us who love the Word of God and who would defend its sufficiency, we often feel like the issue of social justice has been hijacked by those who don't share our high view of Scripture. That's true. So what? The fact that others who do not have a high view of Scripture are showing mercy does not mean that those who do have a high view of Scripture should not.

Further, sometimes issues of social justice have displaced evangelism. No need to defend all sides here; it's just plain enough that some people who will feed the homeless will not open their mouths to explain the gospel to their neighbors. Their defense is that it is better to see a sermon than to give one, better to be a doer than a talker. That approach creates a nonbiblical tension between acts of mercy and the ultimate act of mercy, which is sharing the gospel.

Jesus helped people, and he called them to repent. Jesus hung out with sinners not because he was a great lovable guy but because of holy attraction. They both loved and feared him. He was a friend you could call at midnight, and all the demons of hell feared him. To those close to him he was both familiar and feared. There was unequivocally no distinction between his holiness and his approachability. He was both pure and friendly.

Those errant approaches may throw us. But honesty demands we admit another reason we don't extend justice to those in need: we don't know anyone in need. The American dream may have lodged us in a place where we have no social interaction with those who are the "least of these." If that is the case, what do we do?

There are two important things to remember.

First, Christ expects us to extend justice. "I just never met a poor person" is no excuse. That's right. If we don't know anyone like this, we are to go find them—you know, like God sought us. There is no ridiculous expectation here, just to extend the grace God has extended to us.

Second, remember that ultimate justice is sharing the gospel. So we need to show mercy in practical ways. It's in the heart of God in the passages we mentioned here and many others. But ultimately God is not willing that any should perish. God is concerned with the 55.3 million people that die each year; that's 151,600 people each day, 6,316 people each hour. Most of them die without Christ. Most of them will spend eternity in hell. The good news is that 131.4 million are born each year. These are people to whom God is extending an offer of salvation. These are people for whom Christ died. These are people who can be saved.

Yet there is no record of someone being saved without someone sharing. God is calling them to salvation, and he is calling me to stand between heaven and hell and call them to salvation. So, who in my sphere of influence needs the gospel? That is the meaning in front of the text.

The temptation of course is to sit back and think others will take care of that. You know, the professional Christians (pastors) will take care of this. So, if I harden my heart against those in need, how does God respond to this?

God's Promise: God Reacts to Our Response
JEREMIAH 22:4-10

God's reaction is pretty simple. He will bring the house to ruin that disobeys this command; on the other hand, those who obey will be blessed

(vv. 4-5). The blessing here appeals to the king. The king will be riding through the gates with splendor. One cannot help but think of the parallel passage, Psalm 24:7-10.

> *Lift up your heads, you gates!*
> *Rise up, ancient doors!*
> *Then the King of glory will come in.*
> *Who is this King of glory?*
> *The LORD, strong and mighty,*
> *the LORD, mighty in battle.*
> *Lift up your heads, you gates!*
> *Rise up, ancient doors!*
> *Then the King of glory will come in.*
> *Who is he, this King of glory?*
> *The LORD of Armies,*
> *he is the King of glory.*   Selah

Jeremiah tells the king of Israel that he could be victorious in battle.

Christ is ultimately victorious. This is why David is a picture of Christ. David was a shepherd who left his home to become a warrior. Jesus is also a Shepherd-Warrior who will fight for his people. The kings that sit on David's throne are called to imitate his proficiency in battle and his godliness. Both are essential to being a good king. God promises the blessing of military victory to those who show mercy. Could anything be more counterintuitive? What is the relationship between showing mercy and military victory? The relationship is that victory does not come from horses in battle, but victory comes from the Lord. The Lord gives the victory to those who imitate him and follow him. His trajectory is always reaching down in order to reach up. We go down and then we go up. In the same way, the king is to pursue victory by reaching out to those who are the least of these.

This is odd. It's certainly not taught in any war college or business school. Yet it seems that God brings favor on those who extend mercy. The most obvious New Testament parallel is the explicit promise of Christ that forgiveness will be extended to those who forgive (Matt 6:14; 18:35). God extends mercy to those who extend mercy.

Then in Jeremiah 22:6-7 God makes his reaction specific. The contrast is stark. God considers Judah to be lush like Gilead or Lebanon. These were places that were known for their beauty and their rich resources.[4] Yet if they continued in this way, their "choicest" cedars would be cut down and burned, and they would become a barren wilderness.

It will be so obvious that other people will take notice (vv. 8-9). Public embarrassment will follow this public sin. The kings are so warned. The rest of the passage is specific warnings to specific kings, the sons of Josiah.

Conclusion

What is going on in the immediate context of Jeremiah 22 is bigger than one action. They are reaching a tipping point. They have been accused of idolatry, and now they are being accused of injustice. Again, a love for the heart of God is missing in both sins. The sins are egregious for the actions themselves but also because of what they say about the heart of Israel. Their heart is turned away from God and therefore turned away from others. It's clear enough that they are unwilling to take the elevator trip down to examine their hearts, so God warns them to change their behavior. Exaltation or destruction awaits their response.

In the end it's easy to be dismissive about all of this. The excuses are legion: "God does not care that much about this issue. Think of all the money I give to the church. With that money others can do this. We all have our gifts. I'm good at serving at the church, not so much with people outside the church. I'll be gracious to people after they get here, but I'm not going to go get them."

Yet in one story Jesus destroys all of that. In Matthew 25:31-46 Jesus says,

> *"When the Son of Man comes in his glory, and all the angels with*
> *him, then he will sit on his glorious throne. All the nations will be*
> *gathered before him, and he will separate them one from another, just*
> *as a shepherd separates the sheep from the goats. He will put the sheep*

---

[4] "Gilead and Lebanon were noted for their forests, Lebanon especially for its cedar that was widely valued for construction. David described his palace as a house of cedar (2 Sam 7:2,7). One part of Solomon's palace complex was called the House of the Forest of Lebanon (1 Kgs 7:2-5; 10:17,21), so named for its rows of cedar pillars and beams. The Lord warned that invaders would come and cut down and burn the buildings, as a woodsman would cut down trees. Their beauty would not save them from destruction. So thorough would be the destruction that Jerusalem would be like a desert or an uninhabited town." Huey, *Jeremiah, Lamentations*, 204.

on his right and the goats on the left. Then the King will say to those
on his right, 'Come, you who are blessed by my Father; inherit the
kingdom prepared for you from the foundation of the world.

"For I was hungry and you gave me something to eat; I was
thirsty and you gave me something to drink; I was a stranger and you
took me in; I was naked and you clothed me; I was sick and you took
care of me; I was in prison and you visited me.'

"Then the righteous will answer him, 'Lord, when did we see you
hungry and feed you, or thirsty and give you something to drink?
When did we see you a stranger and take you in, or without clothes
and clothe you? When did we see you sick, or in prison, and visit you?'

"And the King will answer them, 'Truly I tell you, whatever you
did for one of the least of these brothers and sisters of mine, you did
for me.'

"Then he will also say to those on the left, 'Depart from me, you
who are cursed, into the eternal fire prepared for the devil and his
angels! For I was hungry and you gave me nothing to eat; I was
thirsty and you gave me nothing to drink; I was a stranger and you
didn't take me in; I was naked and you didn't clothe me, sick and in
prison and you didn't take care of me.'

"Then they too will answer, 'Lord, when did we see you hungry, or
thirsty, or a stranger, or without clothes, or sick, or in prison, and not
help you?'

"Then he will answer them, 'I tell you, whatever you did not do
for one of the least of these, you did not do for me.'

"And they will go away into eternal punishment, but the righteous
into eternal life."

He compares judgment day to a shepherd who, at the end of the day,
will separate his sheep from his goats. The sheep are analogous to God's
sheep. The goats are not God's sheep. One goes to enteral reward and
the other to eternal damnation that, while prepared for the devil and
not for them, will be their ultimate home.

The odd thing in this story is that the sheep do not understand what
good they did, and the goats do not understand what bad they did. The
difference between the two is mercy: one showed mercy and the other
did not.

Are we to glean from this that all people who do not show mercy
go to hell? No. That would be inconsistent with everything else the
Scriptures say about salvation. Jesus is not trying to work out a fully

developed doctrine of salvation. What Jesus wants to do with this story is explain what mercy receivers look like. Those who receive mercy, give mercy. This is one of their defining features.

It's not that mercy gets us into heaven, but mercy demonstrates that we have heaven in our hearts. Mercy does not merit grace; mercy given exposes a heart of grace. The kind of people who have received mercy are the kind of people who show mercy. It's a hallmark of salvation.

Notice that the criticism God predicts will be leveled against Israel is that they have "abandoned the covenant" (v. 9). The old covenant in its broadest sense covered issues of mercy giving. As the old covenant is enveloped in the new covenant, it's clear from the words of Christ that the call to give mercy is still there. God has not changed. His heart is still open.

Reflect and Discuss

1. What is the heart of God as discussed in this chapter?
2. What about Israel's history should make them acutely responsive to the needs of the alien and the stranger?
3. The challenge to show mercy was given to those who sit on David's throne. How is David an example of showing mercy (22:1-2)?
4. Do you find it ironic that national prosperity is promised to those who show mercy to the least of these (22:4-5)? What is the connection there?
5. How did Jesus emphasize the showing of mercy in Matthew 25?
6. Reflect on the parable of Matthew 25 and make application to your life.
7. Can you think of other passages from the New Testament that affirm this idea of showing mercy to the least of these?
8. If we are not around the poor and the marginalized, then how can we show them mercy?
9. How is showing mercy an evidence of salvation?
10. How is the covenant an example of God's showing mercy?

The Remnant and the Thread

JEREMIAH 23:1-8

Main Idea: The God-Shepherd provides for his sheep.

I.   **Bad Shepherds Scatter the Sheep (23:1-2a).**
II. **The God-Shepherd Brings the Sheep Together (23:2b-4).**
III. **The God-Shepherd Brings a New Leader (23:5-6).**
IV. **The God-Shepherd Brings a New Reputation (23:7-8).**

Good authors always embed clues in their writing. When you start reading a good novel, you pay attention to details because you do not know which details will wind up being significant in the end. After all, if the author is effective, they can weave a theme throughout the whole book. In the end the threads will all come together. The finished product will, like a well-made garment, have central thread that holds the plot together. Details that at first seemed insignificant will, in the end, prove pivotal.

After Jesus rose from the dead, he came up alongside two of his disciples, and something remarkable happened: "Then beginning with Moses and all the Prophets, he interpreted for them the things concerning himself in all the Scriptures" (Luke 24:27). Then later when he sat down with his disciples, he explained things even more explicitly.

> He told them, "These are my words that I spoke to you while I was
> still with you—that everything written about me in the Law of Moses,
> the Prophets, and the Psalms must be fulfilled." Then he opened
> their minds to understand the Scriptures. He also said to them,
> "This is what is written: The Messiah would suffer and rise from the
> dead the third day, and repentance for forgiveness of sins would be
> proclaimed in his name to all the nations, beginning at Jerusalem.
> You are witnesses of these things. And look, I am sending you what my
> Father promised. As for you, stay in the city until you are empowered
> from on high." (Luke 24:44-49; emphasis added)

Jesus opened their minds. What was he doing? He was showing them the *threads* of the Bible. He was saying, "Look, this was the plan all along. I want you to see it."

All the evidence of the New Testament is that they really did understand what Jesus was saying. Taking clues from the conversation of Christ, the New Testament was composed as a commentary on the Old Testament. Think about it.

- The first Gospel, the book of Matthew, has, on average, an Old Testament quotation or allusion in every chapter.
- The strategy of the first Christian sermon (Acts 2:14-36) was to show where the death and resurrection of Christ were prophesied in Joel 2 and Psalms 16 and 110.
- Paul says explicitly in 1 Corinthians 15:3-4, "For I passed on to you as most important what I also received: that Christ died for our sins according to the Scriptures, that he was buried, that he was raised on the third day according to the Scriptures."
- The book of Hebrews is considered a sermon built on the text of Psalm 110.
- The book of Revelation is the most intertextual of all the books of the Bible; it really cannot be understood apart from its constant allusions to the Old Testament prophets.

We could multiply examples, but the point is clear. When Jesus taught them how to read the Bible, he focused on the threads that were holding the whole thing together. This is what scholars refer to as the "compositional nature" of the Bible. Scripture is not a random collection of stories. Rather, it is composed with a specific purpose: to show the glory of God through the exaltation of Christ as he reconciles man to God. When you understand this purpose, you can do what Christ encouraged his disciples to do: see how this theme is developed throughout the book.

While we have not discussed it much thus far, we are now approaching a seminal text in the book of Jeremiah. In this text, like many to follow, we see a specific thread in Scripture. There are many in Jeremiah, but here is an explicit thread that points to the future coming and work of Jesus Christ.

Context

The context of this passage is the reality of wicked shepherds in the land. The shepherds are wicked because they lead people astray. They speak when the Lord has not spoken.

God had promised that he would ultimately give them good shepherds when in Jeremiah 3:15 he said, "I will give you shepherds who are loyal to me, and they will shepherd you with knowledge and skill." This is pitted against the bad shepherds who are under God's judgment. Several times already Jeremiah had prophesied against these evil shepherds:

> For the shepherds are stupid:
> They don't seek the LORD.
> Therefore they have not prospered,
> and their whole flock is scattered. (10:21)

> Many shepherds have destroyed my vineyard;
> they have trampled my plot of land.
> They have turned my desirable plot
> into a desolate wasteland.
> They have made it a desolation.
> It mourns, desolate, before me.
> All the land is desolate,
> but no one takes it to heart. (12:10-11)

Despite this, God affirms that he is their shepherd.

> But I have not run away from being your shepherd,
> and I have not longed for the fatal day.
> You know my words were spoken in your presence. (17:16)

In this context God provides a biting summary of their leadership: they do not gather the sheep; they scatter them.

Bad Shepherds Scatter the Sheep
JEREMIAH 23:1-2A

The shepherding metaphor is ubiquitous in the Scriptures. The hillsides were filled with shepherds tending their sheep. The sheep were well cared for because they were a source of food and clothing. A good shepherd could care for his sheep, understanding that these animals were created to live in a herd. Left alone, a sheep could not care for itself. Once they were scattered, they could not find food and water on their own, and, more seriously, they were vulnerable as prey for the ever-present predators.

The bad shepherds of Israel had not attended to their flock. The shepherds were derelict of duty, and clearly they cared more for their own welfare than they did the welfare of the sheep. They were self-attending but not attentive to the sheep.

Unattended sheep scatter. But remember, this is a metaphor. During Jeremiah's lifetime the people of God went into captivity, to exile, displaced from their homeland. In New Testament times the hillsides of first-century Palestine were scattered with refugees, people displaced from their homeland. God has seen their plight, and he will respond.

The metaphor of a wolf in sheep's clothing stays with us to this day—the idea of someone who is not what he appears to be. The shepherds appeared to care. After all it was their function to care. They just didn't. Here is the good news: every time there is a bad shepherd, the God-Shepherd responds.

The God-Shepherd Brings the Sheep Together
JEREMIAH 23:2B-4

So what does God do when bad shepherds scatter his sheep? First, he deals with the shepherds (v. 2b). They are teachers who are not teaching, leaders who are not leading, and God will hold them accountable.

Second, he gathers a "remnant" out of all the countries where they have been scattered (v. 3). Though mentioned in Jeremiah twice in passing, this remnant will be mentioned eighteen more times, becoming a significant theme in the book.

So, who exactly is this remnant?

God's strategy to gather a remnant who will follow the God-Shepherd is not new; it is a thread that is woven into the whole. When Adam's descendants sinned, God used the small remnant of the family of Noah. When Noah's descendants sinned, God began again, not by destroying the world and starting with a new people, but with a spiritual nation through the offspring of Abraham. Through Abraham God created a spiritual race within the human race.

The spiritual race thrived in their promised land under the leadership of David, was divided after Solomon, and eventually scattered under the leadership of the subsequent kings.

By Jeremiah's time the spiritual race is itself desperately wicked and literally scattered throughout the known world. Yet God is going to isolate a remnant within this spiritual race. This is the people among the people, the true followers of God among the nominal people of God.

After he gathers this remnant, God promises that they will be fruitful and multiply. This is a continuation of God's promise to Abraham. They would have land, and they would have offspring. God also promised new leaders who would keep them free from fear and not one of them would be missing.

Under the leadership of Ezra and Nehemiah, the people would once again enter the promised land. Throughout this desperate situation of disobedience and rebellion, God is keeping his covenant promise to them. They will be in the land, and they will be fruitful.

Yet the greatest promise will arrive with the coming of the Christ.

The God-Shepherd Brings a New Leader
JEREMIAH 23:5-6

"Look, the days are coming"—this is the LORD's declaration—
"when I will raise up a Righteous Branch for David.
He will reign wisely as king
and administer justice and righteousness in the land.
In his days Judah will be saved,
and Israel will dwell securely.
This is the name he will be called:
The LORD Is Our Righteousness."

Jeremiah is not replete with messianic prophecies, but this is a glorious one. So the bad shepherds scatter and destroy the sheep. What is God's ultimate response? He will bring the ultimate Shepherd. He will bring the good Shepherd!

This passage reads much like Ezekiel 34, which criticizes wicked shepherds because they neglected the sheep, allowed them to be prey, and then ate the sheep! God's response was to displace them with the penultimate shepherd-warrior, King David:

> *I will establish over them one shepherd, my servant David, and he will shepherd them. He will tend them himself and will be their shepherd.*
> *I, the LORD, will be their God, and my servant David will be a prince among them. I, the LORD, have spoken.* (Ezek 34:23-24)

This idea of Jesus's being the ultimate shepherd is not lost on the New Testament writers.

- Jesus wept over Jerusalem because they were sheep without a shepherd (Matt 9:36).
- Jesus is the good shepherd (John 10).
- Jesus is the stricken shepherd (Matt 26:31).
- Jesus is the chief shepherd (1 Pet 5:4).
- Jesus is the great shepherd of the sheep (Heb 13:20).

Perhaps the most interesting contrast is that Jesus says he is like a shepherd who seeks sheep and rejoices over them (Luke 15:3-7). In wild contrast to the wicked shepherds of Jeremiah's day who scatter sheep, Jesus seeks after the one that is lost and then brings it home. They scatter. He gathers.

The problem is lost sheep. God's ultimate answer is a new shepherd, and this shepherd-leader is referred to as a Righteous Branch.

If this message is delivered during the time of Zedekiah, then perhaps this is a response to his leadership (Huey, *Jeremiah, Lamentations,* 212). The coming Righteous Branch is in contrast to the leaders who would not bring righteousness to the land. It is interesting that when Jesus ultimately comes to rule the world, he comes bringing right judgment and is described as waging war in righteousness (Rev 19:11). The idea of righteous war seems oxymoronic to us. How could war ever be right? But that way of thinking discounts the way the Shepherd feels about his sheep. He has seen them maligned for so long that he will now bring right judgment. All loving shepherds must fight for the lives of their sheep.

The effect of the presence of the new Righteous Branch is a new reputation.

The God-Shepherd Brings a New Reputation
JEREMIAH 23:7-8

The reputation of Israel will now change. No longer will they be the nation that was saved from Egypt. Their reputation will be updated to be the nation that is regathered back from exile in Babylon.

This really is remarkable. The story of deliverance from Egypt is so profound that several movies have been made from it. The drama of the plagues inflicted, the Red Sea parted, and the Egyptians drowned, inundated in the water of their own defiance, was such a remarkable story that it defines a people—the delivered people. These are the people who, with apologies to Roosevelt, spoke softly and followed a big God. This was not just part of their reputation; it was their reputation.

Yet if God could gather a remnant from all the nations, if he could rebuild them, if he could part the political red tape that kept them in all different kinds of nations, and if he could raise up again what was fallen, then that would be a miracle of biblical proportions. That would be their new reputation.

Conclusion

This is the major thread we need to see. It's possible that you read the Bible backwards. You read the end before the beginning. I certainly did. I knew the story of Zacchaeus before the story of Abraham. I understood the cross and the resurrection before I understood the sacrificial system. Perhaps that's the way it has to be. I need to encounter Christ before I need to understand why he came and how he came. But we do need to understand the whole.

There is a compositional nature to the way God has designed his Word. So we come to Christ, and then we spend their rest of our lives understanding how Christ came to us. It is a massive history behind our salvation. There is a method to the Messiah. Yes, he came for me. But we should be warned that the personalization of our faith can have the unintended effect of ignoring the corporate, national, and even literary nature in which he came. Christ came from the nation of Israel; Christ's coming is revealed in a book. This is not unimportant. We are commanded to read the book, and in doing so we appreciate what the disciples were called to see: that his life is a woven thread that, once seen, can help us understand the whole garment of salvation. It is the thread that holds the whole; it is the thread that came from the remnant.

One can't help read this passage and think of John 15:1-8.

I am the true vine, and my Father is the gardener. Every branch in me that does not produce fruit he removes, and he prunes every branch that produces fruit so that it will produce more fruit. You are already clean because of the word I have spoken to you. Remain in me, and I in you. Just as a branch is unable to produce fruit by itself unless it

remains on the vine, neither can you unless you remain in me. I am
the vine; you are the branches. The one who remains in me and I in
him produces much fruit, because you can do nothing without me.
If anyone does not remain in me, he is thrown aside like a branch
and he withers. They gather them, throw them into the fire, and they
are burned. If you remain in me and my words remain in you, ask
whatever you want and it will be done for you. My Father is glorified
by this: that you produce much fruit and prove to be my disciples.

Perhaps it is mixing metaphors a bit. It's not clear that Jesus is trying to allude to the Righteous Branch title of Jeremiah 23 in John 15, but the relationship is really striking.

Jesus is teaching his disciples to think of their relationship with God like this: The Father takes care of his vineyard. Jesus is the main vine in this vineyard, and then coming from this vine are little shoots, branches. We only have the sustenance and protection of the Father if we are abiding in the Son. We are to abide in him if we want to bear fruit.

Yet the question this raises is, What if someone does not bear fruit? Interestingly, Jesus deals with this *first*. If someone does not bear fruit, that person is removed (v. 2) and then discarded (v. 6), thus this contrast of life and death. Living things produce; dead things wither, die, and are discarded.

While there may be no textual relationship to Jeremiah 23, there certainly is a relational one. Israel had a remnant within the nation. To use the language of John 15 in the great vineyard of God, there were only a few who were bearing fruit. The rest were trimmed; they were cut.

This trimming of the bad and restoring of the good was relationally a precursor to how God would relate to us. He is to this day calling out a remnant of people from the world who will abide in him and allow him to shepherd them.

So for those who want to be in the remnant, there is a thread for that.

Reflect and Discuss

1. How is Jesus the thread that holds Scripture together?
2. Why were the leaders wicked shepherds?
3. Are there other passages in the Bible that speak of good and bad shepherds?

4. What made them bad shepherds (vv. 1-2)?
5. What is the principle difference between the bad shepherds and the God-Shepherd?
6. How are we to understand the new leader of verses 5-6? Who is he?
7. What is the new reputation that the God-Shepherd brings (vv. 7-8)?
8. What exactly is the "remnant"?
9. How is this chapter to be understood on three different horizons?
10. How does this passage relate to John 15:1-8?

Should I Stay or Should I Go?

JEREMIAH 24

Main Idea: Respond to the Lord and be blessed.

I.   The Vision of Jeremiah (24:1-3)
II. Remember the Promise: The Benefit of the Good Fruit (24:4-7).
III. Fear the Curse: The Curse of the Bad Fruit (24:8-10).

Two scientists were gathered in the lab with one purpose: to figure out an odd rat. Originally they were there to test a specific question. They wanted to know how much pain a rat would endure in order to receive what it wanted. The only thing they knew for certain is that the rats hated, absolutely hated, being shocked. So here was the experiment:

The scientists connected a sensor to the rat's brain that could deliver a painful shock. They put food in the corner of the cage, and then as the rat approached the food, they gave it a shock. The rat froze and ran to the other side of the cage. Then it came back to the same place it got shocked. This is the odd thing. The rat did not run *from* the pain; it ran *to* the pain.

They then mixed up the experiment by putting shock sensors in the cage in certain places. Within time the rat identified the places that would bring the most shock and ran to them. Again this was odd. Perhaps they had a broken rat? What kind of sadistic animal would run *to* pain and not *away* from it? But the rat was not the problem. The problem was the scientists.

The scientists had not connected the sensor to the brain in the right place and, as with many great discoveries, stumbled on to something by accident. Instead of connecting the sensor to the brain at the place that delivered a shock of pain, they actually delivered it to the pleasure center. The rat was getting a jolt of pleasure each time it approached the food. The rat was not hurting himself; he was actually experiencing pleasure.

They then gave the rat a shock in close proximity to its food. The rat would ignore food in order to experience the pleasure shock. They then devised a lever so that the rat could shock itself. The rat would press the lever every five seconds. Some rats would do this until exhaustion. So then they took it up a notch to see how much the rat was willing to do to get this pleasure pulse.

They placed two levers at opposite ends of the cage. Both would stimulate the pleasure, but neither could be pushed until the other one was pushed; they had to be released one after the other. Between the two levers was an electrical field that was painful to the rat's feet. The rat ran back and forth pressing the levers all the while scorching its feet. This made no sense. Why was the rat so bent on pleasure at the expense of pain? Why would the rat ignore even food? One rat in the experiment pushed the lever until it fell over exhausted. This is where the experiment took a fatefully interesting turn (McGonigal, *Maximum Willpower*, 106–11).

After a similar test on humans, they finally realized that the sensor was not hooked to a place in the brain that *gave* them pleasure but rather to a place that *promised* pleasure. This led them to wonder, "What if the area of the brain they were stimulating wasn't rewarding the rats with the experience of pleasure but simply promising them the experience of future pleasure? Is it possible the rats were self-stimulating because their brains were telling them that if they just pressed the lever one more time, something wonderful would happen?" (ibid., 110). The rat was not actually experiencing *bliss* but *desire*. Pressing the lever did not satisfy the rat; rather, it let the rat feel like there was a promise of satisfaction coming. In other words, the mild shock gave a promise of more, but that's all. No actual pleasure but the promise of future pleasure.

This might be a good definition of insanity: seeking something not because it is enjoyable but simply because it is a promise of more. It is certainly a good analogy for sin. No Christian, no thinking Christian that is, ever reeled back from sin—with harsh words spoken hanging in the air, the sexual sin just committed—completely satisfied. Why then do we return to sin? Why are we not discouraged from revisiting our sin? Because while sin does not provide actual pleasure, it does tantalize us with the promise of more pleasure.

It's true that sin makes you stupid, but it's also true that sin comes from a stupor. To willfully sin means that we are so anesthetized with self-love we believe the pleasure of sin will actually do something, that it will gratify.[5] Sin does not satisfy; rather, every act of sin is simply the promise of satisfaction. Sin is the willful choice to be promised something that will never happen. Sin really is insane—insanity that helps us understand Jeremiah's words in Jeremiah 24.

Context

God has delivered on his promise of judgment. The people have been deported to Babylon and are under the judgment of God. Yet not all of the people are deported. Some stayed in Jerusalem under King Zedekiah. One would think those who stayed in Jerusalem were blessed and those who were exiled were outside of God's purposes, yet it's quite the opposite. In an odd twist of events, those who are in Jerusalem are in rebellion against God. The exiles are the ones who will be coming back to the land in the future with God's blessing. Those left in the land now are thinking that their presence there is providing them with the blessing they want. They are remaining, but they are in the wrong place.

Sin always overpromises and underdelivers.

Those who are avoiding exile think fighting God's purposes is the best way. God gives Jeremiah a clarifying vision that answers the question, What do we do when we find ourselves under the discipline of the Lord?

The Vision of Jeremiah
JEREMIAH 24:1-3

The king of Babylon deported some but not all of those from Jerusalem. At some unidentified time after this, Jeremiah saw a vision of two baskets of figs that were in front of the temple of the Lord. The Lord asks Jeremiah to identify the two baskets, which represent two extremes. The good figs were *very* good and the bad figs *very* bad. Again, one would think the bad figs were in exile and the good figs were safe at home in Jerusalem. But in God's plan this plays out differently. So what do we do when we are under the Lord's discipline?

---

[5] I'm now thinking of these rats trying to put their lives back together; perhaps in a therapy session of tested rats, all with burned little feet, drinking coffee, huddled in the conference room of a community center and talking about how empty a life of chasing pleasure is: "Hi my name is Steven, I've been off electric shock for three days now . . ."

Remember the Promise: The Benefit of the Good Fruit
JEREMIAH 24:4-7

The benefits of obedience are profound.

God will keep his eye on the obedient exiles and eventually *return them to the land.* Let's stop and think about this for a moment. God had warned this nation not to follow false idols. He sent them prophet after prophet. He gave them the warnings, and they did not listen to them. They did not heed. They did not obey. They turned on their heels and did exactly what they wanted to do. Yet, as they are settling into the life of a refugee—a sentence brought upon themselves by their own disobedience—they are promised that God will not ultimately hurt them but bring them back to the land. This is shocking! God's intention in this exit is to bring them back. Not unlike when they left Egypt, they are going to something better.

The problem is that they have to mentally change the narrative. They had always been the people God delivered from Egypt. They will always be that. Yet now when they are discussed, they will also be the people God led through the exile and back. This is why he prophesied in 23:7-8,

> "Look, the days are coming"—the LORD's declaration—"when it will no longer be said, 'As the LORD lives who brought the Israelites from the land of Egypt,' but, 'As the LORD lives, who brought and led the descendants of the house of Israel from the land of the north and from all the other countries where I had banished them.' They will dwell once more in their own land."

Notice the odd language in 24:5: "I regard as good the exiles." The ones that are exiled are blessed! They are the ones who are considered in line with God's purposes. Why are they kicked out of their home but blessed? Why are they privileged refugees? Because even though they sinned, which led them into exile, God is going to bring them back. God is going to restore them. God is going to heal them and even enhance their influence.

Further, in verse 6 is language that sounds like other language in Jeremiah. God promised, "I will build them up and not demolish them; I will plant them and not uproot them," which reminds of Jeremiah's call to build and to plant (1:10).

God then promised in verse 7, "I will give them a heart to know me, that I am the LORD. They will be my people, and I will be their God because they will return to me with all their heart." This is a precursor to the beautiful language we will see in 31:34. The people will not need external influence to prompt them to know God; they will all want to know God on their own initiative.

So when we are being tried and we are tempted to run, remember that there is a greater promise ahead. But the promise is for those who remain under the discipline of the Lord.

Jeremiah then provides more motivation to obey God. There is both a blessing and a curse here.

Fear the Curse: The Curse of the Bad Fruit
JEREMIAH 24:8-10

The bad figs were inedible. I've never held a basket of rotten figs. I can't imagine it would be pleasant. No doubt the aroma would cause the eyes to water and activate a gag reflex. The contrast between the good and the bad was really stark. It was a perfect metaphor for what God would do to them: make them a disaster, an object of scorn. They would be ridiculed, and they would perish by the sword, famine, and plague, until they were wiped off the surface of the earth. And they would be taken from—watch this—the land God had *given* them. This is a holy and horrible reminder that the covenant was not without condition. They had been in the land God gave them, but they were evicted. They were owners, but they could not be residents. Again, this is a reminder that while God forgives, sin always, always, always, always has consequences. No exceptions.

To clarify, they are in the promised land, where God placed them, the land of the covenant, and they are being punished for that. So what is going on here? Really, why are those who are exiled so blessed and the ones who stayed so cursed? The reason is that those who remained were fighting the purposes of God. Yet they were fighting the purpose of God by staying in the place where they thought they were immune from God's wrath. Patriotism to their homeland had clouded their understanding of God's purposes. They were remaining at home but not remaining under the discipline of the Lord.

The book of Proverbs says a great deal about the discipline of the Lord.

> The fear of the LORD
> is the beginning of knowledge;
> fools despise wisdom and discipline. (Prov 1:7)

Do not despise the LORD's instruction, my son,
and do not loathe his discipline;
for the LORD disciplines the one he loves,
just as a father disciplines the son in whom he delights.
(Prov 3:11-12)

Listen, sons, to a father's discipline,
and pay attention so that you may gain understanding,
for I am giving you good instruction.
Don't abandon my teaching. (Prov 4:1-2)

The notion of discipline is covering two overlapping ideas. The writer of Proverbs is dealing with the idea of parental discipline. The discipline we often think of is self-discipline. The latter is willpower—the ability to control ourselves against the lure of temptation. Two ideas, but they are related in a unique way here.

The discipline of the Lord is always a good thing. It may feel like it hurts, but it always helps, thus the clear instruction not to despise the discipline. Discipline is a form of instruction. If someone gave us the gift of knowledge, why would we ever resent that? In discipline we are being given something we cannot get anywhere else. What's more, no one but a parent loves us enough to bequeath to us this incredible gift of the learning that comes from discipline. In parenting sometimes discipline is punitive, but it is always discipleship. When I type the word *discipling*, my software autocorrects it to *disciplining*, and that's helpful. We discipline in order to disciple.

The person who understands this can, anticipating the Lord's discipline, embrace it by his or her own self-discipline. This leads us to the fascinating yet counterintuitive wisdom of Proverbs 1:23 where Solomon writes,

Turn to my reproof,
Behold, I will pour out my spirit on you;
I will make my words known to you. (NASB)

Do you see the integration here? Turn toward the reproof; move into the discipline. I'm envisioning a child backing into a spanking or putting himself in time-out. This is a teen who gladly hands over the cell phone when the discipline is the loss of privileges. How unnatural.

The verse is also translated, "Turn at my reproof" (ESV), which provides more clarity.

The idea is that when God disciplines us we do not run from it; we turn into it. And then once we have embraced the discipline of the Lord, we turn at it; we pivot at that point and go a different direction. The reason a father would write a son a book filled with short, easily remembered sayings and pithy quotes, and the reason that book mentions the idea of discipline over twenty times in so many different contexts, indicates that this is more than a fleeting idea. Solomon, the wisest of all men, is passing on to his son one of the secrets of life: when God speaks, turn.

Or, to place the verse in the context of Jeremiah 24, when the Lord says go, don't stay. They should have been packing their U-Hauls, but instead they were cutting their grass. They bedded down in the place they should abandon. And God sees. And God disciplines. They sprinted away from God by staying put. They ran by remaining.

Their life becomes a twisted metaphor. On the one hand they are remaining in Jerusalem. This seems like a good thing, yet it is not what God wants at this time. So their remaining is actually running. How odd.

In the last chapter we saw that Jesus was the prophesied Righteous Branch, and we alluded to John 15 where Jesus tells his disciples that if they want to bear much fruit they must remain, abide, in him. Sounds a lot like Proverbs 1:23, doesn't it? If we were to smash the two together, we would have this: Run to the discipline of the Lord and stay there.

Why? Well, to mash the benefits of Proverbs 1 and John 15 together, remaining in the Lord results in hearing from the Lord, and in that way we are fruitful.

So we come back to the twisted irony of Jeremiah 24. Here we have people who are running from God by staying while God says go. This is the perverse idea that they could both rebel and remain. Run by standing still, both static and defiant. But it does not work that way. God is calling them out. Not to go is to reject their calling. It is to run *from* the discipline of the Lord and not *into* the discipline of the Lord.

Conclusion

When the Lord in his sovereignty seems to put on you more than you can bear, when you are facing the challenges of living in his sovereignty or suffering the consequences of your own bad choices, the ever-present temptation is to get wasted. Not necessarily with an intoxicating beverage but with life. When life gets hard, we intoxicate ourselves with a busy schedule, with activity, with life. We can fill the void with food or drink or any number of distractions. But while that may seem to ease the pain momentarily, there is no substitute for listening to the Lord in obedience.

Often the Lord will bring us hard circumstances to get us to move—figuratively or literally. In that moment, remember that waiting is sinning. Move on and follow what God has. We can never see clearly where his discipline is leading us, so we trust him in the move of faith.

Reflect and Discuss

1. What is the significance of the figs' being placed in front of the temple (v. 1)?
2. Compare 24:4-7 with 29:11-12. Is there a connection?
3. Compare 24:4-7 with 31:31-40. What is the connection with this promise and the new covenant?
4. How is the promise of 24:4-7 applicable to us?
5. What were the good figs, and what did they represent (vv. 4-7)?
6. Why were good figs a fitting metaphor?
7. What were the bad figs, and what did they represent (vv. 8-10)?
8. Why were bad figs a fitting metaphor?
9. Consider the implications of Proverbs 1:23. What does this say about our relationship with Christ?
10. Compare Proverbs 1:23 with the metaphor of the vine and the branches in John 15. How do the two relate to each other?

Picturing God's Judgment

JEREMIAH 25

Main Idea: God's punishment is thorough.

I. Evil Families: A Picture of God's Judgment on Judah (25:8-14)
II. Cup of Wine: A Picture of God's Judgment on Other Nations (25:15-29)
III. Lion's Roar: A Picture of God's Judgment on the World (25:30-38)

While the theme of disobedience to God's word is carried from Jeremiah 24, Jeremiah 25 represents a shift. Jeremiah 25 represents the halftime for the book of Jeremiah (Wright, *Message of Jeremiah*, 271). It is, of course, located near the middle of the book. It is twenty-three years since his call, and perhaps the editors want the reader to notice this by inserting that fact here in verse 3. The year is 605 BC, the year Nebuchadnezzar would defeat Egypt and rule over the new Babylonian Empire, and King Jehoiakim would burn Jeremiah's scroll sealing his country's fate.

Not only does the time shift, but the message shifts as well. The first half of the book is written to a people who are seemingly doing well. They need to be told that things are not as good as they appear. In the second half of the book, the prophesied judgments come true, and things are awful. Now the people need to be told that not all hope is lost. Jeremiah's call was,

> See, I have appointed you today
> over nations and kingdoms
> to uproot and tear down,
> to destroy and demolish,
> to build and plant. (1:10)

In the first half Jeremiah was working out his call to uproot, tear down, destroy, and demolish. In the last half he is building and planting. In the introductory chapter we noted this theme: the warning of judgment implies hope. Now that judgment is upon them.

Jeremiah is filled with word pictures. In chapter 24 he used the metaphor of good and bad figs to explain their situation. Chapter 25 could be organized around three principle metaphors: evil families, a cup of wine, and the lion's roar. These metaphors drive home the theme of just how thorough God's judgment is.

Evil Families: A Picture of God's Judgment on Judah
JEREMIAH 25:8-14

This is quite an ironic metaphor. God is summoning the families of the north. This is not the family reunion anyone would want to be part of. Jeremiah is referencing all the families that will mount themselves against Judah on that day.

The judgment on Judah will be so stout that the sound of joy, the wedding songs, and the productive work will be removed from the country (v. 10). The country would serve the king of Babylon for seventy years. The seventy years seems to be related to the same seventy years of 29:10 and later in Daniel 9:2.[6] This was how long they would be in exile and the number of years until Babylon was punished for what it did to the nation.

Notice the irony of verse 9. The nation of Judah would not serve God, so God is summoning his servant Nebuchadnezzar. This wicked king, who could not have known that he was to be a servant of God, will be used by God for God's purposes. We see this theme running throughout the rest of the Old Testament. Even as the curtain closes on the Old Testament in the dramatic events of Nehemiah, Nehemiah is quick to point out that all of this is happening because of the gracious yet strong hand of God (Neh 2:8,18).

In the end, the success of Ezra and Nehemiah makes Jeremiah's life and message so sad. As the curtain closes on the Old Testament, Ezra and Nehemiah experience spiritual awakening, which revives a love for God's Word. They discover the Word, read it, and respond to it. This means that, before the judgment that was coming in Jeremiah's day, they had all the access to God's Word they needed. It was always there. They could have returned. They could have listened. It did not have

---

[6] For helpful discussion of the seventy years, see J. Daniel Hays, *Jeremiah and Lamentations*, Teach the Text Commentary Series (Grand Rapids: Baker, 2016), 184.

to be this way, but their willful rejection of God's word had horrible consequences.

Cup of Wine: A Picture of God's Judgment on Other Nations
JEREMIAH 25:15-29

God has been pictured as many things in Jeremiah, but now God is pictured as a bartender (Ryken, *Jeremiah and Lamentations*, 367). He is pouring a cup of wine that all the nations must drink. There is no escape. This theme also appears in the Psalms. Psalm 75:8 notes, "For there is a cup in the Lord's hand, full of wine blended with spices, and he pours from it. All the wicked of the earth will drink, draining it to the dregs."

Notice the exhaustive nature of the psalm. The cup of God's wrath will be drunk "to the dregs." This is a vivid illustration of the inescapable nature of God's wrath. Not one drop remains when the nations have finished drinking. This means the cup of God's wrath will be emptied. Everyone who drinks from it will be completely drunk with the wine of God's wrath. As a result, "they will drink, stagger, and go out of their minds because of the sword I am sending among them" (Jer 25:16).

The problem they will face is not the act of drinking but the effect of drinking. They will be as dignified and presentable as a drunkard.

What follows is a list of all those who will drink of the wrath (vv. 17-26). The final nation is Sheshach. This was a coded way, by substituting the Hebrew letters, of saying Babel, that is, Babylon. The world's great superpower is not excluded from this judgment.

The reader may have a question about the nature of God's judgment on both Judah and the pagan nations. How could God use the pagan nations to execute his will and then punish those same nations for accomplishing this? This is a New Testament question as well since God brings judgment on Jerusalem through the pagan nation of Rome.

God is not causing the disobedience of anyone, and God is not punishing them even though they have in some manner been obedient or compliant. These are nations that had opportunities to respond to God but have rejected him. They are being recompensed for malicious acts of injustice toward God's people. They carried out those acts without regard for God's opinion about Judah's disobedience. In other words, had Judah been a nation seeking God, these nations still would have wanted to act against them. They were in no sense compliant to God's will. God had simply chosen to leverage their sin for his good.

God is not forcing the pagan nations such as Babylon to sin. They were participating of their own free will. God is allowing their evil to be untempered against his people because it was carrying out other purposes.

In a sense God still does this today. Perhaps the best modern example of this is the country of Romania. Under the evil hand of Romanian dictator Nicolae Ceauşescu, the people of Romania suffered greatly, especially the Christians. Christian pastors were treated as enemies of the state. They were persecuted, abused, and in every way marginalized. Why God allowed this evil to continue is something we will never understand. However, we can see the effects. After Ceauşescu was removed from power and the Romanian Revolution occurred in 1989, the church flourished. In fact, the largest evangelical church in Europe and the largest evangelical university in Europe are in, of all places, Romania! Romanian believers are among the strongest on the continent. Few believers in history have faced greater persecution; few have displayed such spiritual prosperity. The evil in this man's heart God chose to use for his own purposes. God demonstrated his sovereignty by facilitating evil for good—something he still does to this day.

Lion's Roar: A Picture of God's Judgment on the World
JEREMIAH 25:30-38

The judgment that is coming now extends from Judah to the nations, to the whole world. Note how inclusive the language is: "all the inhabitants of the earth" (v. 30), "to the ends of the earth" (v. 31), "from nation to nation" (v. 32), and "from one end of the earth to the other" (v. 33).

Since God's judgment is coming on all the nations, the only response is to mourn. Jeremiah speaks with burning poetry (v. 34). Verses 35-38 spell out why they should mourn: escape is impossible. In the end God's judgment will sweep the entire earth.

Conclusion

One might ask, isn't judgment an Old Testament theme? This is not in the New Testament and certainly not something we can relate to, right?

The reality is that the judgment of God is a thread woven through all of Scripture. Paul notes in Romans 1:18, "For God's wrath is revealed from heaven against all godlessness and unrighteousness of people who by their unrighteousness suppress the truth." And later, concerning the end of the age, John says of the one that worships the beast and the false prophet, "He will also drink the wine of God's wrath, which is poured full strength into the cup of his anger" (Rev 14:10).

The wrath of God that was poured on the nations that rose against Judah will be poured out on others. This is because God has not changed. Judgment is an expression of his holiness as it responds to those who reject him. He is still holy, and he is still rejected. Therefore his judgment is still very much alive.

Scripture is clear that not one sin that has been or will ever be committed will not be punished. Daniel Hays offers a simple and clear illustration one could use in preaching and teaching this text (see *Jeremiah and Lamentations*, 191–92). If you stood before your congregation and held a ball about as high as your head you could ask them what would happen if you dropped it. (In a typical crowd some prompting for response might be necessary.) The livelier crowd will respond immediately that the ball of course will drop, which you demonstrate as you let go. Then you could ask, What if we were to do this a hundred times, how many times of the hundred will it drop? The answer is of course a hundred out of a hundred. After all, it's a natural law. It will happen. Every time.

God is clear. The wrath of God is revealed against *all* unrighteousness, no exceptions. No sin you have committed will be immune to God's wrath. Jesus is pictured in Revelation as having laser-like eyes (Rev 1:14). He knows everything because he sees everything. Everything. No one, no person, no man, no woman will escape his wrath.

God is bound by his own knowledge to know all things and to punish all expressions of sin against him. This is why there is no way for us to get right, no way for us to reconcile the wrong we have done against God. If we stopped sinning today, we would still need forgiveness for all the things we have done in the past. This is a situation we cannot fix.

Enter Christ. Christ stood before the Father and drank the full cup of God's wrath. Knowing the power and depth of God's wrath, he prayed in Luke 22:42, "Father, if you are willing, take this cup away from me." This was an educated prayer. He knew what he was about to endure. God's wrath would be in no way tempered. Christ was taking on himself the sins of the world. Yet out of obedience to the Father, and considering our salvation, he drank every last ounce. When Jesus put down the cup of God's wrath, not a drop was left. He consumed all of it.

The weight, the grief, was all clear to Christ, so he prayed, "Nevertheless, not my will, but yours, be done."

When sinners look at the cross and walk away, they are saying in effect, "I do not fear tasting the wrath of God from which Christ drank. I think I can handle that." What Christ endured is unspeakable. We only talk of a cross and a whip and thorns and beatings because these physical acts are the best ways we have of explaining this. In reality what Christ experienced is so much worse than we can describe because the anguish was as much emotional as physical. No one has at any time been more troubled than Christ was at that moment.

Sadly, many wink at what made Christ weep. He sweat drops of blood, yet it is ignored as so much religious talk. This is sad. This is real.

There is a word of warning here for the believer. The only way to sin is to ignore the cross. The greatest deterrent against sin is to meditate on his sacrifice for us. To say it another way, he endured horrible agony so we would not have to suffer but also so we would not have to sin.

Philip Graham Ryken (*Jeremiah and Lamentations*, 367–75) insightfully outlines Jeremiah 25:15-38 this way:

A Bitter Cup for Every Sinner
A Bitter Cup for the Nations
A Bitter Cup for Christ
A Sweet Cup for the Christian

Since Christ took of the full wrath of God, we can come to the Lord's Table. We can come to the Lord's Table and drink. We drink of his blood as a symbol of the reality that he drank of God's wrath. What was to him the bitter cup is to us the sweet wine of salvation. By this atoning elixir we are healed.

Reflect and Discuss

1. Explain the shift that is taking place in Jeremiah starting with chapter 25.
2. How is chapter 25 a working out of Jeremiah's call in Jeremiah 1:10? What does this have to do with the divisions of the book?
3. The sounds of joy were removed (v. 10). What are the sounds of joy for your culture, and what would it be like if they were removed?
4. How is God like a bartender (vv. 15-29)?
5. What do you think of when you think of God's wrath?

6. Is there a difference between God's punishment and his judgment?
7. Explain the difference between punishment and judgment in the context of a new covenant believer.
8. How can God use pagan nations to execute his will?
9. Can you name another time in the Old Testament that God used people who did not acknowledge him as God to accomplish his will?
10. Explain how the lives of Ezra and Nehemiah complete the promises God made through Jeremiah.

The Parenting of God

JEREMIAH 26–28

Main Idea: The sovereign God of hope is serious.

I. **God Is Hopeful (26).**
   A. Jeremiah preaches in the temple (26:1-6).
   B. Death is threatened (26:7-10).
   C. Jeremiah is spared from death (26:11-24).
II. **God Is Sovereign (27).**
   A. The metaphor of the yoke and the prophecy (27:1-11)
   B. Prophecy to Zedekiah (27:12-15)
   C. Prophecy to the priests (27:16-22)
III. **God Is Serious (28).**
   A. Hananiah's false prophecy (28:1-4)
   B. Jeremiah's response (28:5-9)
   C. Hananiah breaks the yoke (28:10-11).
   D. Jeremiah responds (28:12-16).

The grocery cart wheel ebbs slightly to the right. You try to correct it, wondering why, in the twenty-first century, there is not a better solution to the grocery-cart-wheel problem. You have a mental list of things to buy. Your success as a grocery shopper depends on your getting everything in your cart at a good price and in a reasonable amount of time. It is not an impossible challenge, but it is a challenge, and you are up for it.

With all that you are multitasking in this moment, there is something that demands more of your attention and mental energy than anything else. It's the twenty-seven pound two-year-old sitting in the cart. Toddlers are adorable. You think so, and any smart person agrees. If someone stops to tell you so, it won't hurt your feelings. You don't ask a lot of the child. She has snacks; she is content since your grocery run is strategically placed at a time when she is well fed and rested. You don't need her to cross off things on your list or compare prices to online options. You don't demand anything of her but this: she cannot under any circumstances embarrass you.

In your more honest moments you wish this did not bother you. You wish that your parenting were not influenced by what others think. You wish that you did not want the approval of perfect strangers. Yet we don't live that way. Public perception still weighs on us as if we were in junior high all over again. We know, we just know, that the moment our baby cries the perfect parent will bob along down the aisle with her perfect, nonslobbering, athletically conditioned, baby Mozart, and she *will* judge us. Even if she does not know us, acknowledge us, or even see us, we just know she is judging us. How dare she!

So when parenting toddlers, we have this agreement: I will feed, clothe, and love you. You are only asked not to embarrass me in public.

It seems this is how the other prophets of Israel thought about Jeremiah. He is an absolute, perfect embarrassment to them. You have the sense as you read these passages that the others around Jeremiah are cringing. Every time he opens his mouth he does something more embarrassing than the last time. Why does he do this to himself in public?

Context

These three incidents have specific historical markers. The first takes place in the beginning of the reign of Jehoiakim and the other two during the reign of Zedekiah. During the reign of these two kings, the attitudes of the people and the priests have not changed. The people have the wrong attitude because they have the wrong leaders.

What they do not see is that this embarrassing prophet is actually bringing the exact message they need to hear. Sometimes the thing we think is the most embarrassing is revealing to us something about the heart of God.

And this makes me wonder: Does God parent us like this? When we act up, how does God respond? Does he cringe at our behavior? No. God fears no one's approval. He is not embarrassed by us, and this is really the point of this passage. At every turn God is not about behavior modification. He is not trying to get us to be better. If you read these chapters closely, you see that God is trying to teach them something about himself.

In the first two narratives God is sending Jeremiah to teach them about his character. God is sending because God is teaching. In the last narrative we see Jeremiah responding in a way that demonstrates he has already learned these lessons. So, what do we learn about the character of God from these stories?

God Is Hopeful
JEREMIAH 26

Jeremiah Preaches in the Temple (26:1-6)

God commands Jeremiah to go and to stand in the court of the temple and deliver a hard message. The message is delivered and the response is horrific. While people gathered around to hear the message of the prophet, the people wanted to kill Jeremiah.

Death Is Threatened (26:7-10)

He is spared from death, but it will not be the last time he is threatened with death or physically abused.

Jeremiah Is Spared from Death (26:11-24)

Jeremiah's defense is clear enough: he is simply saying what God sent him to say. The people respond to this. As much as they do not like his message, there is still a sense of respect for the prophetic mantle. His life is spared because they reasoned, "This man doesn't deserve the death sentence, for he has spoken to us in the name of the LORD our God" (v. 16).

God Is Sovereign
JEREMIAH 27

The Metaphor of the Yoke and the Prophecy (27:1-11)

Jeremiah effectively used the metaphor of the yoke. Yet it is as troubling as it is helpful. They were told to put their necks under the yoke of Babylon. Babylon hated God and tortured and abused God's people, yet they were to submit to them.

Prophecy to Zedekiah (27:12-15)

Accepting this metaphor had to be especially painful for King Zedekiah. He was told to submit to this foreign nation. Few things in Scripture seem more counterintuitive. Zedekiah's land was the promised land. This was the inheritance from God to the children of Abraham. This land was won at the price of great sacrifice and military conquest under Joshua and sustained under David. This land was a royal wonder under the hand of Solomon. And to complicate things, Zedekiah has a host of prophets telling him to stay. To obey God, Zedekiah must deduce that they are trying to deceive him or that they themselves are deceived (vv. 14-15).

Still, he was told also to put his neck under the yoke. Why? Because to submit to the foreign king was in reality to be saved. Think about how merciful this is on the part of God. He promises to bless his obedient people. Initially, they do not obey, so he gives them opportunities to repent over hundreds of years. When they still do not repent, he tells them, through the prophet Jeremiah, that he will destroy the land. Yet God gives them one last opportunity to repent when he allows them to escape to Babylon. They can walk off and avoid the destruction.

To be clear, they could not avoid the discipline. Those who did not submit to the discipline would be destroyed. Their disobedience had consequences from which they would not recover.

Sadly, as we know from the rest of the book, Zedekiah rejects the discipline of the Lord and is destroyed. He would not embrace the yoke, so he was dealt the rod.

There is an interesting passage in Jeremiah's songbook, the book of Lamentations. In 3:27 he says it is good for a young man to "bear the yoke while he is still young." In other words, he must bear down now under God's discipline if he wants to bear up later in life. This is the advice Zedekiah was unwilling to take. In this way Jeremiah and Zedekiah are opposites. Jeremiah is bearing a heavy yoke now and God's favor later. Zedekiah is rejecting God's yoke now and will bear his anger later.

Prophecy to the Priests (27:16-22)

Jeremiah has a word to those who were trying to deceive. They submitted a positive message about the future of their ritual temple implements, but Jeremiah promised that all of it would be taken back to Babylon.

God Is Serious

JEREMIAH 28

Hananiah's False Prophecy (28:1-4)

Contrary to Jeremiah's prophecy, Hananiah tells the king exactly what he would want to hear: that God had broken the yoke of Babylon.

Jeremiah's Response (28:5-9)

Jeremiah is sympathetic. He wants this prophecy to come true. However, he is cautious and warns Hananiah the prophet that only when a prophecy comes true is a prophet vindicated.

Hananiah Breaks the Yoke (28:10-11)

Hananiah breaks the yoke off of Jeremiah in a public demonstration of his message. Again, the hope is that it comes true.

Jeremiah Responds (28:12-16)

Jeremiah has a new message: the wooden yoke will be replaced by an iron one. Jeremiah only spoke after God had spoken. Now he knows the truth, and he is willing to speak the truth. Hananiah will pay the ultimate price because he "preached rebellion against the Lord."

These three narratives have a specific function in the book of Jeremiah. Taken as a whole, they carry the narrative of the book along by showing just how bad the times were when a prophet is treated like a criminal. In doing so, they also show how far the people of God are from the heart of God.

Conclusion

We began by talking about the paranoia of public embarrassment when other people see us dealing with an uncooperative child. However, often the shoe is on the other foot. Those of us who see a child acting up in public have been there. We know exactly how the parent feels, so even if the parent appears to be perfectly content and have it all under control, we cringe for them. We are embarrassed for them.

This is the irony: Jeremiah is faithfully following the direct words of God himself. So even though the whole world looks at Jeremiah and cringes, God does not. Everyone is embarrassed for God, but God is not embarrassed. Jeremiah's Father approves of his public behavior. This is all that matters.

A mentor of mine often said, "The only person we have to please in life is God." While we might at times feel like a lonely prophet, rarely is the whole world actually against us. Yet Jeremiah rarely had a friend to lean on, to confide in, and to stand with him. He had no private emissary for his public shame. But this is no matter. He is obedient to God, and that is enough.

So when we look in the mirror, we may ask if we can say that. Jeremiah is not passive. He is aggressive. He is not just looking out for his own interest but for the interest of others (Phil 2:4). He is speaking the truth in love (Eph 4:15), and he is being a good steward of his assignment (Matt 25:21). God was pleased with him when no one else was. So Jeremiah could sleep well at night. He had pleased the only one who mattered.

Discuss and Reflect

1. Why was the metaphor of the yoke so critical?
2. Is there a connection between Jeremiah 28 and Lamentations 3:27?
3. Based on the king's unwillingness to listen to Jeremiah, what future actions is he likely to take?
4. What are we to do when someone preaches a message contrary to Scripture?
5. Is there a connection between this passage and the warnings to the teachers, such as James 3:1?
6. Could it be that the new false prophet is not a person but a feeling?
7. If our culture establishes that truth is in ourselves, and we hear something preached that makes us feel uncomfortable, could we not conclude that the preacher should not have a hearing? Would that conclusion be valid?
8. What would it look like if a preacher stood today and called out the false prophet of hearing things that just make us feel good?
9. What kind of courage was demanded of Jeremiah to call out Hananiah and prophesy that he would die?
10. With the exchanges of Jeremiah 26; 27; and 28, why is it that the people, especially the king, will not respond to the message? Why do they love the false prophets?

Thriving in Exile

JEREMIAH 29

Main Idea: God tells us now what he will do later so we will not be overcome with the present.

I. **Thrive in Exile (29:4-9).**
II. **Thrive in Exile Because of Future Deliverance (29:10-14).**
III. **Those Who Refuse God's Discipline Are Warned (29:15-31).**

As the words populate themselves on the screen in front of me, what is interesting is that this is not so interesting. The fact that characters that were not there a millisecond ago are now present does not strike me at all. That is just the way things are. Communication has changed through the years.

Communication theorists suggest that there have been major shifts in communication. These could be sliced in many different ways, but think about it this way. Communication has shifted

- from oral to written,
- from written to print,
- from print to broadcast,
- from broadcast to digital.

These are all seismic shifts. However, the most significant shift in communication was doubtless the first shift, from an oral culture to a written one. The reason this was so significant was because of presence. When something was written down and then reread at another time, it separated the presence of the messenger from the message itself. You could argue that all forms of communication are attempts to get back at that original form; they are attempts to make the nonpresent person present. The messenger "re-presents" the original speaker. The limited functionality of visual phone calls reminds me at once how amazing technology is and how the trillions of dollars spent have yielded something profoundly mediocre at re-presenting presence. Spending time with my wife cannot be replicated by seeing her face pixilated on a tiny screen.

Yet the letter described in Jeremiah 29 is different. This letter represents the heart of God. God's word is always accompanied by God's presence. He is invisible, yet he makes his presence known in the word he communicates to his people through his prophets. In this written letter we have a metaphor for the nature of the written Word of God. God is invisible, yet he writes to us through his Word. He speaks to us. When he does, he is near. His presence is in his Word. This word communicated through Jeremiah will contain a message of encouragement to the exiles and a message of warning to those who are still in rebellion. So here we have a profound word, a word that carries perhaps the most notable passage in the book of Jeremiah.

Context

The leaders of the country are now refugees. They are living exiled from their home. Jeremiah is writing to them, but the text also indicates that his emissaries might have received an audience with the king of Babylon himself (v. 3).

So here is God's word of encouragement to them.

Thrive in Exile
JEREMIAH 29:4-9

God gives them clear directives: build houses, provide for yourselves, and have families. In other words, they are to have the posture of presence. God is saying they are to spend their time not moping about what was lost from the old country but actually thriving in the new land. There is no question that they are exiles, and there is no question that they are to act well in this situation.

Being a foreigner has deep roots in our faith. Abraham was praised because

> by faith he stayed as a foreigner in the land of promise, living in tents
> as did Isaac and Jacob, coheirs of the same promise. For he was looking
> forward to the city that has foundations, whose architect and builder is
> God. (Heb 11:9-10)

This is a great metaphor for what it means to be a Christian. A believer is, by definition, exiled from his ultimate home in heaven. First and foremost we are citizens of the kingdom we cannot see. This is why the language of those who are displaced in this life is so appropriate for us. We are strangers, foreigners, and aliens. We are in this life but not of this life.

So the counsel is appropriate for us: like Abraham we are to thrive in this land even though it is not our home. But the directive is even more specific. They were not just to thrive personally but also to "pursue the well-being of the city I have deported you to. Pray to the LORD on its behalf, for when it thrives, you will thrive" (v. 7). Perhaps this is an extension of the promise to Abraham that they were to bless all nations. They were to pray for the prosperity of the country that exiled them for the practical reason that when the country prospered they would as well.

The section ends with a warning against the false prophets. This assumes the false prophets were encouraging them to do something other than be supportive of their host country. Perhaps they were advancing a nationalism that, while well intended, did not seek the best for the land they were occupying.

This posture might strike us as odd. Are they to act like nothing is wrong? Of course not! They are in fact exiles. The markets they patronize are different from what they are used to. The ground yields different crops; the customs are different. Everything seems to be different. God never asks us to pretend.

But there is a specific reason they should seek to thrive in exile: the promise of future deliverance.

Thrive in Exile Because of Future Deliverance
JEREMIAH 29:10-14

The motivation for their behavior is that their home was temporary. Like Abraham their biological and spiritual father, they were to look for something more.

God had already prophesied that the time of the exile would be fairly short (25:11-12). Babylon would fall, and the people would be restored. As mentioned earlier, this is remarkable. The people have disobeyed God, and his discipline is punitive, but it is also restorative. He is taking them out to bring them back in.

Then God gives them the glorious promise that his ultimate plans were not for destruction, but to give them "a future and a hope" (v. 11).

The Lord assured the people that what had happened was not a series of unplanned, accidental events. He said, "I know the plans" (lit. "I, I know"; emphatic in Hb). His plan was not intended to hurt them but to give them "hope and a future" (perhaps a hendiadys, "a hopeful future"). He encouraged them to pray, for he would listen to them. (Huey, *Jeremiah, Lamentations*, 254)

This would have been at once encouraging and tough. How do you accept that God is giving you a hopeful future when you have no home, when all of your memories are tied to a land that you are not sure you will see again, when you have just walked hundreds of miles to be displaced among a strange people, when you are a blessed people living in a pagan land, and when you are literally under the judgment of God? That is a hard ask for humans. But God is not asking them to trust the plans.

The assurance is not in the plans; it is in God's knowledge of the plans (v. 11). God knows. So that they may focus on the present, he tells them now what he plans to do later.

Now we see the importance of the letter. God assures us in our present by telling us now what he plans to do later. This is always his pattern.

- He told Abraham that later he would have offspring, a land, and a blessing (Gen 12:1-3).
- He told David that later he would have an everlasting kingdom (2 Sam 7:8-17).
- Jesus told his disciples that later they would have a home in heaven (John 14:1-6).
- We are told that later we will reign with him (2 Tim 2:12).

God's promises are glorious, but they are future. God tells us now what he will do later so we will not be overcome by the present.

God does not promise to alleviate all suffering in this life. He rather gives us his promise in his Word that ultimately the fake kingdom in which we are citizens will be displaced by the real kingdom of heaven. All injustices will be righted, all will worship Christ, and Jesus will bring an end to all war and bring judgment on all those who have come against him and his bride. This will happen. This may not change my present, but it changes my hope. What is at stake for the country of Judah is not whether God will act but whether they can trust him until he does. Future blessing does not negate present pain. But more importantly, present pain does not negate future blessing. The fact that I cannot see the finish line does not mean it does not exist; it just means I am not in a position to fully see what is actually there. God is here, even when he is invisible.

So I do not slacken my stride, I don't sit down or lie down, I don't embrace the life of laziness toward the present or remorse for the past, and I don't swelter in the heat of my present situation until I wilt in hopelessness. I don't turn an aid station along the racecourse into a finish line.

No, we run by faith. We run toward a finish line we cannot see to a God we cannot see because his invisibility is not a worry to us. We are running by faith. His concern is not his plan; his concern is our faith in it. God tells us now what he will do later so we won't focus on the present.

By the way, since he knows the plans, this means the most valuable asset is not the plans; the most valuable asset is the Person who knows them. We don't know the plans, but we know the Person. He knows the plans, so run by faith into his presence.

And now we are back to how sweet this letter actually is.

Please don't miss this. The letter is not scribbled off in a hurry with thoughtless words. No, these are the words of God to them. Remember, with his word comes his presence. Now we know why this is so important. If we have his presence, we have his plans because he is the one who knows the plans.

Those Who Refuse God's Discipline Are Warned
JEREMIAH 29:15-31

The following section is as scary as the previous section was glorious. God warns those who, as we saw in chapter 24, are left behind (29:15-19). Then he warns the false prophets who try to subvert the work of God (vv. 20-23). The closing of the chapter is a series of three letters concerning Shemaiah, a false prophet who rejected the word God was giving to Jeremiah.

It's difficult, of course, to blame those who would not believe. After all, who wants to believe that God's very plans involve hardship, pain, and suffering? Would it not be more logical to assume God wants me to have a happy life? After all, if God wants me to have a happy life, any enemy of my happiness is the enemy of God. Yet the book of Jeremiah exists to show that this is patently false. God has plans that involve suffering. God has plans that involve pain. God has mysterious plans in which he uses the evil of the enemy for our good. And *these are his plans.*

Conclusion

The lesson is twofold. First, sometimes God plans to use evil to accomplish good. God is not at all pleased with the activity of the Babylonians. In fact, he will punish them. Sometimes God plans to use bad things, even bad people with bad intentions, to accomplish his purposes. Second, when he does, we must yield to those plans. This is what it means to stay under the discipline of the Lord.

We began by suggesting that God's Word to us is God's presence with us. We saw in God's encouragement to Israel that he has plans and that he tells us now what he will do later so we won't focus on the present.

The secret then is not to know the plans but to know the Person. This affirms what Jeremiah said in 9:23-24:

> This is what the LORD says:
> The wise person should not boast in his wisdom;
> the strong should not boast in his strength;
> the wealthy should not boast in his wealth.
> But the one who boasts should boast in this:
> that he understands and knows me—
> that I am the LORD, showing faithful love,
> justice, and righteousness on the earth,
> for I delight in these things.
>   This is the LORD's declaration.

Our confidence is in God. Our confidence is in God because he knows how things will transpire, and he is working his plans toward a good end. If God tells now what he will do in the future, the most important thing is the mind of God that comes from the presence of God.

Reflect and Discuss

1. How are these chapters an encouragement to those in exile?
2. Why would God tell them to thrive in a nation whose people did not know or love God (v. 7)?
3. Is there anything relatable in verse 7? What are practical ways we can seek the welfare of our cities?
4. How does Hebrews 11:9-10 relate to our attitude as believers in this present state of affairs?
5. Compare the New Testament idea of being an "alien" to the Old Testament idea of Israel as strangers and aliens.

6. Jeremiah 29:11 is perhaps the best-known passage in the book. How is it commonly understood? Do you understand it differently after reading this chapter as a whole?
7. Discuss the pattern of future promises in the Scripture.
8. Describe the warnings of verses 15-31. Why were these warnings rejected?
9. If the nation were to embrace the future promise, what dreams in the present would have to die?
10. Is this death to self relatable to the New Testament idea of the crucified life? Can you name any New Testament verses that affirm this idea?

Restored

JEREMIAH 30

Main Idea: God can restore us in our darkest desperation.

Introduction: God Tells Jeremiah to Write a Book (30:1-3).
I.   God Defends the Defenseless (30:12-17).
II. God Restores (30:18-22).
III. God Brings Justice (30:23-24).

In chapter 30 everything changes. After the hard passages of the first half of the book, now comes hope and redemption. The entire tenor of the book changes—from dark prophecy and hard judgment to hope. The impression of the following passages is the hug a parent gives a child after severe discipline. Christopher Wright observes the shocking nature of this transition and how it relates to the prophecies that have already been spoken:

The Message of Jeremiah:

- 30:8 echoes the prediction of Hananiah in 28:4,11. Hananiah got the timing wrong, but even though Jeremiah predicted an iron yoke (unbreakable by any human force), God would ultimately break the yoke of Israel's oppressors.
- 30:9 reverses the ending of the line of Davidic kings in 22:30, promising a new David (as also in 23:5-6, repeated in 33:15-16).
- 30:11 answers the hope and prayer of 10:24, that God would discipline but not completely destroy.
- 30:12-17 answers the cry of the wounded at 8:22 and 15:18, while 30:17 answers the question at 15:5.
- 30:18 promises a rebuilding that reverses 9:19, while 30:19-20 reverses the depopulation of 9:21-22 and 10:20.
- 31:3-4 answers the nostalgic, bittersweet honeymoon memory of Yahweh in 2:2 with the promise of a fresh wooing of his bride ('you' is feminine singular).

- 31:6 answers the forlorn question at 8:19 and 14:19, as to whether the Lord would be present in Zion.
- 31:8 transforms *the land of the north* from a source of impending invasion (1:14-15, etc.) into the source of coming restoration.
- 31:9 anticipates people praying to the God who now listens, who had earlier refused to do so in 11:14.
- 31:12-13 transforms the ending of all social joy in 16:9 into a new celebration.
- 31:18-19 answers at last God's own question in 8:4-7 as to why his people never turn to him in repentance, with the promise that they will.
- 31:31-34 promises a new covenant that will transcend the broken one of 11:1-8. (Wright, *Message of Jeremiah*, 301–2)

It is clear that Jeremiah 30 and 31 are the oasis in the arid judgment of the first 29 chapters. They provide the hope that is needed and the promise of a better future. Jeremiah 30 reminds us of Psalm 30:1-5:

> *I will exalt you, LORD, because you have lifted me up*
> *and have not allowed my enemies to triumph over me.*
> *LORD my God, I cried to you for help, and you healed me.*
> *LORD, you brought me up from Sheol;*
> *you spared me from among those going down to the Pit.*
> *Sing to the LORD, you his faithful ones,*
> *and praise his holy name.*
> *For his anger lasts only a moment,*
> *but his favor, a lifetime.*
> *Weeping may stay overnight,*
> *but there is joy in the morning.*

It also calls to mind Psalm 103:8-10:

> *The LORD is compassionate and gracious,*
> *slow to anger and abounding in faithful love.*
> *He will not always accuse us or be angry forever.*
> *He has not dealt with us as our sins deserve*
> *or repaid us according to our iniquities.*

However, as we will see, this renewed hope is not the next thing on the horizon. There will be judgment before the hope. Just as in the previous chapter, the hope and future will come after the judgment.

Introduction: God Tells Jeremiah to Write a Book
JEREMIAH 30:1-3

Jeremiah is told to write a book. So after all the judgment God has communicated through his prophet, now God wants the hope documented. Jeremiah 31–33 contains the content of the book Jeremiah was told to write. It is a book of encouragement and hope. He is writing to explain how their fortunes would be restored and how they would possesses the land.

While we have mentioned this before, it is encouraging to turn to the books of Ezra and Nehemiah to see how this restoration played out. They really did find what God promised. The contents of Jeremiah become a reality in the restored Jerusalem that God brings.

God Defends the Defenseless
JEREMIAH 30:12-17

These verses are typical of the type of word pictures Jeremiah likes to use. Jeremiah describes the situation with three metaphors. First, he is suggesting they are so bad they are sick patients with a terminal disease. I have often wondered when people had cancer two hundred years ago what they thought. No remedy, no cure, and no hope. Or perhaps even today it is like that in a majority-world country where there is disease with no cure.

Second, they are also like a defendant with no lawyer. This is another tragic metaphor. There are those who need justice, but justice will not be served because they have no one to defend them. They are at the mercy of the court.

Finally, the nation is like an abandoned lover. No one will come to their rescue. They have plenty of lovers but none who will come to their aid. They are a pariah because God's judgment is on them.

Then there is a reversal of fate. God takes all of their enemies, plunders them, and sends them into exile. Then, in one of the most beautiful verses in the book, God says,

> But I will bring you health
> and will heal you of your wounds—
>   this is the LORD's declaration—
> for they call you Outcast,
> Zion whom no one cares about. (30:17)

There is no one to heal their wounds so God becomes their healer.

If there was ever a passage that so exquisitely sets up New Testament theology, it is Jeremiah 30. We are people who are diseased with sin (Rom 6:23); we are people who have no one to stand in our defense (Rom 8:31-39), and we are people who are without hope in the world (Eph 2:1).

Yet God, after our many rebellions, treats us in salvation in the same way he treated Judah. Because of Christ, we are healed from the disease of sin. Because of Christ, we have him to stand in our defense. Because of Christ, we have hope that we are actually a part of the bride of Christ and forever wed to him.

The desperation of my situation was not fake; it was real. Without Christ I was genuinely destitute. Yet the power of the gospel is stronger than my plight. My life with Christ is the light that overcomes the darkness that was my life without Christ.

This gospel-centric way of reading Jeremiah is not forced, as the next section demonstrates.

God Restores
JEREMIAH 30:18-22

The picture of restoration in this section is rich and encouraging. Notice the language of completeness: "every city . . . every citadel." With all that God has taken away, he will also give. This is not a temporary restoration; this is a complete restoration. Yet we know how this ends: God does allow the city to be rebuilt under the leadership of Ezra and Nehemiah. The exiles do return. There is a future and a hope. But then the city is once again given to Roman occupation and destroyed in AD 70. So how, in any reasonable sense, is this fulfilled?

Brueggemann's suggestion, that a text such as this is to be viewed in a promissory sense and not a predictive sense, is helpful (*To Build, to Plant*, 42). That is, the focus here is not *when* and *how* this will be fulfilled but *that* it will be fulfilled. This is more promise than prediction.

There is a sense that this will be fulfilled in the prophet's time, relatively speaking. The exiles do return to Jerusalem. There is also a spiritual sense in which this is fulfilled in the time of Christ when he restores all things spiritually and brings an invisible, but real, kingdom. Finally, this is fulfilled in the new Jerusalem that John sees coming down (Rev 21–22). In that moment all the promises of the prophets are ultimately fulfilled.

This is what theologians call the "horizons" of prophecy (see Wright, *Message of Jeremiah*, 304). There is the horizon of the time of the prophet, the horizon of the coming of Christ, and the final horizon of the new heavens and the new earth. The challenge of interpretation is to understand on which horizon the text is to be viewed.

One could say that all things are fulfilled in relation to Christ and the gospel message. The prophets anticipate Christ, Christ comes, and then his obedience to the will of the Father executes the plan to consummate all things by Christ. This is to reverse the language of Colossians 1:16: "Everything was created by him . . . through him and for him." The Old Testament is *for* Christ, the New Testament is *through* Christ, and the Revelation is a reality *by* the obedience of Christ. Anticipation, execution, and consummation.

God Brings Justice
JEREMIAH 30:23-24

The final section is sobering. It reminds God's people that the coming storm cannot be stopped. Yet even this judgment is an expression of his integrity. Jeremiah writes,

> *The LORD's burning anger will not turn back*
> *until he has completely fulfilled the purposes of his heart.*
> *In time to come you will understand it.*

The harshest fulfillments of prophecy still remind us that God keeps his word. He is immutable. He always makes a promise to protect the weak and bring justice on the oppressors.

Conclusion

Jeremiah 30 is a text of hope in a dark time. God had promised them immediate hope and ultimate hope, but the ultimate hope would come on another horizon altogether. Let's end at the beginning.

God made all things in the creation and then destroyed all things in the flood. However, Noah was too much like his father Adam, and the legacy of sin and separation from God simply proliferated with the race. God then started over with a new race—a physical race of people but a people who would be his through a covenant instituted by God. God initiated this covenant through Abraham in Genesis 12:1-3.

> *The LORD said to Abram:*
> *Go out from your land,*
> *your relatives,*
> *and your father's house*
> *to the land that I will show you.*
> *I will make you into a great nation,*
> *I will bless you,*
> *I will make your name great,*
> *and you will be a blessing.*
> *I will bless those who bless you,*
> *I will curse anyone who treats you with contempt,*
> *and all the peoples on earth will be blessed through you.*

Notice the three parts of the covenant: God would give them a land, make them numerous, and make them a blessing to all people.

One way to understand Scripture is the progression of how God kept the three parts of the covenant.

A Great Nation

When the famine forced the young family into the land of Egypt, they could not envision what would transpire. They would go in a family of seventy and emerge a nation of a few hundred thousand. They prospered so much that the Egyptian government was afraid they would rise up and force them into slavery.

A Land

After the exodus from Egypt, and their subsequent rebellion-induced wilderness wandering, they received the land God promised them. This was the land of Canaan.

A Blessing to All the Nations

It is at this point hard to see how they are a blessing to all nations. The answer is, of course, that they are a blessing to all the nations through the promised one, the Messiah. Jesus would come for every tribe and tongue. He would be a light to the nations (Isa 49:6), and all people would worship him (Phil 2:10; Rev 4–5).

As mentioned, Jeremiah 30 touches these horizons. There are promises that will be fulfilled a few years after they were declared by

Jeremiah, some not until the time of Christ, and others still not until the new Jerusalem comes down. One way to view this would be through cycles of bondage and freedom.

Time	Promise Fulfilled	Fulfillment
Bondage in Egypt	Great Nation	1/3
Bondage to Freedom	Great Nation Promised Land	2/3
Bondage to Ultimate Freedom in Christ	Great Nation Promised Land Blessing to All Nations	3/3

Jeremiah is prophesying in the time that only two-thirds of the promise is complete. The Messiah has not yet come to bring all things to himself. Jeremiah's message of restoration would not be completely fulfilled in the lifetime of those listening to the message.

Today the Abrahamic covenant is fulfilled, but not completely. In a real sense the covenant promise to Abraham was a missionary covenant. The blessing to the nations is a message that has not yet reached all the nations. The covenant, in this missionary sense, is more fully complete when we extend the missionary call to the world.

Discuss and Reflect

1. Describe the shift that takes place in chapter 30.
2. What is the significance of this restoration considering the trajectory of the whole Bible?
3. Is there a metaphor for salvation here? Can we speak of God's restoring his people and draw an analogy with salvation?
4. How does the book of Nehemiah help us understand the fulfillment of the hope that is promised?
5. How is God's promise to bring judgment on the wicked (vv. 23-24) strangely encouraging?
6. What does it mean that this passage is fulfilled on three horizons?
7. How do these horizons find their fulfillment in Christ?
8. Explain the chart showing cycles of bondage and freedom.
9. Describe how Jeremiah 30 echoes the Abrahamic covenant.
10. Why are the covenants in a sense "missionary covenants"?

God Restores

JEREMIAH 31:1-30

Main Idea: God restores fully what was devastated completely.

I. **Invitation: God Is Husband (31:3-6).**
II. **Provision: God Is Father (31:7-9).**
III. **Protection: God Is Shepherd (31:10-14).**
IV. **A Heart of Responsive Obedience (31:15-22)**

Some regard the hymn "The Love of God" to be one of the greatest hymns ever penned.

> The love of God is greater far
> Than tongue or pen can ever tell;
> It goes beyond the highest star,
> And reaches to the lowest hell;
> The guilty pair, bowed down with care,
> God gave His Son to win;
> His erring child He reconciled,
> And pardoned from his sin.
> > *Refrain:*
> > O love of God, how rich and pure!
> > How measureless and strong!
> > It shall forevermore endure—
> > The saints' and angels' song!
> When years of time shall pass away
> And earthly thrones and kingdoms fall,
> When men who here refuse to pray,
> On rocks and hills and mountains call,
> God's love so sure shall still endure,
> All measureless and strong;
> Redeeming grace to Adam's race—
> The saints' and angels' song.

This third verse is recognized as one of the most profound hymns of all time.

Could we with ink the ocean fill
And were the skies of parchment made,
Were every stalk on earth a quill
And every man a scribe by trade,
To write the love of God above
Would drain the ocean dry;
Nor could the scroll contain the whole,
Though stretched from sky to sky. (Lehman, "The Love
   of God")

It almost seems strange to talk about love in the book of Jeremiah.
Yet, after chapters and chapters of judgment, there is a shift from condemnation to consolation. If you are thinking that it's like a parent disciplining a child, then you are right, but there is more. This is not a subtle
shift; it is a massive shift, like the shifts we observed in chapter 30. The
shift in the way God feels about them is concisely stated in verses 1-2:

> *"At that time"—this is the LORD's declaration—"I will be the God of
>   all the families of Israel, and they will be my people."*
> *This is what the LORD says:*
> *The people who survived the sword*
> *found favor in the wilderness.*

These are the people who found favor with the Lord. So what is the
favor of the Lord? It is not based on natural giftedness or worthiness. If
you look at the favor God showed to Joseph or to Ezra, you see that his
favor is a divine decree. He simply chooses to bless one person. That's
clear enough. However, if you look at the lives of people on whom God's
favor rested, you notice that while it is powerful, it is also fragile. The
people who had the favor of God sustained throughout their lives are
people who recognized this and honored God with their obedience.
   Joseph had the favor of God, and he was faithful to God during dark
times. Ezra had the favor of God, and he sought God when the times
were the most difficult. So God's favor is at the sovereign discretion of
God, yet it seems it often rested on those who had active faith to seek
favor from God. In other words, the favor of God is *God's* favor. It is not
ours. It belongs to him. The people who recognize that favor belongs
to him are the people who enjoy it the most. This is fascinating. The
people who think it is *their* favor often do not have it ultimately. This is
the position Israel is in. They had the favor of God for a time, and they

thought it was theirs by right. God then turned against them because of their sin and withheld his favor for a season. Now he is showing his favor to them again.

The text helps us understand how to respond to God when he turns his favor toward us. So how is God turning his favor toward Judah?

Invitation: God Is Husband
JEREMIAH 31:3-6

The new language that is used is startling. Even though they are far away from the physical place they called home, God is still present. "Removal from God's land did not mean removal from his love" (Huey, *Jeremiah, Lamentations,* 269).

The love that is expressed in verse 3 is both poetic and lavish. He uses the language of a husband's love for his bride. He loves them "with an everlasting love." His love has never ceased and will never cease. They did not initiate the love of God, nor did they ever deserve it. It was initiated by God, and he will consummate the love. It will never go away.

But there is more. He references "faithful love" (Hb *chesed*). This is the strongest expression of God's love for Israel. It is his love and his faithfulness together. There is nothing subtle or implicit here. The mood of the text is initiation. God is doing something different from what he has done before. Yet this is not a completely new thing; it is a return.

What God envisions in the ensuing verses is nothing less than a restored Israel. They will return from exile and, more importantly, their love for God will be restored.

God is their husband. It's a new day.

Provision: God Is Father
JEREMIAH 31:7-9

Beyond the initiation of the love relationship, God then promises that the nation of Israel should be celebrated because God is going to gather the people together, even the most vulnerable among them, and he will console them. This is the spirit of this poem: consolation. And the consolation is not simply emotional. God will console them with provision. They will come back and find that they have water and a smooth path.

Note that the metaphor switches. In the first passage God was the groom to the bride. In this passage he is the Father of his firstborn.

Again, this seems like an astonishing reversal. If you are reading through the book of Jeremiah in one sitting, something that is highly recommended, you will find the contrast shocking. God is the one who was saying there was no more hope. It's all over. It's done. Now he is saying he will be the Father to his firstborn.

God as Father is a helpful mental image. Imagine a son in his late adolescence who rebels to the point that he distances himself from his parents. It is done. Their relationship is destroyed. When the son initiates repentance, the parents, perhaps cautiously at first, reciprocate with trust and affirmation. No one blames them for being cautious. They do not want to be taken for granted again, and they do not know, ultimately, how this will work out.

Unlike that scenario, God knows exactly what will happen. His spokesman prophesies as much. Yet God is not initiating a new chapter in their relationship like the parents in that story; he is returning to the way things always were. In fact, this is similar language to that which God commanded Moses to use with Pharaoh in Exodus 4:22-23:

> And you will say to Pharaoh: This is what the LORD says: Israel is my firstborn son. I told you: Let my son go so that he may worship me, but you refused to let him go. Look, I am about to kill your firstborn son!

God is still a husband who loves his bride, and he is still a father who provides for his children. It's a new day.

Protection: God Is Shepherd
JEREMIAH 31:10-14

God as Father will not only provide for his children, but he will protect them as well. God is like a shepherd who guards his flock. A part of this blessing is protection.

As a result, their mourning will be turned to joy. The nouns in this passage are telling: *joy, consolation, happiness, abundance,* and *goodness.* God is going to bless them, and he is going to bring all of this to pass. This is wonderful consolation.

Notice that he is like a shepherd in verse 11 because "the LORD has ransomed Jacob and redeemed him from the power of one stronger than he." This makes perfect sense. If the sheep could take care of themselves, then they would not need a shepherd. They would be on their own. They would be fine. If the enemies of the sheep were other sheep—which is both unlikely and comical—they would be fine. However, the enemy is greater than they are, and they lack the means to take care of themselves. God is going to deliver them from the hand of the Babylonians. It will be accomplished in a way they never could have predicted. It will be glorious, and they will return home.

Shepherding is a difficult task. A shepherd not only needs to work hard; he must be discerning as well. He needs to know when and where to lead the sheep to water, when and where to lead the sheep to greener pasture. He cannot be too demure with the errant sheep, and he cannot be too deferential with the sheep that are easy to love. He must strike the balance of a tender warrior. He is to take up the challenge with both compassion and vigor.

God protects them. It's a new day.

When God loves, provides, and protects, how are we to respond?

A Heart of Responsive Obedience
JEREMIAH 31:15-22

For the first time in the poem, there is dialogue. There is a remarkable twist in this passage, namely, the response of Israel to this new development. Read this telling response in verses 18-19:

> You disciplined me, and I have been disciplined
> like an untrained calf.
> Take me back, so that I can return,
> for you, Lord, are my God.
> After my return, I felt regret;
> After I was instructed, I struck my thigh in grief.
> I was ashamed and humiliated
> because I bore the disgrace of my youth.

What you see, for the first time, is a broken heart. God has been railing against his people for having hard hearts—for having hearts that are turned toward false gods. Now for the first time their hearts are sensitive to the Lord.

God loves like a true husband, provides like a father, and protects like a shepherd. The thing is, these characteristics have always been true of him. What has not been true, to this point, is that the heart of the people can be moved. Finally, they are beginning to respond to God.

Conclusion

This passage reminds us of Micah 6, where God, frustrated by the rebellion of his people, says that he will put them on trial before the whole world. In Micah 6:1 God says,

> *Now listen to what the LORD is saying:*
> *Rise, plead your case before the mountains,*
> *and let the hills hear your complaint.*

God then asks in verses 2-5 just precisely how he has offended them. What exactly has he done? Then in verses 6-7 they respond that perhaps they should do something dramatic to appease God and restore their relationship. The people in the mock courtroom respond,

> *What should I bring before the LORD*
> *when I come to bow before God on high?*
> *Should I come before him with burnt offerings,*
> *with year-old calves?*
> *Would the LORD be pleased with thousands of rams*
> *or with ten thousand streams of oil?*
> *Should I give my firstborn for my transgression,*
> *the offspring of my body for my own sin?*

That might do it! What if we bring bulls or calves or something dramatic like this? Then God brings them back to reality by saying,

> *Mankind, he has told each of you what is good*
> *and what it is the LORD requires of you:*
> *to act justly,*
> *to love faithfulness,*
> *and to walk humbly with your God.* (v. 8)

In other words, you know what to do. You know. You know that I do not want some elaborate response to my call. Rather, I want a heart of responsive obedience.

So there is a shift in the passage. However, the shift is not so much in God's posture but in Israel's posture. God is not changing the way he feels; he is simply verbally remembering the way he has always felt. The real change comes in the people who are finally affirming their love for

God. Their hearts are soft. They are tender. Or to say it in the language of the chapter, they are ready to be loved, to be fathered, to be the sheep to the Shepherd. For the first time in a long time, they are ready to receive the love God has always had for them.

Reflect and Discuss

1. What are the three metaphors used to describe God in Jeremiah 31:2-30? In what ways do these metaphors portray God's character?
2. The love that is expressed in verse 3 is both poetic and lavish. Did Israel initiate this love, or does the love emanate from God?
3. Why is there a shift from condemnation to consolation in this passage?
4. What is the favor of the Lord? How does Jeremiah understand this term? How should we interpret it today?
5. Is God's favor based on human merit, natural ability, or self-worthiness?
6. What kind of love does God give to Israel in this passage?
7. What is the spirit, or emotive tone, of the poem in 31:7-8?
8. When God loves, protects, and provides, how are we to respond?
9. Why does God value a heart of obedience over religious performance and activity?
10. Is there a thematic connection between Jeremiah 31 and Micah 6? If so, what is the connection?

Something New

Main Idea: God is making something new.

I. **New Day: The New Covenant Will Be Different from the Old Covenant (31:32).**

II. **New Distinctives: The New Covenant Will Have Four Distinctives (31:33-34).**
   A. Internalized word (31:33)
   B. Personal God (31:34)
   C. Personal instruction (31:34)
   D. Permanent forgiveness (31:34)

III. **New Permanence: The New Covenant Will Be Permanent (31:35-37).**

IV. **New City: Jerusalem Will Be Rebuilt (31:38-40).**

From the moment the piece of forbidden fruit slid from Eve's hand and landed softly on the lush soil of the perfect garden, we have been waiting for something new. The Lord chased after Adam and then chased them out of the garden (Gen 3:8-9,21-24). Everything was lost, and the only hope was that the woman's offspring would come and bruise the head of the serpent (Gen 3:15). Some members of her offspring were types of the one who would rend time and come to make all things new. The partial newness came first in the form of a man named Noah.

God re-created all things from a new starting place. Yet Noah's family was wrought with the same problem as Adam's family (Gen 9). Noah shared DNA with Adam, and he shared a genetic disposition to ruin things, to make things old again. So we see the Adamic race building a tower when God had actually told them to disperse and multiply. God used the inauguration of diverse languages to force a scattering into the whole world (Gen 11:1-9). God wanted to make all things new, and this newness came in the form of a man named Abraham.

Abraham was called of God to bring new things. He was called to be the progenitor of a new spiritual race of people. God promised them land, offspring, and blessing (Gen 15; 12:3). None of this could be physically seen full orbed at the time; rather, it was to come. He was walking and living in faith toward a trajectory of newness he would never see with his eyes. The land would come through another man, Moses.

Moses would lead God's people out of the bondage of Egypt and to the threshold of the promised land (Exod 3). The people led out of Egypt would suffer at the hands of their own rebellion and never see the promised land (Num 14:20-24).

Once Israel was in the promised land, the period of the judges and then the kings would follow. Solomon's sin would lead to a divided country, and many other sinful kings came after him, leading the people astray. This brings us up to Jeremiah's time. Now the people are exiles. If they ever wanted something new, this was the time.

They understand the weight of their sin. They understand the consequences of sin so deeply that they grieve and repent, as we saw in chapter 29. They finally get it. And then, in chapter 30, their prospects reverse. The God who was bent on destroying them now wants to restore them. He promises in 29:11 that he has a future and a hope for them. Jeremiah 31:31-40 is an explanation, a more explicit commentary, on Jeremiah 29:11. The future and the hope for Israel is this: a new covenant with them.

In order to understand this, you have to understand the background to get at the weight of what he is saying to them. You must understand the power of the covenant for their collective national consciousness. It was profound. You also have to understand what this means for us today. It is fascinating, so let's get at it. Here is God's declaration of something new and what it means.

A New Covenant (31:31)

> *"Look, the days are coming"*—this is the Lord's declaration—*"when I will make a new covenant with the house of Israel and with the house of Judah."*

It is extremely difficult to fully express how powerful the idea of *covenant* was to God's people. God was always making promises, all the way back to the time of Adam and Eve. It was his way of communicating with us. God promised Adam death when he sinned. God promised Adam and Eve curses with a hint of blessing when they exited the garden. When Noah landed on the ground, God promised that he would never again flood the earth. Yet the idea of covenant crystalized when God appeared to Abraham in Genesis 12:1-3.

The LORD said to Abram:
Go out from your land,
your relatives,
and your father's house
to the land that I will show you.
I will make you into a great nation,
I will bless you,
I will make your name great,
and you will be a blessing.
I will bless those who bless you,
I will curse anyone who treats you with contempt,
and all the peoples on earth will be blessed through you.

God promises three elements of the covenant: land, offspring, and blessing. Later in Genesis 15:18 the covenant is made explicit: "On that day the LORD made a covenant with Abram, saying, 'I give this land to your offspring, from the brook of Egypt to the great river, the Euphrates River.'"

Abraham receives the covenant. The covenant is renewed in Moses, and later it is affirmed to David. Before they were taken into exile, Judah was living in the blessings of the Davidic covenant. Perhaps now they wondered if the covenant was still active. After all, it seemed that God had forgotten them. Then, right in the middle of their mess, God does not affirm the covenant. He does not come in and say he wants to re-up what he said in the past. What he said was not confirmation of something old. This was the promise of the inauguration of something new. This is new. Again, this was a shocking reality to their system.

We see all this clearly, of course, from the vantage point of living after the coming of Christ. We can see how God's plans were fulfilled in the person of Jesus. Jesus referred to the cup at the Lord's Supper as representing the new covenant: "In the same way he also took the cup after supper and said, 'This cup is the new covenant in my blood'" (Luke 22:20). The cross of Jesus was a promise of salvation for all who would believe. And, unlike the old covenant, this new covenant would never fade away.

Paul makes this explicitly clear in 2 Corinthians 3:7-11, where he compares the new covenant with the old.

Now if the ministry that brought death, chiseled in letters on stones,
came with glory, so that the Israelites were not able to gaze steadily

*at Moses's face because of its glory, which was set aside, how will
the ministry of the Spirit not be more glorious? For if the ministry
that brought condemnation had glory, the ministry that brings
righteousness overflows with even more glory. In fact, what had been
glorious is not glorious now by comparison because of the glory that
surpasses it. For if what was set aside was glorious, what endures will
be even more glorious.*

The new covenant is more glorious than the old because the new
covenant has a glory that will not fade. Paul uses the fading glory of
Moses's face as a metaphor for the fading glory of the old covenant.

At the time the message of Jeremiah is recorded, all of this is still to
come. God gives them details about what this new covenant will look like.

New Day: The New Covenant Will Be Different from the Old Covenant
JEREMIAH 31:32

God begins with a reminder of the covenant that was broken. The language of marriage here is a reminder of how tragic the faithlessness of his
people really was. They rejected the one who loved them and who wanted
to protect them. Instead of fixing them, however, he will establish a new
covenant that deals with such transgression in a similar but new way.

New Distinctives: The New Covenant Will Have Four Distinctives
JEREMIAH 31:33-34

Internalized Word (31:33)

The word that was spoken to them was an external word that needed to
be internalized. He is prophesying about a day when the Word would
be in their hearts.

Personal God (31:34)

Notice the personal language used here. God will be theirs, and they
will be God's. This is a righting of the wrong of faithlessness he mentioned earlier. Even though they had been faithless, God is going to
make all of this right.

Personal Instruction (31:34)

The people Jeremiah was speaking to knew the word from the elders and teachers. The scribal culture will soon begin with Ezra, and for the next few centuries learning from teachers in the synagogue would be their way of life. Yet this promise would be fulfilled in the person of Christ, and from then on the Word would be in the hearts of all the members of the sacred community of faith.

Permanent Forgiveness (31:34)

The forgiveness that would come in the new covenant would be permanent. Jeremiah invites Judah to imagine that forgiveness is purely an act of grace that can never be taken away (Eph 2:8-9). This is the promise of the new covenant.

New Permanence: The New Covenant Will Be Permanent
JEREMIAH 31:35-37

This beautiful poem speaks for itself. It describes the permanence of the new covenant as being as fixed as the order of creation, as regular as the cycles of nature, and as immense as the universe. A new-covenant believer cannot read these words without thinking about the power of God to keep eternally all those who are in Christ.

New City: Jerusalem Will Be Rebuilt
JEREMIAH 31:38-40

This did indeed take place. Starting in 538 BC, groups of exiles returned to Jerusalem and rebuilt the city. So the prophecy was fulfilled in the fairly near future. Except it wasn't. The promise of verse 40 is not just rebuilding but rebuilding in a way that the city "will never be uprooted or demolished again." In AD 70 the temple was destroyed again. We might surmise that Jeremiah was getting a bit carried away; perhaps he was speaking in metaphor or hyperbole. However, another more probable explanation helps us understand this entire passage. Let's leave the immediate question about the rebuilding of Jerusalem to look at the larger question of when this new covenant will be totally operative.

The best way to understand the fulfillment is to understand it as fulfilled at three different intervals, if you will (see Wright, *Message of*

Jeremiah, 334–39). The first interval is the immediate. Jerusalem was restored and the people taken back into the land.

In the second interval we see this new covenant as fulfilled in the life of Christ. As we noted, Christ himself borrowed the language from this verse when he said, "This cup is the new covenant in my blood" (Luke 22:20). If someone reads the New Testament first then reads this passage in Jeremiah, several themes jump out as explicitly fulfilled in the work of Christ and in the church he established. First, the law is indeed written in our hearts. The Holy Spirit of Christ came to bring to remembrance everything Jesus had taught his disciples. The Word is now in us bearing fruit as we *abide in* his words (John 5:38; 8:31; 15:7; 1 John 2:14). The Word of God is now a witness within us.

The second promise is of personalization and possession. God will belong to us, and we will belong to God, made real by the abiding presence of the Holy Spirit. Peter clearly expresses this idea of possession when he amalgamates several Old Testament prophets in 1 Peter 2:9-10:

> *But you are a chosen race, a royal priesthood, a holy nation, a people for his possession, so that you may proclaim the praises of the one who called you out of darkness into his marvelous light. Once you were not a people, but now you are God's people; you had not received mercy, but now you have received mercy.*

The promise that we will need no teachers does not, of course, negate the teaching ministry of the church but rather affirms it. The work of teaching is explaining the Word of God in a way that resonates and affirms the inner work of the Holy Spirit. In other words, the Holy Spirit is the teacher, and he uses teachers and preachers as instruments to open the eyes of understanding to the truth. In seeing the Word of God, we see the Son of God; and in seeing the Son of God, we understand the Father. This is the power of the inner witness of the Spirit.

Finally, there is the promise of forgiveness, a promise ultimately fulfilled in Christ (Rom 3:23-26).

This leads us back to our discussion of the temple and the timeline. We know that because of the power of Christ, who will return as our royal Messiah-Warrior, the enemy will be defeated and New Jerusalem will come down at the end of the age (Rev 21:9-27). This is the city of our eternal home.

When one considers all that is involved in the fulfillment of Jeremiah 31:31, it is breathtaking! This new covenant describes so much more than the events of Jeremiah's life and time. This text serves as a hinge on which so much of salvation history turns. Yet the original audience could not have known that at the time. They were simply receiving the encouragement for the moment. And this speaks to how God works so often. We simply have grace for the moment.

Conclusion

Think back to the moment when God instituted the covenant with Abraham. Think about how much information God tells Abraham. Think about it: God tells him, in a dream, these magnificent details:

> Then the LORD said to Abram, "Know this for certain: Your offspring will be resident aliens for four hundred years in a land that does not belong to them and will be enslaved and oppressed. However, I will judge the nation they serve, and afterward they will go out with many possessions. But you will go to your fathers in peace and be buried at a good old age. In the fourth generation they will return here, for the iniquity of the Amorites has not yet reached its full measure."
> (Gen 15:13-16)

Oh my! These are details no one in the world knew but Abraham: slavery, bondage, judgment, and deliverance. God is saying to Abraham, "I am giving you a lot of details that are going to happen before I fulfill my promise." This leads us to two interesting facts about God's promises.

God Often Gives a Lot of Information

God gave Abraham enough information to act and more. At that point he was the only person alive who knew the scope and sequence of God's plans. So too with us. We don't feel like we have all the information, but we have all the information we need to obey. More than enough really. Walking with the Lord is not a matter of information; it is a matter of obedience. And it seems, as a matter of curious observation, that the people who know the most of God's plans are those who are acting on what God already said. Why did God trust Abraham with so much information? We can only guess. But the guess would have to factor in the reality that few people were as responsive in their obedience as Abraham.

God Does Not Give Us All the Information

But with all that God tells Abraham, he stops after the exodus. Think of it in terms of the Bible. We are still thinking about the implications of all that is in the Bible. The thousands of words, the promises of the psalms and the warnings of the prophets, and the glorious consummation that comes at the end of the sixty-six books in the book of Revelation! What a story! Yet God just gives Abraham the story up until chapter 12 of the second book. That's it. This means Abraham was acting on what seemed like a lot of information, but he did not know the whole story. Maybe he thought he did, but he didn't. God does not finish the story. He rarely does. He gives us all the information we need to walk as far as he wants us to go. And that's all.

So we read in Jeremiah 31 of the wonderful promise of a new covenant. We cannot help but think of the promise fulfilled in Jesus. The word *fulfilled* is in past tense. We are reading this chapter with the end in mind. We can't help it. We are living its fulfillment. Yet what you must realize about all of this is that it was, at the time, not clear. We look at this arc of newness and see the wonderful way the plan seems to fit together. So maybe the faith element is lost on us. At the moment the weeping prophet of doom is giving this good news, they can only believe it by faith. When times were good, they had a difficult time believing things could be bad. Now that times are bad, how will they do with the news that times will be good again?

You see, at this moment all is lost. Literally. Homes, families, comfort, civilization. The people are refugees. When they were cascading down the crescent of their own bad choices, when the memory of lost idols was so fresh they could see it, when being in exile was so awful, perhaps they lacked the capacity to see this; they did not know what was on the horizon and just how glorious it was. In this moment they had to walk by faith. And, of course, so do we.

This makes me wonder: What is all the rest of my life going to be like? What are the surprises of grace? What discipline will the Lord put on us? What discipline will we need to put on ourselves? What challenges? What joys? We just do not know. We need some type of assurance, some type of promise—you know, like a covenant. And there we have it. The words of the steely prophet are words for me. God has done something new. We're living it. But the faith, needed by Israel to believe in what would come, is the faith I need to believe in what has already come. We are in the new covenant. God has done something new, and he has given us all the information we need to obey. Yet, praise God, we don't know it all. There is a glorious mystery to the newness of God—the mystery that calls us to walk by faith.

Reflect and Discuss

1. Compare and contrast the old covenant and the new covenant. What are the differences? What are the similarities?
2. Where did the old covenant begin, and with which historical figure in the Old Testament did it begin?
3. Name the four distinctives of the new covenant. Discuss them.
4. Second Corinthians 3:1-7 compares the new covenant with the old. Discuss the metaphor used to describe the fading glory of the old covenant.
5. Do you agree that the best way to understand the fulfillment of the new covenant is to understand it as fulfilled at three different intervals? What are these three intervals?
6. Do we have enough information to obey God fully today? Why or why not?
7. Abraham is often viewed as a man of faith. Why did God withhold certain details from Abraham and still expect him to walk by faith?
8. Is the information that God gives us proportionate with our willingness to obey it?
9. Discuss this statement: God often gives us a lot of information, but he does not give us all the information.
10. How should we preach the old covenant in light of the new covenant?

Of Prayer and Promises

JEREMIAH 32–35

Main Idea: Praise frames prayer when God's promises are perplexing.

I. **Promises Can Be Perplexing (32:1-15).**
II. **Praise Frames Prayer When Promises Are Perplexing (32:16-25).**
    A. Praise: Acknowledge that nothing is impossible for God (32:16-17).
    B. Praise: Acknowledge that God is faithful and just (32:18-19).
    C. Praise: God redeems (32:20-23a).
    D. Confession for the guilt of the past (32:23b)
    E. Laying before God the problem of the present (32:24-25)
III. **God Responds to Perplexing Prayer (32:26-44).**
    A. Judgment still stands (32:26-35).
    B. God will gather his people (32:36-44).
IV. **God Responds with Promises (33).**
    A. Peace and renewal (33:1-13)
    B. New priest and a perfect King (33:14-26)
Conclusion: Promises Made and Promises Broken (34–35)
    A. Great faithlessness
    B. Great faithfulness

Faith is the practice of delayed gratification for a promised outcome. This is true with parenting. It is rarely gratifying to tell children no, to warn them, or to rebuff them with discipline. Yet this is exactly what we must do. It is best for them to "bear the yoke in their youth" (Lam 3:27). If children do not learn to bear down now, they will not be able to bear up later. The most loving thing we can do is prepare them for this reality by stretching them to do well now, even if this is indeed a stretch. Faith is a matter of delayed gratification.

This is true financially. It rarely seems practical to invest in the kingdom of God and be divested of the kingdom of this world. It makes more sense to invest all we have in this life and not worry about what we cannot see. Yet Jesus loves us too much not to slap us in the face with this truth over and over again. We gain huge reward when we are divested of this life and invest in the life to come (Luke 16:1-13). He knows we cannot serve God and money, so he calls us to serve God alone by investing our money in the kingdom. The truth is that this investment pays off in massive ways. It is more real than any earthly investment because it is permanent. It can never be taken away (Matt 6:19-20). Faith is a matter of delayed gratification.

This is true in leadership. It would make sense to take vengeance on our enemies right away, to run over people to get what we want, and to manipulate facts to our tactical advantage. Yet Christ calls us to lead by serving and by loving (Matt 20:25-28). This counterintuitive leadership has as its goal investing our best resources, our time and service, in other people, not in ourselves. The goal of this leadership is to make as many other people successful as possible. The payoff is huge, but it is often seen in the next life and not in this life. Faith is a matter of delayed gratification.

If we do not realize that faith is a matter of delayed gratification, the promises of God can seem perplexing. You see, the health-and-wealth preachers are right about some things, just not the timing. God does promise us complete and perfect health—just not now. God promises us unlimited financial wealth—in the next life. God goes even further by promising complete justice over all our enemies—at an undisclosed time.

For those of us who want to see cause and effect, a relatively quick return on our investment, the promises of God can be perplexing. This is exactly the situation Jeremiah finds himself in. He is faced with stepping out and trusting God when nothing makes sense to him.

Sometimes following God makes perfect sense. This is not one of those times. This is when Jeremiah will put himself out there financially with only his trust in the word of God. However, when we trust God, risk is, in a sense, no risk. We risk more by disobedience than by obedience. So Jeremiah is wise to trust God in this way.

Promises Can Be Perplexing
JEREMIAH 32:1-15

It is clear to Jeremiah that God has moved on. Judgment is coming in the form of persecution, captivity, and eventual exile of Judah. Babylon is taking on Jerusalem (v. 2), and Jeremiah is in jail. He is there because the king is tired of the prophecies he is speaking against his reign

(vv. 3-5). Jeremiah is shut in with nothing to do but think about how God is moving in this situation. He has no next move—until the Lord speaks to him, that is. The Lord tells him to buy a field when the opportunity presents itself, which it does very soon (vv. 6-8).

He buys the field and completes the whole legal transaction necessary for the field to be purchased (vv. 9-15).

So this is interesting. This is not exactly what you call a seller's market. It would be like going to a Middle Eastern country today, one ravaged by a dictator, and just before he occupies the land, you invest in real estate. No one is thinking Jeremiah is investing wisely. So why is he doing this? Well, because he is a living demonstration of the promises of God.

This sounds like a massive act of faith, and it is. Yet in reality it is not too different from what we do on a day-to-day basis. We all must invest in our faith knowing that, when we invest in the promises of God, the returns only make sense in the long run, rarely in the short term.

This is like a child who will eat all her cake except the icing because she knows that the icing brings greater satisfaction. She is willing to wait for a greater reward. Yet there is something deeper about this with Jeremiah. He is actually willing to bank his confidence in God because he has banked his whole life and ministry on God. This is not simply an act of faith; this is a public demonstration of willingness to put up or shut up. He cannot talk a big game and then be afraid to invest in the land that one day will be active and viable again.

This is why verses 9-14 describe an elaborate process of counting the money, weighing the money, sealing the deed, and putting it up for safekeeping. This is a sign that the future prosperity of the land was indeed coming.

So what do you do when you need to trust God in a big way? Well, you pray.

Praise Frames Prayer When Promises Are Perplexing
JEREMIAH 32:16-25

Jeremiah prays a model prayer for when the work and will of God seem confusing. This prayer could be its own lesson or sermon. Let's look at the anatomy of a prayer that is prayed in a moment when we need to trust God but find that his promises are perplexing.

Praise: Acknowledge That Nothing Is Impossible for God (32:16-17)

Jeremiah does not have his questions answered. That will be clear in a moment. Yet he begins with the fact that, even though it is impossible for him to understand exactly what is going on, nothing is impossible for God.

Notice what he is specifically praising God for: that nothing is impossible. This is significant because he has really put himself out there in this real-estate transaction. He wants God to know that he gets it. He just extended himself, but that is in the category of nothing—not a thing God cannot conquer.

As a preacher I'm tempted to stop here and make a list of all the things that are impossible for us. But since *everything* is on that list, I'll just let you make your own list.

What are you worried about? Got it in your mind? It falls in the "nothing" category. Nothing is impossible for God! Nothing. Now you might want to put down the book and praise him for the reality that nothing is impossible for him. Many things are impossible for me; nothing is impossible for God.

- This is why he asks us to pray so lavishly in John 14:14. Nothing is impossible.
- This is why we are to pray expectantly in James 1:6. Nothing is impossible.
- This is why we are to ask boldly in Luke 11:5-8. Nothing is impossible.
- This is why we are to ask persistently in Luke 11:9. Nothing is impossible.

You see, every time I pray, the thing I pray for falls into the "no thing" category. Everything I ask is nothing for God. What is something for me is nothing to God.

In the end this is why Jesus said in John 14:14, "If you ask me anything in my name, I will do it." We can ask anything because everything is nothing for God.

Praise: Acknowledge That God Is Faithful and Just (32:18-19)

Now that Jeremiah has established God's power to do all things, he rehearses how faithful God has been in the past, yet he also acknowledges that God is just. Sin has consequences.

Praise: God Redeems (32:20-23a)

His final praise rehearses how good God has been to redeem the Israelites from their disasters in the past. A New Testament believer adds to this note of praise that God paid the price for our sin ultimately when Jesus extended himself for our sin on the cross. Jesus came with signs and wonders, Jesus died with outstretched arms, and Jesus will return with greater terror. Jesus will lead us to the final promised land. Jesus is redemption.

This prayer begins with praise. This is not insignificant. Prayer that begins with praise is a significant theme in Scripture. The ultimate expression of this is the psalms, where praise is explicitly mentioned more than 130 times! How significant is it that the model for singing in the Old Testament has as its dominant theme the concept of praise to God?

Perhaps this is why the first thing Jesus taught us to pray was,

> *Father,*
> *Your name be honored as holy.*
> *Your kingdom come.* (Luke 11:2)

The idea that the praise of God and the first request for the coming kingdom are together is not insignificant. Since God is worthy of all praise, it stands to reason that his kingdom, his will, his rule, should be seen and manifested above ours.

In the ministry of Jesus, he healed people, and then God was glorified. Note how many times the connection is made. God is praised, and we ask that his kingdom come; and when it does, it draws more praise to him. Jesus explained this relationship in John 13:31-32 when he prayed, "Now the Son of Man is glorified, and God is glorified in him. If God is glorified in him, God will also glorify him in himself and will glorify him at once." Prayer that begins with praise as its goal will end in praise as its result. This is why we cannot pray for selfish things (Jas 4:2-3).

In the early church the call to send out missionaries came after worship. Look at the remarkable sequence of Acts 13:2: "As they were worshiping the Lord and fasting, the Holy Spirit said, 'Set apart for me Barnabas and Saul for the work to which I have called them.'" Clarity comes from worship. Leadership from God comes from worship of God. Again, prayer that begins with praise as its goal will end in praise as its result.

So when Jeremiah begins his prayer with praise, he is standing in the arc of a long trajectory throughout Scripture. Prayer that seeks results and clarity begins with praise.

Confession for the Guilt of the Past (32:23b)

Again, this follows the pattern of the Lord's Prayer. We are taught by our Lord to seek forgiveness from sin. In this case Jeremiah is not checking something off a list. This is an important part of the discussion. God can do all things, yet we are prone to sin, as demonstrated by our past.

Laying before God the Problem of the Present (32:24-25)

Now he comes down to the problem. The problem is that he had been called to do something that did not make sense. The practical lesson here is that Jeremiah did not sin by bringing his problem to God. God can handle honest prayers. If God does not squelch David for the seemingly over-the-top imprecatory prayers in Psalms, it stands to reason that he can handle it when we confess that we do not know why he is asking us to do what he is asking us to do. We are not only allowed *but commanded* to bring our problems to God. Anything at all.

There are times we throw up prayers of desperation to God. He hears them. This is not that. This is a thoughtful prayer that shows a pattern of lavish praise, clear confession, and then honest petition. Yet note that a pattern is not a formula. That's not the point. The fascinating thing about this prayer is not that it guarantees certain outcomes; rather, the fascinating thing about this prayer is that it is consistent with so many other things the Scriptures teach us about prayer.

God Responds to Perplexing Prayer
JEREMIAH 32:26-44

God's response to Jeremiah's prayer is twofold: He will discipline, and he will gather.

Judgment Still Stands (32:26-35)

God begins by affirming that Jeremiah is correct: nothing is too hard for him (v. 27). So nothing has changed. He will hand this city over to the Babylonians (v. 28).

It is almost as if God turns the question back to Jeremiah. "Do you really believe what you have just prayed? Then, Jeremiah, pay attention as I crush the reality you once held on to; watch as the narrative of a favored people who were untouchable is ruined before you without any hope. And then watch as I create a new redemptive reality."

The new reality is that, while the judgment still stands, God will bring about a new redemption.

God Will Gather His People (32:36-44)

This is the new reality: "a permanent covenant" along the lines described in chapter 31 and a future restoration to the land. The everlasting covenant is ultimately fulfilled in the new covenant given in Christ. The first fulfillment is the restoration of Jerusalem; the complete fulfillment is the covenant that is new in Christ and the ultimate city that is to come. So we see here a distinct covenant with Israel that is affirmed, and the continuation of that affirmation is expressed in the church, God's new covenant people.

In the following chapter God responds with clear promises.

God Responds with Promises
JEREMIAH 33

The conversation begins with these remarkable words to Jeremiah in 33:3: "Call to me and I will answer you and tell you great and incomprehensible things you do not know." God responds with specific promises.

Peace and Renewal (33:1-13)

God promises in the most poetic of terms that he will restore Israel. You can feel the joy and almost hear the wedding music (vv. 7-11).

New Priest and a Perfect King (33:14-26)

God then promises that the Davidic line will continue, and the Levitical priesthood will as well (vv. 17-18). What a wonderful promise!

Jeremiah has been given some perplexing problems to deal with. Now he has received promises that affirm what God told him previously. They also give him hope that his seventeen shekels was money well spent.

In the shadow of this great promise is a story of both promises made and promises broken.

Conclusion: Promises Made and Promises Broken
JEREMIAH 34–35

The following chapters illustrate great faithlessness and faithfulness.

Great Faithlessness

Zedekiah and all his officials promised to free the countrymen they had enslaved, but then they reneged on their promise (34:10-11). This angered the Lord. Zedekiah was supposed to proclaim liberty to the captives. He did not re-present God, who loves to free enslaved people. Instead, he selfishly reimposed the oppression.

Great Faithfulness

By way of contrast, the Rechabites are used in chapter 35 as an illustration of faithfulness. After being tempted to drink wine, they reply that they have remained steadfast for generations within the instructions of their ancestor. They are now the archetype of faithfulness to God. The king, sadly, is the antitype of faithfulness. He perfectly demonstrates what not to do.

Zedekiah did not demonstrate the capacity of faith. He could not bear up under the long-term vision that is needed to be a man of faith. Faithful people are often saying no to what makes sense in the immediate present in order to believe what they cannot see. This is why we are called to pray for the kingdom to come: we are looking to a city we cannot see. This is why the poor in spirit are blessed: they are divested of this life in order to embrace the life to come. As an example, the Rechabites kept their word to God even when God's leadership in their lives was perplexing.

The applications to our lives are legion. It's not hard to think of a dozen ways in which our time, our money, our abilities, and our resources are typically used to invest in the short term and not the long term—the eternal perspective. This is one reason God in his mercy will create situations for us like he created for Jeremiah. These situations demand that we face the perplexity of his promises. It is only there that we get it. The school of confusion graduates faithful people if they learn to praise. Praise frames prayer when God's promises are perplexing.

Reflect and Discuss

1. Several examples regarding faith as delayed gratification were given in the introduction. Can you name them?
2. "Faith is the practice of delayed gratification for a promised outcome." Do you agree with this definition of faith? If so, why?
3. What is the correlation between prayer and praise?

4. In what way did Jeremiah display faith when he purchased a field (32:6-8)?

5. What is the return on investment when we invest in the purpose and plan of God?

6. What actions should we take when we need to trust God in important situations?

7. Should prayer begin in praise? Why or why not?

8. How should we view Luke 11:5-8; 11:9; John 14:14; and James 1:6 in light of the truth that nothing is impossible for God?

9. God often calls us to actions that do not make sense to us. Reflect on such a time in your life when God called you to act on faith. How should the fulfilled promises of God in the past influence your future decisions?

10. Take a moment and pray. Begin your prayer with praise.

Deadly Defiance

JEREMIAH 36–38

Main Idea: Obedience costs, but defiance toward God's word is deadly.

I. **The Story of the Book (36)**
   A. Scene One: The scroll is read (36:4-10).
   B. Scene Two: The scroll is read before the secretary (36:11-19).
   C. Scene Three: The scroll is read to the king (36:20-26).
   D. Scene Four: The second edition (36:27-32)
II. **Jeremiah in Prison (37)**
   Setting: Zedekiah is willfully deaf (37:1-2).
   Scene One: The king seeks out Jeremiah (37:3-10).
   Scene Two: Jeremiah is imprisoned (37:11-21).
III. **The Story of the Pit (38)**
   Setting: Jeremiah upsets the wrong people (38:1-5).
   Scene One: Jeremiah is thrown into the pit (38:6).
   Scene Two: Jeremiah is delivered (38:7-16).
   Scene Three: The king's counselor (38:17-28)

Nothing about ministry is easy. Life is tough and ministry is tougher. Sometimes we do not know which way is up. Sometimes we feel unfairly treated. Sometimes desperation is so thick it follows us like a fog in a demented cartoon. Careless words, caustic people, and friends who act like enemies are things those committed to a life of ministry will all have to face.

What makes this bearable is the call of God, of course; the knowledge that we are set apart for this makes any other type of life unthinkable. Yet something else sustains us: the life of the sheep. One can only imagine that the difficulty of walking sheep to water, protecting them from wolves, and retrieving them when they are errant is tempered by the sight of a ewe lamb just learning to take her legs. The travails of the hard days mix with the joys of the good days giving us hope. So there it is. A life of long days and monotonous days sprinkled with days of inexplicable joy. This is the life of a minister.

What we have here are three stories that seem unconnected. However, they carry a central theme: a willing and obedient prophet and two defiant kings. On the surface the stories seem to answer a question about the high cost of obedience to God. In the end they also answer the question about the even higher cost of disobedience.

The Story of the Book
JEREMIAH 36

Scene One: The Scroll Is Read (36:4-10)

The word Jeremiah receives is read to the people on a day of fasting. This would have been a day that there was a significant crowd, ensuring that his message has a large audience.

The motivation for the reading is fascinating. In verse 7 we find the hopeful words of Jeremiah to Baruch:

> *Perhaps their petition will come before the LORD, and each one will turn from his evil way, for the anger and fury that the LORD has pronounced against this people are intense.*

We might think this is ridiculous. After all Jeremiah has been through, why is he expending emotional energy on the false hope that the people will repent? It seems naïve at best. Yet this is also God's perspective. God has been consistently hopeful that they would repent. Compare Jeremiah 26:3 with 36:3:

> *Perhaps they will listen and turn—each from his evil way of life—so that I might relent concerning the disaster that I plan to do to them because of the evil of their deeds.* (26:3)

> *Perhaps when the house of Judah hears about all the disaster I am planning to bring on them, each one of them will turn from his evil way. Then I will forgive their iniquity and their sin.* (36:3)

God's optimism is like a gentle ray of light breaking through the rock of their hard hearts. He is trying to get through to them and offering them every opportunity to repent.

Scene Two: The Scroll Is Read before the Secretary (36:11-19)

The scroll causes quite a stir and is read before all the king's officials. They tell Baruch and Jeremiah to hide, and they hold on to the scroll.

Scene Three: The Scroll Is Read to the King (36:20-26)

Eventually the scroll finds its way into the courtyard of the king. The plot thickens! It is wintertime and the king is in his winter house enjoying a fire. As the scroll was read, the king would cut off columns of the scroll and throw them into the fire.

From the bonfire of the vanities during the times of Savonarola, book burning has a long and rich history. However, the point here is not purity in literature or censorship; the point here is clear defiance. Look carefully at verses 24-25:

> *As they heard all these words, the king and all of his servants did not become terrified or tear their clothes. Even though Elnathan, Delaiah, and Gemariah had urged the king not to burn the scroll, he did not listen to them.*

The problem was that they were not scared. This is disconcerting because Jeremiah's words were scary. The king and his servants were so full of themselves that they were not willing to fear what should have evoked terror. The editor wants us to see this clearly when he emphasizes that they did not tear their clothes, which would have been a sign of contrition. Even after being urged by others not to burn the scroll, the king continued to do so. He was completely defiant to the words of God through Jeremiah.

It is interesting to look at the other characters in this story.

The friends of the king (Elnathan, Delaiah, and Gemariah) were good friends: they were scared because the king was not scared. Good friends help us identify strains of bad in our hearts based on our attitudes and emotions. They warned against where the king was going.

The king in the story is representative of so many people in the book of Jeremiah who were defiant toward God's word. Perhaps the most vulnerable position we can be in is when we outright reject God's word. This is the definition of wickedness according to Psalm 1—the person who does not submit himself to God. When we reject God's Word, we reject the means by which he will purify us (Eph 5:26). We miss the direction and comfort that comes from knowing God's Word (Ps 119:50). We miss the peace of God (Ps 119:165). All of these things we forfeit when we do not have a love for God's Word.

When we do have a love for the Word of God, we hate falsehood: "I hate and abhor falsehood, but I love your instruction" (Ps 119:163). To love the Word is to hate the things that challenge it, so then by default we are loving what is wrong and hating what is right! The person who rejects the Word of God cannot really know the truth about so many things because he or she rejects the source of truth, which is God.

Worst of all, the person who rejects the Word of God rejects Christ himself. Christ is the image of God (Col 1:15); he is the Word (John 1:1-5); and he is made known to us through the Word. The Word of God leads us to the Son of God. To reject the Word is to reject Christ, and to reject Christ is to reject the Father. This is why in Proverbs 4:7 Solomon would plead with his son,

> Wisdom is supreme—so get wisdom.
> And whatever else you get, get understanding.

This idea that wisdom came from God, and further that we should respond to the wisdom of the Lord in humility and reverence, was not unfamiliar to the king. He knew this. Therefore, those standing with him—and the author of Jeremiah—want us to see that he is defiant against what he knew to be right.

How does he act so brazenly against the word of God? Well, there seems to be an implicit alibi in the text: the prophet. God's holy word is delivered to the king. The king rejects the word, and then the king finds a way to excuse his disobedience: blame Jeremiah. I do the same thing. The conviction of the Lord will be coming to me from his Word, and I mentally drift to reasons I do not want to obey. Good reasons. Justifiable reasons. I can always blame the preacher; I don't like what he is doing or the way he is saying it. Like the king, I need to cover the tracks of my disobedience.

So after hearing these words, the king decides to take out Jeremiah and Baruch. However, God hides them (36:26).

Scene Four: The Second Edition (36:27-32)

And this is where the story gets interesting. Jeremiah publishes a second edition. What's more, this second edition has more information than the first (v. 32)!

In the end Jeremiah escapes unharmed, the people who warn the king have a clear conscience, and the judgment prophesied against the king does not change—in fact, it gets stronger. A defiant heart has stoked the fires of God's wrath. It always does. Defiance against God's Word is deadly.

Jeremiah in Prison
JEREMIAH 37

Setting: Zedekiah Is Willfully Deaf (37:1-2)

Zedekiah is the new king, but tragically it is said, "He and his officers and the people of the land did not obey the words of the LORD that he spoke through the prophet Jeremiah" (37:2). Nevertheless, the weight of impending doom eventually bears so heavily that the king seeks out Jeremiah.

Scene One: The King Seeks Out Jeremiah (37:3-10)

The king requests prayer and receives an interesting answer. The prayer is not a prayer of repentance; it is a prayer for deliverance. However, it was the greatest military strategy possible. In the world of warfare, what you want is battle awareness, and this is exactly what the king heard from Jeremiah. God told Jeremiah that the threat of Egypt would remove the Chaldeans from their siege, yet the removal of the siege was only temporary.

Scene Two: Jeremiah Is Imprisoned (37:11-21)

Jeremiah is imprisoned based on false accusations. After a series of events and a long period of time, he petitions to get out of the dungeon and is sent to the court of the guard where he stays.

So now the king is positioned in the best way possible. He has the greatest intelligence anyone could provide from the most intelligent source. This is shocking. He asked for prayer and he gets the prayer, plus he gets military intelligence! Yet he did not want it.

This short story is a metaphor for what is going on in the whole book. God is offering wisdom and counsel, and they are, each time, summarily rejected. The price that will be paid for this attitude is high. Right now it appears that only Jeremiah is paying a high price, but this is about to change.

The Story of the Pit
JEREMIAH 38

Setting: Jeremiah Upsets the Wrong People (38:1-5)

Jeremiah is still prophesying that the city will be destroyed and that all those who stay in the city will be doomed. His message is no more popular than when he first proclaimed it. Jeremiah has not changed. He has heard a call from God, and he keeps preaching until God tells him to stop. Nothing has changed with Jeremiah, but the people—well, that is a different story. The constant message has changed something in their hearts, namely, their tolerance for the message. It's gone. They are fed up. Throughout the book you see a general rejection of Jeremiah's message, but in this passage the officials have had enough. They appeal to the king who, in a tone similar to Pilate's at the trial of Jesus, gives them the green light to do what they wish.

Scene One: Jeremiah Is Thrown into the Pit (38:6)

They take Jeremiah and throw him down a well. They have found a cistern that is dried up, and they place him down in it. The cistern has no water, just mud. As the prophet is lowered to the bottom of this cistern, his feet sink down into the thick mud. We can imagine it was deep and narrow. No way down, up, around, or out. He is stuck. I've felt stuck before in life but just metaphorically. Jeremiah is stuck literally.

Perhaps it is not an accident in the text, but in reading this we can't help but think of the initial criticism God had against Israel in 2:12-13 when God said,

> Be appalled at this, heavens;
> be shocked and utterly desolated!
>   This is the Lord's declaration.
> For my people have committed a double evil:
> They have abandoned me,
> the fountain of living water,
> and dug cisterns for themselves—
> cracked cisterns that cannot hold water.

The people reached up and cut off the source of eternal, never-ceasing, living water. They reached down and dug wells that could not hold water. So it's a little more than interesting that they find an empty well so quickly. It's a perfect place to stick a prophet. They do not want to hear from God, so they cut off the supply of God's living word by sticking him into an empty well.

And then silence. The prophet cannot be heard. He is muted. Their desire for their broken word is stronger than their desire for the living word.

Scene Two: Jeremiah Is Delivered (38:7-16)

The deliverance of Jeremiah is significant. The story will surface again when his deliverer, Ebed-melech, is rewarded by God for putting his trust in God. When Jerusalem falls, God will say to Ebed-melech,

> But I will rescue you on that day—this is the LORD's declaration— and you will not be handed over to the men you dread. Indeed, I will certainly deliver you so that you do not fall by the sword. Because you have trusted in me, you will retain your life like the spoils of war. This is the LORD's declaration. (39:17-18)

Ebed-melech will be rescued because he rescued the man of God. We all need people to lift us out of a pit, but the reading of 38:7-9 hints that something more is going on. Ebed-melech is not just trying to make friends. He is not trying to help someone out. He is exercising faith in God. It is the other side of 1 Samuel 16:7. Man could only see the Cushite servant; God, however, was looking on his heart.

Scene Three: The King's Counselor (38:17-28)

Then, oddly perhaps, in a breath Jeremiah goes from down in a pit into the king's palace. This was the nature of the prophet's life. The king wanted a private consultation with Jeremiah. So, as a counselor to the king, Jeremiah has an opportunity to shape the future of the kingdom. In that moment he does not equivocate. He tells the same truth that he has always being saying. However, in the presence of the king, he does not miss the opportunity to press the king to respond. He tells him specifically to surrender and obey (vv. 17-18,20). Surrender to God, surrender to his will, which means surrender to the king of Babylon.

This appeal given in the private quarters of the king is in shocking contrast to what is coming. In chapter 39 the king will be caught trying to escape. He will be subjected to gruesome torture, his officials and sons killed, and his palace burned. It seems that the king thought escape was an option. It was not. Surrender was the only means of keeping his life, though it would mean losing the kingdom. The refusal to surrender still meant he would lose his kingdom, and he would lose so much more.

This is the question we face: How much do we want to lose? If we surrender to God, we lose. We give up. We die. Yet, if we don't surrender to Christ, we give up so much more. The different price tags on these surrenders are what bring these stories together.

Conclusion

While these stories may seem different, they really are much more alike. In the first narrative King Jehoiakim is so defiant against the word that he cannot weep when the destruction is foretold. In the second story the replacement king will not listen to Jeremiah either, and Jeremiah is persecuted. In the final story the new king is given an opportunity to change, an opportunity to humble himself. Will he do so? That question will be answered in the next chapter. For now it's enough to gather this simple truth: defiance against God's word is deadly.

Defiance cost King Jehoiakim an opportunity to repent, an opportunity to live. In the second story defiance cost Zedekiah a chance to repent, and in the final story defiance against the word appears as if it is going to cost Zedekiah everything.

We began by discussing the nature of the call to ministry. It is in fact a costly call. If you choose to follow Christ, it will take a certain toll on your self-perception. We ask, Who am I in a world that does not know what to do with Christ? It will cost financially, as you will not be living for the kingdom of this world. It might cost you the love of family and the respect of peers. It will cost you the toll of being misunderstood. All of these things we can of course bring on ourselves; that is never justified. Yet all of these things we have to willingly embrace; that is to be expected. There is a high cost to obedience. Jeremiah had his book rejected, was lied about, and then was tortured in a pit. Obedience has its price. But so does disobedience.

As the curtain closes on their narratives, the high cost of defiance against the word is clearly much greater than submitting gladly to the word.

This reminds us of one of the strangest stories Jesus ever told, that of the rich man and Lazarus, in Luke 16:19-31. The rich man is apparently blessed; he has everything in life. He has everything but respect for God's Word and love for others. Lazarus is apparently cursed; he has nothing. He has no money; he has no health. The two could not be more different. Yet Jesus throws a massive twist in the story when in the first scene the two die, and the rich man goes to hell and the poor man goes to heaven. The listening audience would have been shocked! Wealth, for the audience to whom Jesus was speaking, was a sign of blessing, and poverty a sign of cursing. How could that be their destiny?

It's the most extreme role reversal they could imagine:

- The rich man was feasting while Lazarus begged; now Lazarus is feasting while the rich man begs.
- The poor man wanted what the rich man would not give; now the rich man wants what the poor man cannot give.
- The rich man gorged himself daily while Lazarus starved; now Lazarus is feasting while the rich man wants a drop of water.
- The rich man was so blessed and Lazarus was so cursed; now we see the reality: Lazarus was blessed and the rich man was cursed.

In the end of the story, the rich man needs Lazarus's help, which is ironic: Lazarus was the rich man's only problem; now the rich man sees Lazarus as his only solution.

This story helps illustrate suffering. The suffering the poor man endured on earth was horrible, excruciating, real, and temporary. The pain the rich man felt after death was eternal. If you can pan out far enough, you can see that the high price for following Christ is much less than the higher price of defying him.

Life is hard and ministry is harder, but it comes with a reward. The story in Jeremiah gives the sense that the prophet could not imagine disobeying God, and the kings could not imagine obeying him.

Obedience costs, but defiance toward God's Word is deadly.

Reflect and Discuss

1. What is the connection between the three stories in Jeremiah 36–38, which initially seem unrelated?
2. How is a rejection of the Word a rejection of Christ himself?
3. In what way does obedience cost? How is disobedience to God's word deadly?
4. Does the king in the story (Jer 36) represent the people who are defiant against God's word? If so, how?
5. Agree or disagree: We are in a most vulnerable position when we reject God's Word.
6. In what way does a love for God's Word produce within us a heart that despises evil?
7. In chapter 37 the king asked Jeremiah to pray about deliverance, not repentance. What is the difference between these two types of prayer?

8. Is the short story in Jeremiah 37 a metaphor for what is going on in the whole book? What is God offering Israel, and in what way does Israel reject this offer?

9. What do we, as Christians, lose when we surrender to God? What do we lose when we refuse to surrender to God?

10. Defiance cost King Jehoiakim and Zedekiah an opportunity to repent. What is the high cost of continuously rejecting God?

The Fall and the Fallen

JEREMIAH 39–41

Main Idea: We fall when we don't kill the beast of pride.

I. **The Fall (39:4-10)**
   A. Capture and judgment (39:4-5)
   B. Torture (39:6-7)
   C. Destruction (39:8)
   D. Exile (39:9-10)
II. **The Rescue (39:11-14; 40:1-6)**
III. **The Deliverance (39:15-18)**
IV. **The Fallen (40:7–41:18)**
   A. Gedaliah appointed governor (40:7-15)
   B. Gedaliah assassinated by Ishmael (41:1-8)
   C. Ishmael routed (41:11-18)
Conclusion: How Did He Get So Low?
   A. Creation of an echo chamber
   B. Rejected counsel
   C. Prideful heart

Then there was the fateful day. It happened. We have been reading for thirty-eight chapters of God's pending judgment. Now the judgment falls.

When Rome fell, it was the most cataclysmic collapse of a world power. Politically, nothing greater happened before or since that time. It was so profound that it still is in our collective minds the metaphor for a great power falling. Many remember the collapse of the USSR, although that was more of a reshuffle. Many more will remember the fall of the regime of Saddam Hussein. Yet evil in the Middle East continues to exist to the point that it is hard for us to keep up with the constant character changes that still have elements of evil and totalitarian rule.

However, the fall of Jerusalem is unique. For those on the inside it seemed sudden. The flow of this narrative is that King Zedekiah is caught by surprise with all of the activities of the moment. Yet one cannot forget that this was long in the making. Ever since the superficial reforms of Josiah, Jeremiah had been predicting that this time would come. The only people who didn't expect this to happen were those willfully rejecting the message. Yet the main reason this was unique is that this is an act of God. God is using unwitting evil powers to accomplish his will. This is something that has been in the mind of God for a long time.

The Fall
JEREMIAH 39:4-10

The fall is described in horrific terms of capture, judgment, torture, destruction, and exile.

Capture and Judgment (39:4-5)

When King Zedekiah and his guard saw that the Babylonian contingent had broken into the city, they attempted to escape to the south; nevertheless, they were captured, arrested, and sentenced. This fulfilled the downside of Jeremiah's prediction in 38:17-18 when, in a private conversation, Jeremiah told the king exactly what would happen if he surrendered and what would happen if he did not.

> Jeremiah therefore said to Zedekiah, "This is what the LORD, the God of Armies, the God of Israel, says: 'If indeed you surrender to the officials of the king of Babylon, then you will live, this city will not be burned, and you and your household will survive. But if you do not surrender to the officials of the king of Babylon, then this city will be handed over to the Chaldeans. They will burn it, and you yourself will not escape from them.'"

If Zedekiah had surrendered as God had directed him to do, there would have been much less destruction. He had every opportunity to surrender, but he did not. He kept doing what he wanted to do the way he wanted to do it. There was no stopping him. There was no stopping the Chaldeans either.

From the capture came torture.

Torture (39:6-7)

Zedekiah's sons were killed, his nobles were killed, and perhaps he wished he had been killed, but instead he was blinded. They did not take his life but his ability to see life.

Destruction (39:8)

The Chaldeans next burned down the king's palace and the people's houses and tore down the walls of Jerusalem.

Exile (39:9-10)

The Babylonians deported all those who remained in the city—those who had assumed God wouldn't let Jerusalem fall (ch. 7). The description is horrific and poetic. There is a descent from invasion to capture, execution, destruction, and exile. Zedekiah woke up a king and went to bed a prisoner, destined to die alone at the hands of his captors.

Yet in the midst of the story is a note of rescue and deliverance.

The Rescue
JEREMIAH 39:11-14; 40:1-6

Why Jeremiah is shown favor in this situation is uncertain. He is captive, but he is treated in a manner well suited to a faithful man of God, and he is eventually taken to the home of Gedaliah. We can only speculate that the Babylonian king had heard about Jeremiah and wanted to treat him well since what he had been saying surely did, in fact, come to pass.

The Deliverance
JEREMIAH 39:15-18

The story of Ebed-melech the Cushite is an interesting insertion here. Why is it included? Remember, he is the one who saved Jeremiah from the cistern (ch. 38). However, God did not save him for this act alone. No, God saved him because "you have trusted in me" (39:18). Whatever the reason for the insertion here, it stands as a massive contrast to the king. Here is a foreigner who is willing to risk his life for Jeremiah. Like Rahab, here is someone who trusted in God. This trust was illustrated by the fact that he had both faith and works.

The Fallen
JEREMIAH 40:7–41:18

It is often true in organizational life that some things, when they fall, keep falling. Someone is kicked while down. Inertia of problems takes over, and an organization cannot seem to recover. This is the way it was after the land was decimated.[7] This is the case with Jerusalem. Jerusalem has not *fallen*. Technically it is *still falling*. Chapters 40–41 record the tragic story of the first attempt at governance after the departure of Zedekiah. This narrative moves in three scenes.

Gedaliah Appointed Governor (40:7-15)

In the previous portion (vv. 1-6), Gedaliah was quickly appointed governor, and Jeremiah had opted to stay in Jerusalem with the governor. However, Jeremiah is not mentioned in this portion of the story.

The city is smoldering. It is a mess. There is no sense of direction and purpose. Yet, as a calm after a storm, there is a sense of tranquility. The people who were left and not taken into exile have gathered summer fruits and wine (vv. 10,12), and they have returned from all the places they had been driven during the conquest. It actually seems like a happy time.

Yet the happiness is short-lived.

Gedaliah Assassinated by Ishmael (41:1-8)

A rumor persists that there is an assassination plot against the governor. It is so strong that Johanan suggests that the would-be assassin, Ishmael, be executed as a preemptive strike. Gedaliah foolishly believes well of Ishmael. He could not have been more wrong. Ishmael takes ten men and strikes down the governor and his men while they are eating (41:1-3). But the terror does not stop there. Ishmael murders almost eighty men who were coming to worship.

Ishmael Routed (41:11-18)

Finally Johanan took men and pursued Ishmael. Ishmael escaped and fled. The decimated city was now further reduced to a small remnant. The king has been captured, the city has been burned, the replacement governor is dead, and a massacre of worshipers has followed. Now the warnings of Jeremiah do not seem so hollow.

Conclusion: How Did He Get So Low?

Jeremiah had prophesied that Zedekiah would be taken and that the city would be burned. This did not have to happen. Days before the

---

[7] This story within the story could stand alone but seems tied thematically with the fall of Jerusalem.

destruction, the wicked king heard counsel from the godly prophet, and even after all that God had said had been rejected, he still offered the king one more chance: surrender.

We mourn the loss of Jerusalem and cringe at the foolish pride of the king. Still, we have to admit, it's tough when your only option is surrender. There was no way to save face. There was no way to look good in this situation. If he had taken the surrender route, he would have had to stand and say to his people publicly that he had been wrong. That *never* happens. When is the last time you heard a sitting monarch admit that his entire foreign relations policy has been wrong and that he needs a course correction? It's just inconceivable. What would that even sound like? Here is the speech Zedekiah never gave:

> Look, I was wrong. We had an approach to survival that was "stand our ground and pretend that defeat is not going to happen." We were wrong. Based on the latest intelligence, we believe defeat is going to happen. Destruction is imminent. If we try to escape or defend ourselves, the situation gets worse. We will surrender. Yet, in surrendering, we are entrusting our fate to the God who ultimately promises to deliver us.

As hard as it would have been to give that speech, the lost, tortured, blinded Zedekiah would have given anything to turn back time and obey God. Again, I don't want to be too hard on Zedekiah. I have not been in that situation. Yet I do wonder, How did he get to that place in which he was so defiant toward God? We knew that the fall was coming, but this did not have to happen this way. God made that clear enough. So why did it? The answer could be called "The Anatomy of a Fall." Here are a few obvious things.

Creation of an Echo Chamber

The king was living in a veritable echo chamber. You've heard that term before. The term *echo chamber* is used to describe a hollow enclosure that, based on the shape of the structure, allows sounds to reverberate. These can be used by scientists to test sound waves or by musicians to produce certain effects. The simple idea is that the sound is not lost. The voice once spoken comes back.

Metaphorically the term has come to describe an individual or a church, business, university, institution, news outlet, or other group that has created its own environment in which all they can hear is the sound of their own voice. The voice of the speaker is so loud that it is the dominant voice, and any other realities are ambient noises and little more than distractions to the main voice. We see this effect throughout the lives of these kings. They surrounded themselves with people who were only willing to tell them what they wanted to hear. There is usually safety in a multitude of counselors, yet the multitude is not effective if they are motivated by anything less than the truth. If they are motivated by a false sense of loyalty, or even a false sense of love, they have not helped when they have not told the truth.

This is why it was a shocking act of grace when God allowed the king to step outside his echo chamber. For some reason the king knew he was not getting the whole truth, so he stepped out to take counsel with Jeremiah (38:14-28). He heard another voice—the voice of truth—but it didn't matter; he would not respond.

Rejected Counsel

Over and over again in Proverbs, the wisest king Israel ever had gave his son the advice to listen to counsel. Solomon made clear that the success or failure of his son rested on his willingness to receive counsel. Look at the insightful words of Proverbs 1:1-7:

> The proverbs of Solomon son of David, king of Israel:
> For learning wisdom and discipline;
> for understanding insightful sayings;
> for receiving prudent instruction
> in righteousness, justice, and integrity;
> for teaching shrewdness to the inexperienced,
> knowledge and discretion to a young man—
> let a wise person listen and increase learning,
> and let a discerning person obtain guidance—
> for understanding a proverb or a parable,
> the words of the wise, and their riddles.
> The fear of the LORD is the beginning of knowledge;
> fools despise wisdom and discipline.

While we do not know about all of Solomon's sons, we do know about his successors to the throne. They rejected the voice of God who was graciously trying to protect them. While we are reading this text, sometimes I feel like I am watching an old movie in which I know people are in danger and I can't help but yell at the screen. This is Zedekiah.

Why won't he just listen to all the obvious lessons? The answer is the root sin of pride.

Prideful Heart

As Bill Elliff said, "Pride is the mother of all sins" ("The Sin that Prevents Revival"). Pride was driving Zedekiah's rejection of counsel. Pride produces someone who can hear but not listen. The pride of his heart had a physiological effect: it caused his ears to filter out everything he did not want to hear. The echo chamber was not around him; it was in him. The echo chamber was created by a heart that did not want to respond to God. This is the key issue. We all struggle with pride. Yet when pride is in the heart of a leader, the implications are more profound. The pride of his heart caused him the loss of family, officials, eyesight, and kingdom (39:6-7).

His blindness is a metaphor for what he could not see all along: his pride was killing him. It wasn't supposed to be this way. He was going to exile, but he could have surrendered. He could have saved his life and the lives of those who were with him. It's more than ironic that he died blind. He was a great king. All he is now is a metaphor.

This picture of Zedekiah scares me. It scares me in the way a mirror does when you do not know it's there—you know, when you scare *yourself*.

A pride monster is inside of me because it is I. We're attached. Occasionally I take credit for something God has done. It's food for the monster. At other times I feed the monster from compliments I send down to him and not up to God. Over time he grows so strong that I just imagine he is real. My self-perception is perverted by the organism I keep feeding until, once permeated by the beast, I cannot listen to those who could challenge him. I will only listen to those who want to feed him. He is *so* demanding.

Christ came to heal us, and we are only whole when the beast is slain. He cannot be kept in the corner and ignored. It doesn't work like that any more than you would pluck an animal from the wild and let him roam your house.

No, the pet of pride kills and destroys, so the most loving thing you can do for your God and for those you lead is to kill the beast. Kill the beast. Kill the beast.

This is precisely what Zedekiah did not want to do. He did not kill the beast; he coddled the beast. Once fed and cultivated, the beast roared and took everything. The officials, the sons, the eyesight were simply the beast roaring out of control, insatiable, wanting more. He fed the beast that killed him. I understand because I do too.

So, as we saunter through the story of the tragic fall of Jerusalem, as we walk through the rubble and ponder the mysteries of God, we feel sympathy for a blind man who is so much like us.

Reflect and Discuss

1. Reflect on the main idea of this text: "We fall when we don't kill the beast of pride." Is this true of your own heart?
2. The irony of the fall in Jeremiah 39 is that, although well predicted, it took the people by surprise. Why?
3. What are some of the terms used to describe the horrific fall of Jerusalem?
4. Does our success or failure rest on a willingness to receive godly counsel? Why or why not?
5. Discuss and reflect on these statements: Pride is the mother of all sins. Pride drives rejection of counsel. Pride produces someone who can hear but not listen.
6. Pride is a beast that rises up within us. What must we do to defeat the monster of pride?
7. In what ways are our hearts like proverbial echo chambers?
8. The book of Proverbs says that "pride comes before destruction" (Prov 16:18). Name the specific acts of pride that led to the fall of Jerusalem.
9. The text gives three consequences of Zedekiah's prideful heart. Name them.
10. Compare and contrast the wisdom of Solomon and the wisdom of his successors.

Blinded by the Light

JEREMIAH 42–45

Main Idea: When God shows us the way, tragically we can choose to be blinded by the light.

I. **Jeremiah's Last Words to Judah (42:1–43:7)**[8]
   A. God's word requested (42:1-6)
   B. God's word received (42:7-22)
      1. First alternative: Stay in the land (42:10-12).
      2. Second alternative: Go to Egypt (42:13-22).
II. **Jeremiah's Last Words in Egypt (43–44)**
   A. God's word rejected (43:1-7)
   B. The pharaoh dethroned (43:8-13)
   C. The warning delivered (44:1-14)
   D. The people defiant (44:15-19)
   E. The future determined (44:20-30)
III. **God's Words to Baruch (45)**

Among the most fascinating of Jesus's miracles is the sixth sign miracle recorded by John. It is fascinating for the detail in which John tells the story, and even more fascinating in that John details the reactions of all those who were standing around Jesus.

The miracle happens in John 9:1-5 when Jesus's disciples question him about a man's blindness:

> *As he was passing by, he saw a man blind from birth. His disciples asked him: "Rabbi, who sinned, this man or his parents, that he was born blind?"*
>
> *"Neither this man nor his parents sinned," Jesus answered. "This came about so that God's works might be displayed in him. We must do the works of him who sent me while it is day. Night is coming when no one can work. As long as I am in the world, I am the light of the world."*

---

[8] The outline for this chapter is taken from Wright, *Message of Jeremiah*, 395–407.

Jesus's response answers the question but points to a deeper reality: a time is coming when darkness will fall. For us darkness means so much less than it did then. With no electric lights, darkness meant the end of productive work. John the writer wants us to see the insight of Jesus. Jesus is using this teachable moment to affirm that (1) a particular sin did not cause this guy's blindness, but (2) his blindness is for the glory of God, and (3) darkness is coming, but that's OK because (4) Jesus is the light of the world.

In other words, Jesus is saying, "Really guys, don't be concerned about the blindness of this man; be more concerned with your own spiritual insight: don't be blind to the truth that I am the light."

Jesus healed the blind man. The light of the world caused the blind man to see the light that was always around him. Perhaps no supernatural miracle was so spiritually natural. Perhaps no miracle was as metaphorical as this one. And the disciples were not the only ones who could not see it. When the blind man's friends saw it, they did not believe him. Almost with a sense of ironic comedy, John records,

> His neighbors and those who had seen him before as a beggar said,
> "Isn't this the one who used to sit begging?" Some said, "He's the one."
> Others were saying, "No, but he looks like him."
> He kept saying, "I'm the one."
> So they asked him, "Then how were your eyes opened?"
> He answered, "The man called Jesus made mud, spread it on
> my eyes, and told me, 'Go to Siloam and wash.' So when I went and
> washed I received my sight."
> "Where is he?" they asked.
> "I don't know," he said. (John 9:8-12)

The neighbors cannot see it. They are not unlike the disciples. The man who had sight for the least amount of time can see more than those born with sight. That is often true spiritually. The deepest insights often come from the freshest eyes.

The Pharisees cannot see it. When he is brought to them, there is again an almost comical exchange. John records in verses 13-17 that they are fixated on the fact that he was healed on the Sabbath! Really. I am not confident the blind man was particular. It's hard to pass up a life-changing miracle even if the timing is not right.

So they call his parents. His parents see it but because of the social pressure can't admit it. They have to hold their hands in front of them and feign blindness so as to avoid persecution (vv. 18-20).

When the Pharisees return to question the formerly blind man, he simply says, "One thing I do know: I was blind, and now I can see!" Again, we have another comical interlude by John:

> Then they asked him, "What did he do to you? How did he open your eyes?"
>
> "I already told you," he said, "and you didn't listen. Why do you want to hear it again? You don't want to become his disciples too, do you?" (vv. 26-27)

They didn't. They were blind and wanted it that way.

Jesus finds the man.

> Jesus heard that they had thrown the man out, and when he found him, he asked, "Do you believe in the Son of Man?"
>
> "Who is he, Sir, that I may believe in him?" he asked.
>
> Jesus answered, "You have seen him; in fact, he is the one speaking with you." (vv. 35-37)

"You have seen him." Of course he has. Jesus opened his eyes. The point was not lost on the Pharisees:

> Some of the Pharisees who were with him heard these things and asked him, "We aren't blind too, are we?"
>
> "If you were blind," Jesus told them, "you wouldn't have sin. But now that you say, 'We see,' your sin remains." (vv. 40-41)

The shocking thing about this story is all the blindness. The one man who was healed exposes all those who were blind all along! Sometimes a healing exposes further sickness. Sometimes when the light is adjusted in a room we are able to see just how dark it had been all along. We know that is axiomatic, yet in John's story this was taking place in the presence of the one who is the light of the world. Truly the disciples, the parents, and the Pharisees were blinded by the light, which is crazy because they were always waiting for a Messiah. Yet, when God sent the Messiah, they were not sure if they really wanted what they had asked for. This is what is going on in Jeremiah 42-44.

Context

A remnant is left in Jerusalem after the exiles have been taken away. The remnant desperately wants to be saved, so they ask Jeremiah to look, to see their condition, and to tell them God's instruction (Jer 42:2-3). The question is, Do they really want illumination? When God gives them insight in the way they should go, will they be responsive to it?

Jeremiah's Last Words to Judah
JEREMIAH 42:1–43:7

God's Word Requested (42:1-6)

God told Jeremiah over and over again how to lead the people. They now are in the exact position God wanted them to be in all along: they desperately want to hear from God. However, the problem is that it is too late for them to receive the benefit of receiving from God what he wanted to give them all along: peace during this transition. The transition was coming. God had already set the moving date. God had gladly provided them a way of escape, a way they did not take. So they will submit to God's plans—we all do eventually—they will just do it without the benefit of God's blessings.

God's Word Received (42:7-22)

After the people prayed for ten days, God finally answers their prayer. He presents them two alternatives.

First alternative: stay in the land (vv. 10-12). The first alternative they have is to stay in the land and obey God. They are commanded not to fear the king of Babylon.

Notice the logic of this affirmation. First, don't fear the king that you fear (v. 10). This is as compelling as it is comical. Stop fearing what you fear. This is a command not to have an emotion. Stop feeling this way. This seems ridiculous to our modern sensibilities in which we are taught that the greatest violence we can do to ourselves is not to emote anything! We should always express every emotion in real time! After all, why even have social media if that were not the case? But God says to stop fearing what you are fearing. If this were not possible, he would not have commanded it.

So, is he telling them to play mental games and just pretend that the threat is not real? Not at all! The command to reign in the emotion of fear is based on solid truth. Here it is:

- Believe God's word—he will rebuild you (v. 10).
- Believe God's presence—he is with you (v. 11).
- Believe God's sovereignty—the king will have compassion (v. 12).

Here, at the beginning of the narrative, is an invitation to respond to the character of God. Of course, the choice to respond to the character of God is also a choice not to react to circumstances around them.

Second alternative: go to Egypt (vv. 13-22). The second alternative is to disobey God, leave, and go to Egypt. This is what the people want. They have a heart that is bent toward disobedience. Tragically, the God who wanted to give them a future and a hope is now prophesying terror for those who disobey (v. 18).

God is saying that wrath and punishment will take place "just as" it took place in Jerusalem. God is helping them with a mental picture. He is asking them to visualize what it had been like in Jerusalem a few days before. That is what waited for them in Egypt. Why would they not see this? Why did they only see what they wanted to see?

Jeremiah's Last Words in Egypt
JEREMIAH 43–44

God's Word Rejected (43:1-7)

After all the warnings, they act on their disobedience. They make their decision and choose to go to Egypt. Occasionally in the book of Jeremiah, massive movements and decisions are summed up in tight little concise statements.

Verse 7 is an example: "And they came into the land of Egypt, for they did not obey the voice of the Lord" (ESV).

That's it. They heard the voice. They did not obey the voice. This is the disobedient relocation. So close to God they could not see him. They were blinded by the light.

The Pharaoh Dethroned (43:8-13)

Egypt is a world superpower. The people want to go there. God is telling them to stay in Judah. They are going to practice the deadly combination of selective hearing with a selective memory. Taken together, a selective memory with selective hearing can weave just about any narrative one wants. And the people reject God's word that Egypt is a no go.

God warns them that he is not hurting them; he is actually protecting them from coming disaster. The pharaoh will be dethroned, and

Egypt will be overrun by the Babylonians. Egypt will be taken out; and, as a dramatic example, even the famous Egyptian landmarks will be broken (v. 13).

The Warning Delivered (44:1-14)

God appeals to the people and asks them to see his patience. Even though the people have rejected him time and time again, he still sent prophets to warn them. Since they still refuse, God warns them that they would not survive in Egypt. God, who had been for them, is now against them. Why do they want to go to Egypt? The reason is that they cannot see what they do not want to see. They see Egypt as a symbol of prosperity and security. They could have in Egypt the best the world has to offer: peace, comfort, security. This logic made perfect sense—it always does—except that it's false. They just did not want to see the truth.

The People Defiant (44:15-19)

The people respond tragically: "As for the word you spoke to us in the name of the LORD, we are not going to listen to you!" They are so blinded they believe this calamity has come because they have not been sacrificing to the queen of heaven. In the world of logic this is called a *non sequitur*. This is Latin for, "It does not follow." Yes they stopped sacrificing, and yes they have fallen on hard times, but the two facts are not connected. They are only connected because, in the defiance of the people, they want them to be connected. They want anything but the light of the word.

The women then insist that what they did was done with their husbands' permission. This is a fascinating insertion. According to the Levitical code the husband could veto a vow that was improper (Num 30:3-16). So the women are saying that they worshiped a false god with their husbands' permission! In other words, they were taking a page out of Adam's book by blame shifting. However, you cannot do the wrong thing the right way.

The Future Determined (44:20-30)

Jeremiah reaches a different conclusion. He notes that in reality these sacrifices to the queen of heaven were causing all the problems they were experiencing (v. 23).

God promised, through the words of Jeremiah, that those who sought refuge in Egypt were on a fool's errand. No refuge would be found there. There was no hope in fleeing to Egypt. Why? Because in the same way that Zedekiah was taken out, the Egyptian pharaoh would be removed as well (v. 30). God was not the king of Egypt. That would be beneath him. He was not merely the king; he was the kingmaker. Israel then had a significant tactical advantage because God allowed them to see things no one else could see. They had insight no one else had. The problem is that sometimes God allows us to see, but we just can't see it. We do not have a vision of what it would be like to walk in the light.

Recently I asked my young children what they would do if they could time travel. This is a remarkable fantasy! Any time. Any place. My eight-year-old replied that she would time travel forward and skip all the homework of third grade. My eleven-year-old replied that she would take money and travel back to the time when ice cream was a nickel (something I assume she heard from her grandmother) and buy tons of ice cream. Think of this! They could meet the great leaders of the world. They could stand on the beaches of Normandy or see Rome in all her glory. They could see the first Olympic games in Greece or walk with the disciples. Instead they go for skipping homework and cheap ice cream. Why can they not see all the possibilities?! I know, I know, I have some parenting to do. But did I mention they are eight and eleven? The great vistas that lay before them are invisible because they want sweets and free time. They are blinded by their own immediate desires.

As a pastor I have seen this numerous times but in far more serious ways. A couple is shown what the ravages of divorce will do to their family, but in that moment they do not want to see it. They just want the immediate false freedom from their marriage. A man is tempted to be unfaithful and ruin the most precious stewardship any man could ever have, but he will trade that beauty for a few moments of pleasure. An opportunity to live and die with integrity cannot be seen because a student just wants a quick grade, so he cheats in school. The truth is that the horizons of our sight are blocked by the urgency of our desires. Sin is so blinding that it is like the low-hanging lights that keep us from seeing the stars.

God's Word to Baruch

JEREMIAH 45

In this short chapter God affirms that disaster is coming upon the land. Yet God has mercy. He will spare the life of Jeremiah's friend Baruch. He had been taken off to Egypt (43:6), and he shares Jeremiah's despondency over the whole situation. Evidently this was a young man with promise, yet now he is relocated with nothing to show for it.

Kidner notes, "This little chapter speaks volumes of the 'quick-eyed love,' the 'severe mercy,' and the 'never-failing providence' of God" (*Message of Jeremiah*, 135). God is protecting Baruch. Baruch is, in this sense, the opposite of the false prophets and of King Zedekiah. He does put his neck under the yoke, and he is spared.

Conclusion

So at the end of the story the people ask for insight, reject the insight, and continue in the way they were going. One would think that after seeing your nation demolished and brought to ruin, your leadership carted off, and your way of life forever altered, you would be more spiritually responsive.

Why did they act this way? Why did they want to stay blind when God was lighting their way? The reason is that they were blinded by physical realties. When life was good in Jerusalem, the spiritual reality of the prophet's words did not match the physical reality that they were comfortable in their homes. Life was good. This is the same reason Jesus called us to divest ourselves of the world and to live for the world to come: the appearance of prosperity does not match the reality of spiritual desperation. If we cannot see that, then we are spiritually blinded.

We don't naturally go there. God has to press this on us. This is why, in another shocking passage about blindness, God wrote to the church at Laodicea:

> For you say, "I'm rich; I have become wealthy and need nothing," and you don't realize that you are wretched, pitiful, poor, blind, and naked. I advise you to buy from me gold refined in the fire so that you may be rich, white clothes so that you may be dressed and your shameful nakedness not be exposed, and ointment to spread on your eyes so that you may see. As many as I love, I rebuke and discipline. So be zealous and repent. See! I stand at the door and knock. If anyone hears my voice and opens the door, I will come in to him and eat with him, and he with me. (Rev 3:17-20)

This is why, in a strange way, the persecution is good. The suffering is good. The homelessness is good. When we are without a home in this world, we are miserable, poor, blind, and naked—and we know it. The problem is not when we are these things; the problem is when *we do not realize* we are these things. Israel is finally in a place of seeking God. Yet the moment is lost because with all the light God gives them, they still reject him. It is odd that we reject healing. We resent sight. We forgo understanding and wisdom.

So there is something worse than blindness; it is spiritual blindness. The reason is that people who are spiritually blind do not know it. They keep moving forward, making a mess out of so much because they are not aware of what they cannot see. The only thing worse than being blind would be being blind and thinking you could see. Being blinded by the light.

Reflect and Discuss

1. The metaphor of the yoke is used many times in Jeremiah/Lamentations. What does it symbolize?
2. What were Jeremiah's last words in Egypt?
3. What would happen to Pharaoh?
4. In what way was the nation blinded by the light?
5. Why are the people defiant in chapter 44?
6. Why was it foolish to flee to Egypt?
7. What does chapter 45 tell us about Baruch?
8. In what way is Baruch different from Zedekiah?
9. In what ways can persecution and suffering be good?
10. Reflect on the different characters in this chapter. Where do you see yourself? Where do you see the people of this generation?

God's Word to the Nations

JEREMIAH 46–51

Main Idea: God punishes those who hurt his children.

I. **Egypt (46)**
II. **The Philistines (47)**
III. **Moab (48)**
IV. **Smaller Nations (49)**
    A. Ammon (49:1-6)
    B. Edom (49:7-22)
    C. Damascus/Syria (49:23-27)
    D. Kedar/Arabia (49:28-33)
    E. Elam/Persia (49:34-39)
V. **Babylon (50–51)**

The weight of the text of Jeremiah predicts doom for Israel. They have long neglected God as their source of hope and have dug cisterns that hold no water. As a result, God has used the nations that come against them as his means of discipline. Now God is going to punish those nations. That might surprise us.

However, what should not surprise us is that God defends those who are his own. This is a consistent theme throughout Scripture. God is perennially focused on those who have no ability to defend themselves. Both the Major and the Minor Prophets deal with the issue of social justice.

The first dispute in the Christian church concerned poor widows who were neglected (Acts 6). The precursor to church infrastructure was created to help those who were disadvantaged. The book of James offers a stinging rebuke of those who neglect the needy. In fact, James uses compassion on the needy as an example of works that accompany true faith (Jas 1:27).

Here is the most shocking instance of God's defending his own: in the end of it all, Jesus will come back to lovingly wed his bride the church. Then, after the marriage supper of the Lamb, Jesus will defend his bride. When a battle ensues, the army, perhaps the believers standing with Christ, is arrayed in white—garments that have not been stained with blood. Christ has the bloody garment because he has already entered the battle on behalf of the church. This is why it is said of him that he comes back to bring righteous judgment (Rev 19:11). He is the perfect Judge, and he is coming back to make things right.

Jesus is said to have laser-like eyes (Rev 1:14; 2:18; 19:12). That is not an indication of brute strength. Rather, the eyes are a means by which a person knows things. We acquire knowledge though what we see. Jesus sees all; therefore, he is in a perfect position to execute right judgment. There is so much injustice in the world, but Christ sees it all and will one day make all things right.

Perhaps we did not think of the problems of Israel this way, but God does. Even though Israel is under his discipline, he still wants to protect those who are defenseless, especially those who are his own. So now God is passing judgment on those who have abused his children. He is serious, and the judgment is significant.

As I am writing this, I am texting my brother about how glorious it is when, in the midst of wrestling with a text of Scripture, the main idea of the passage comes to us with clarity. Some texts are difficult, and the main idea must be rooted out by prayer, begging, and even fasting. But not so much these passages. It's pretty clear. God is bringing the smackdown on the nations that have abused Israel. Their wickedness has sealed their fate, and now what has always been implicit is explicit: God punishes those who hurt his children.

Egypt

JEREMIAH 46

As mentioned in the previous chapter, Egypt was a picture of all that was good in the world. There was wealth, prosperity, and security. Thus, the allure to go there and settle down was strong.

This chapter has two prophecies concerning Egypt. The first prophecy comes from the reign of Jehoiakim when, in 605 BC, Nebuchadnezzar defeated the Egyptians (vv. 2-12). Egypt was hurt. The second prophecy concerns after the fall of Jerusalem, when Egypt is attacked by Nebuchadnezzar. The prophecy targets those trusting in political power more than in God. This is why God's children were warned not to go there in the first place: Egypt will be severely punished (vv. 25-26).

The prophecy ends with a wonderful affirmation of Israel (vv. 27-28). Israel will be saved; Jacob will return. Therefore, they do not need to be discouraged. They will be both disciplined and delivered. This, as we saw from previous chapters, is what God always wanted, namely, for them to stay under the discipline of the Lord, to turn toward it. In the end the discipline will come. They must learn to bear down under it.

The Philistines

JEREMIAH 47

The metaphor of rising waters was not difficult to grasp for those living in the area. The dry, desert environment lacked continual rainfall, but when the rains came, they rarely had a place to run off. Very quickly the water in the gullies and gorges would rise. This is what makes Jesus's first parable, the parable of the wise and foolish builder, so provocative. The foolish builder did not anticipate the rising waters that would gather faster than he could react (Matt 7:24-27).

In the same way, the Babylonian Empire would rise and engulf the Philistines. Later, hope will be prophesied for the Philistines but not now. They have met the end of God's mercy and will be engulfed by the Babylonians. The helplessness, the baldness, perhaps is best summarized in verses 6-7, where God's sword will not rest until it has accomplished its purpose.

Moab

JEREMIAH 48

When we read the name *Moab*, our minds wander to Ruth the Moabitess. She was an ancestor of King David and was featured in the lineage of the Messiah in Matthew 1:5. This makes more sense when we understand that Moab was close to Judah, perhaps the closest neighboring nation. They were destroyed not because they came against Judah but because of their pride, complacency, and confidence in idols. Verse 42 says Moab "has exalted himself against the LORD." Wright notes two themes in this prophecy: (1) pride and complacency, and (2) mourning and lament (*Message of Jeremiah*, 422–23).

Yet the chapter has a remarkable ending in verse 47. God promises restoration to a people that are not his people. One cannot help but read this and consider how much love God has for all the nations—that he is compassionate beyond measure.

Smaller Nations
JEREMIAH 49

Chapter 49 comprises prophecies against other nations.

Ammon (49:1-6)

The first prophecy is against Ammon. They were trusting in the false god Milcom/Molech. The worship of Molech was marked by the grotesque practice of child sacrifice (32:35; Lev 20:1-5). Yet again, as with Moab, the prophecy ends with a promise to restore their fortunes.

Edom (49:7-22)

Edom comes under awful condemnation by God. Unlike the prophecies to Moab and to Ammon, there is no hope or promise of restoration.

Damascus/Syria (49:23-27)

Damascus is so helpless they are described in terms of the distress of giving birth. Once the labor pains have started, the situation is painful until it is over (v. 24). Yet, in verse 25, God takes delight in this city. Again, this is the promising note that God is not limited in his love. He can take delight in whomever he chooses.

Kedar/Arabia (49:28-33)

The position of these cities, with their natural defenses, would give them a sense of security. Yet, against the wrath of God, their natural defenses were a vain thing in which to trust.

Elam/Persia (49:34-39)

The interesting thing about these nations is that, unlike the others, they are far away geographically from Judah. Yet God is insistent that no country is going to fall outside the purview of his judgment. This includes the world's biggest superpower, Babylon.

Babylon

JEREMIAH 50–51

This massive prophecy against Babylon shows that God's reach is not limited. He will judge all. The other significance of this prophecy is that it shows an egalitarian nature to the judgment of God. God is going to demonstrate that he is no respecter of persons. In the judgment on Babylon, he will both vindicate his bride and punish her oppressors.

This prophecy is divided into six movements and six themes.

1. Six Movements
   a. Movement One – 50:4-20
   b. Movement Two – 50:21-32
   c. Movement Three – 50:33-46
   d. Movement Four – 51:1-33
   e. Movement Five – 51:34-44
   f. Movement Six – 51:45-53
2. Six Themes
   a. The violence of Babylon will be avenged.
   b. The arrogance of Babylon will be brought low.
   c. The gods of Babylon will be powerless to save them.
   d. The land of Babylon will be devastated by enemies from the north.
   e. The fall of Babylon will signal the restoration and return of Israel.
   f. The fate of Babylon carries cosmic significance. (Wright, *Message of Jeremiah*, 428–40)

What is notable about this prophecy is that it returns us to chapter 1, where we discussed the hope shining through the judgment.

In 50:6 God again refers to his people as sheep, setting the tone for this entire passage. They have been lost sheep with bad shepherds. God is going to punish Babylon and redeem his people. The chapter could be summarized in 50:34: God's strong redemption will be based on his strength.

The contrast between those punished and those delivered is found in 51:18-19 when Jeremiah writes first about the Babylonians,

They are worthless, a work to be mocked.
At the time of their punishment they will be destroyed.
Jacob's Portion is not like these
because he is the one who formed all things.
Israel is the tribe of his inheritance;
the LORD of Armies is his name.

Conclusion

Throughout all of this the end game for God is not punishment. God will demonstrate that he is a greater power than others. He will also demonstrate that what they put their faith in, if it is not in him, is a weak thing in which to trust. However, ultimately what God is after is fulfilling the promise of restoration to his people. What is really at stake is what is coming at the end of 2 Chronicles, when King Cyrus decides to let his people back into their promised land.

This is significant because here in this promised land God will restore Israel, and he will bring about the fulfillment of his promise to bring the Messiah. This is the ultimate plan. Overstating the significance of this fact would be impossible. God is showing mercy to Israel because he wants to provide a place for the coming Messiah who will offer redemption for the world. And, in the midst of this, God is giving hints of mercy to the Gentile nations who do not fear his name. One cannot read this without thinking of John's vision in Revelation 7:9 of a throne room in which every tribe and tongue will be joined in praise for God. God's heart was not just for a people. God's heart was for a people so that they could be a blessing to the nations.

This is the fulfillment of the promise made to Abraham that through him all the nations of the earth will be blessed:

I will make you into a great nation,
I will bless you,
I will make your name great,
and you will be a blessing.
I will bless those who bless you,
I will curse anyone who treats you with contempt,
and all the peoples on earth
will be blessed through you. (Gen 12:2-3)

So there are two remarkable lessons here.

God Is Covenantal but Not Tribal

God was always promising his covenant people that he would fulfill the promises of his covenant. He promised to do exactly what he said he would do, and he would do it in the way he said he would. His promises to his people were clear. They were a nation set apart. This national identity has stayed with Israel to this day.

Yet woven into the words of the prophet Jeremiah are these big hints that the reach of God's mercy is bigger. These notes are covert yet conspicuous; they are hidden in plain sight. Since the clues were not acknowledged, the people that came later—the Pharisees and the scribal culture that emerged during the return to Jerusalem—just couldn't get it. The Gentiles were so far out of the reach of God's mercy, to their way of thinking, that it was wrong to associate with them at all.

This is a crucial point as we read the Gospels. One might think Jesus is against organized religion or against people who were supported by the ministry. But Jesus is not against the Jewish faith; he is against the leaders who perverted it. This is why he says, "Do not think that I will accuse you to the Father. Your accuser is Moses, on whom you have set your hope" (John 5:45). Jesus said that the father of their faith would not be proud of them but would accuse them! This is for many reasons, but one reason is that they had made the covenantal faith tribal. They could not see the signs. God was blessing them so that they could in turn be a blessing to the nations.

If Jesus were to return today, I do not think he would condemn all people who practiced his faith, but he would clear his throat and have something to say to those who were so fixated on the maintenance of their own tribe that they had no love for outsiders. Since I am not God, I do not know who will be in heaven and who will not be. For this reason I should share my faith with all those around me, assuming that they are going to be a part of the covenant. We call everyone to repent; we treat all people as pre-Christian until we know otherwise.

All believers in Christ should see the blessings in their lives as a gift given to bless others.

> May God be gracious to us and bless us;
> may he make his face shine upon us   Selah
> so that your way may be known on earth,
> your salvation among all nations. (Ps 67:1-2)

God Disciplines but Does Not Cast Off Forever

The wonderful thing about this exile is that God is actually removing his people from disaster. Perhaps in reading the first few chapters this is lost on us, but now in reading what God is doing to Babylon, it becomes clearer. God did not cause the exile because he hated his people. He did not tell them to avoid Egypt because he did not love them. Rather, one of the reasons for the exile was to protect them from the destruction that he was going to bring on Babylon and Egypt. You have this sense, now reading to the end of the book, that God was pushing his people aside as he is now dealing harshly with the enemies of his people. Again, the most concise statement of this is found in the lament song of Lamentations 3:25-33.

> *The LORD is good to those who wait for him,*
> *to the person who seeks him.*
> *It is good to wait quietly for salvation from the LORD.*
> *It is good for a man to bear the yoke*
> *while he is still young.* (Lam 3:25-27)

Here it says that the discipline of the Lord is good. Of course it is good! If they had stayed under the discipline of the Lord, Zedekiah would not have been tortured and killed, the city would not have been destroyed, and lives would not have been taken. The discipline of the Lord is hard, but it is good.

Those of us in the new covenant use more explicit language to describe the goodness of God. Romans 8:28-29 tells us that everything works out for the good purposes of God, making us like the person of Christ. This does not mean all things immediately seem good. It does mean that all bad things, in this case the discipline of the Lord, can be thought of as good—not in the vain hope that right thoughts will create better realities but in the reality that the Lord's discipline is always teaching us to bear down so that we can later bear up.

No soldier in boot camp wants boot camp. No soldier in battle can be there without boot camp. The training is indispensable. So our hope as believers is not the removal of suffering; God is too loving for that. The hope of believers is that God never intends to waste a sorrow. No tear unused. No hardship left behind. He rescues each one.

The encouragement continues in Lamentations:

> *Let him sit alone and be silent,*
> *for God has disciplined him.*

Let him put his mouth in the dust—
perhaps there is still hope.
Let him offer his cheek
to the one who would strike him;
let him be filled with disgrace.
For the Lord will not reject us forever.
Even if he causes suffering,
he will show compassion
according to the abundance of his faithful love.
For he does not enjoy bringing affliction
or suffering on mankind. (Lam 3:28-33)

God was sending them into exile temporarily. He told them this over and over again. The Lord will not reject forever. His discipline of his children is severe, but it is not eternal. Yes they were under his discipline, but the discipline of the Lord is so good that he causes us to be able to bear up under it. He is so good!

Reflect and Discuss

1. In what way did God punish those who hurt Israel?
2. Egypt was a picture of all that was good in the world—wealth, prosperity, security. Yet Egypt incurred the wrath of God because they trusted in their self-manufactured political power. What lesson can we learn from Egypt's mistake(s)?
3. Christian discipline is inevitable. How do Christians "bear up" so that they will not be "torn down"?
4. Wright notes two themes in the prophecy of Moab: (1) pride and complacency, and (2) mourning and lament (Jer 48). Why does God restore a people who are not his people?
5. Discuss the six themes of the prophecy given to Babylon and the universal principles we, as Christians, can apply today:
    a.   The violence of Babylon will be avenged.
    b.   The arrogance of Babylon will be brought low.
    c.   The gods of Babylon will be powerless to save them.
    d.   The land of Babylon will be devastated by enemies from the north.
    e.   The fall of Babylon will signal the restoration and return of Israel.

    f.   The fate of Babylon carries cosmic significance.

6. In what way(s) does God show mercy to Israel during the exile?

7. Discuss this statement: God is "covenantal" but not "tribal." Do you agree?

8. Do these passages imply that Christians should reject organized religion?

9. In what way does God discipline believers but not cast them off forever?

10. Do you believe that the discipline of the Lord is a good thing? If so, why?

Hope in the Worst of Times

JEREMIAH 52

Main Idea: God's plans are in process, so we wait through suffering.

I. **The King Is Fallen (52:1-11).**
II. **The Temple Is Fallen (52:12-16).**
III. **The People Are Taken (52:17).**
IV. **Jehoiachin Is Free (52:31-34).**

I t was the best of times, it was the worst of times." Thus begins Dickens's *A Tale of Two Cities*. The line is remarkable for its sheer beauty and symmetry and for the fact that it accurately summarizes what the reader will find in the rest of the book. Indeed, that opening line is so powerful that often its context is lost. In its immediate context it makes more sense while also demonstrating the remarkable giftedness of its author. Dickens wrote,

> It was the best of times, it was the worst of times, it was the age of wisdom, it was the age of foolishness, it was the epoch of belief, it was the epoch of incredulity, it was the season of light, it was the season of darkness, it was the spring of hope, it was the winter of despair, we had everything before us, we had nothing before us, we were all going direct to Heaven, we were all going direct the other way—in short, the period was so far like the present period, that some of its noisiest authorities insisted on its being received, for good or for evil, in the superlative degree of comparison only. (*A Tale of Two Cities*, 1)

The novel is set in the events leading up to the French Revolution, a revolution that, in hindsight, was a good revolution. The nature of the events that lead up to revolutions, the clumsy nature of those revolutions, and the jagged realties that necessitate them, made this the worst of times.

Perhaps Jeremiah could have related. His time was the best of times. God was protecting his people through discipline. He was propelling them back to the promised land by taking them from the promised land. He was leading them in by first leading them out. He was giving them a future and a hope but first exile and desperation. It was good precipitated by bad. However, the composer of the book ends it in a minor key. It is low, but it is not discordant. The note he sounds is consistent with the hope-through-judgment theme that drives the book. The book ends with a recounting of the fall of Jerusalem, and it develops in four movements.

The King Is Fallen
JEREMIAH 52:1-11

In this passage we see great disparity. Zedekiah is rebelling against the king of Babylon, yet we know what is really happening. In chapter 38 he was given a private audience with Jeremiah. God blessed him with a confidant in the hour he needed it the most. He rejected Jeremiah, he rejected God, and eventually he rebelled against the king of Babylon. It is not every day that rebellion against a wicked king is rebellion against God. However, the presence of Nebuchadnezzar did not cause his heart to be cold; rather, it revealed a heart that was already cold against God.

The Temple Is Fallen
JEREMIAH 52:12-16

The tragedy of the lost temple would mean more for the first readers than we can imagine. They were not just reading about a demolition of bricks but of their faith.

It was not their fault that their faith was visual. God commanded it to be so when he carefully instructed the way the temple should be orchestrated. Perhaps this is why it was all so confusing. They were demolishing what God had planned. God commanded that the temple be constructed. God commanded that the capitols be arranged in certain ways. God laid the blueprint for the outside and specified the décor for the inside. This was his vision, realized by his people. So, how could it be God who allowed this destruction to happen?

The answer of course was that all of this was instigated by Israel's own rebellion. God was overseeing the exile of his people and the destruction of his temple in a way that would eventually lead to the furthering of his plan.

The People Are Taken

JEREMIAH 52:17

The leading people of the city are taken and killed. Over the next few waves of exiles, 4,600 become deportees. Jerusalem is empty. The population of Babylon increases. Now what they really need is an exodus. They need a Moses to lead them out. And in God's timing they will have one in the form of Ezra. Ezra will begin the scribal culture, he will seek the heart of God through the Word of God, and then, eventually, he will be used of God to extract his people. Yet for now the city is decimated, and the people are scattered.

Jehoiachin Is Free

JEREMIAH 52:31-34

It is much like the flavor of the book to include some of the "best of times" in the midst of the worst of times. In the midst of this horrendous tragedy, thirty-seven years into the exile, Jehoiachin is set free. The king of Babylon is even kind to him and, remarkably, "changed his prison clothes" and carried him financially the rest of his life.

It's almost like Jehoiachin is the prototype, the model, the beta test, for the thousands who will later cast off the bondage of the exile. They will return to their country, and they will be free.

There was a day when Jehoiachin woke up a prisoner and went to sleep a free man. One day he ate prison food, and the next he dined at the king's table. This little hint, this little clue, subtly embedded at the end of the book, is a hope for a people who will come out of exile and all be set free.

The people would return to the land, they would provide space for the coming Messiah, and they would be the people who would welcome the one who can cause all exiles to come home and all prisoners to be free. It was no comfort to them at the time, but it is of enormous comfort to us that, one day, Christ will cause all the chains of this earth to fall and we will be free in the heavenly home for which we were created.

Jehoiachin is a part of this. He is in the story that leads to the ultimate story. The action of his life is the action that God is using to make all of us part of his story. And that's what we can't miss here.

Conclusion

What is remarkable here are all the verbs. This is a recounting of the
actions that have taken place in Babylon's battle against Jerusalem:

Zedekiah (vv. 1-3)
    Reigned
    Did evil
    Rebelled
Babylon regarding Jerusalem (vv. 4-7)
    Advanced against
    Laid siege
    Broke in
Zedekiah (v. 7)
    Fled
    Left
    Made his way
Babylon regarding Zedekiah and his officials (vv. 8-11)
    Pursued
    Seized
    Passed sentence
    Slaughtered
    Blinded
    Bound
    Brought to Babylon
    Kept in custody
Babylon regarding the temple (vv. 12-19)
    Entered
    Burned
    Tore down
    Broke in pieces
    Carried to Babylon
Babylon regarding the people (vv. 15,24-30)
    Deported
    Took (x 3)
    Put to death
Evil-merodach regarding Jehoiachin (vv. 31-34)
    Pardoned
    Released
    Spoke kindly
    Gave a portion

In this dense summary the verbs tell the story of a king in rebellion, a city being taken, people who are exiled, and a king who receives mercy. Yet, with all of this action, it is easy to forget that God is controlling it all. Even all the evil done to Jeremiah was done with God's oversight. God knew it would take a strong prophet to withstand all that he had asked him to do, so he made him stronger through suffering.

The most quoted verse of the book of Jeremiah is probably 29:11, which reads, "'For I know the plans I have for you'—this is the LORD's declaration—'plans for your well-being, not for disaster, to give you a future and a hope.'" However, the passage is really only hopeful in its context:

> For this is what the LORD says: "When seventy years for Babylon are complete, I will attend to you and will confirm my promise concerning you to restore you to this place. For I know the plans I have for you"— this is the LORD's declaration—"plans for your well-being, not for disaster, to give you a future and a hope. You will call to me and come and pray to me, and I will listen to you. You will seek me and find me when you search for me with all your heart. I will be found by you"— this is the LORD's declaration—"and I will restore your fortunes and gather you from all the nations and places where I banished you"— this is the LORD's declaration. "I will restore you to the place from which I deported you." (29:10-14)

Note three things about God that are implied in this passage and that help us understand the ending to this book.

God's Promises Are Fulfilled in God's Time

He is not just saying they have a hopeful future. That is only part of it. He is saying, "Despite the fact that you will be isolated for seventy years, you will have a hopeful future." He will restore them but not at the moment. God is always on time, but he is rarely early. All that he promised would come true but not until seventy years had passed.

God Brings Hope through Suffering

He is the one who sent them into exile. With all the action verbs of this chapter, this is something God is doing. God is allowing them to be punished as a result of their rebellion. Yet God is giving them a hopeful future *through* exile. And this is what he always does. To every believer God gives a hopeful future *through* suffering. There is no resurrection without a cross. There is no victory without waiting. There is no glory without pain. There is no heaven without the suffering of this life. This brings us to the bigger picture of the book.

God's Plans for Us Are Part of a Larger Process

Jeremiah existed to call a nation back to repentance. That nation would not repent, so God allowed them to go into exile. Yet even the exile was redemptive because they would come back to the land. The return was something new, yet it was in the same trajectory of God's plan. God was in the process of fulfilling his promise to Abraham. He was in the process of fulfilling his promise to Moses. He was in the process of fulfilling his promise to David for an everlasting kingdom. All that Judah was experiencing and all that Jeremiah was experiencing was not wasted. It was all bringing about a plan.

This plan would culminate when the Messiah, the Righteous Branch, would come for his people. He would come to his own, and his own would reject him. He would be led like a lamb to the slaughter for his people, even though they rejected him. All of the pain Christ experienced, all of the isolation he felt from his Father, all of this was allowed by the hand of God in the process of the plan. This was God's plan to bring peace to the world—peace through suffering.

This was God's plan for Judah: security through exile, peace through suffering. This is God's plan for us. This is the way of God. God allowed all of this suffering, "For everyone who calls on the name of the Lord will be saved" (Rom 10:13).

Praise God that there is life in suffering! This is the hope of judgment.

Reflect and Discuss

1. Why is patient trust a necessity in times of suffering? In what way does suffering build character, according to Jeremiah?
2. Discuss the theology of hope and judgment as portrayed in Jeremiah 52.
3. Jeremiah 52 provides four movements in the fall of Jerusalem. Name them.
4. Discuss how the action verbs in this passage relate to the four movements of the fall of Jerusalem.
5. Does the interpretation of the well-known promise in Jeremiah 29:11 change in light of Jeremiah 52?

6. Do you agree with this statement: "God is always on time, but he is rarely early"? Why or why not?
7. How does God bring hope through suffering? Think about how he's given you hope when you were hopeless.
8. Was there a redemptive focus in the exile? If so, explain why.
9. What does this passage teach us about remaining hopeful through suffering?
10. In what way does God show his providential care for Israel through this text?

Lamentations

Introduction

Why study a book of laments?

First, this is life. Unlike made-for-TV movies, real life rarely resolves itself cleanly. The paper-thin veneer of "a perfect Christian life" is a modern invention crafted with the tools of Western consumerism. The idyllic life, untouched by pain, is simply not in the Bible or in the long history of the church. That's good news. The incongruence we find in our lives is what God knows. After all, it is only comforting that God is with us if we are in fact walking the valley of the shadow of death.

Suffering *is* in the Bible. It's clear. In Scripture, real haziness is seen more than pretend clarity. Nothing hidden. A whole book dedicated to regretful weeping, Lamentations is not an appendix to Scripture; it is Scripture. Lamentations is Scripture because lament is not tacked on to our lives as something to be hidden. It's right out there in the middle. God chose not to hide the plaintive cries of the confused. This illustrates that the inspired Word of God is bent toward human suffering. Therefore, understanding this book honors the great suffering that took place by a displaced nation, and Lamentations gives us the rhetorical tools to weep with displaced people around the world today. Lamentations: this is their story, this is their song.

It would not be too much to say that I have found myself in this book. It's not that I can identify with the deep agony of the prophet but that in my own suffering I find a surprising comfort in knowing that life in God's world is not all so neat. The untidiness of this book is therapeutic. It reminds me that the unresolved questions of life are in a sense an answer in themselves.

Second, this is God's work. What we see in this passage is the heavy hand of discipline on those he loves. I serve that God. I love that God. I have given my life to the God who caused tragedy to fall on those he loved and, what's more, allowed the journals of those who resent him to be in his book. The book that guides my life is filled with complaints! We've got to understand this. And this understanding leads to so many questions: What kind of God is this? Does God still discipline his children like this? Will we ever feel like Jeremiah felt in this lament?

Am I insulated from the lament? Am I insulated from what caused the lament? We need to wrestle with the questions in this book.

But there is a *third* reason I also find strangely comforting. *Lament is an experience of everyone God is using to fulfill his covenant promises.* Let's think about this in terms of the old and new covenant.

Dealing with Discipline

If one were to look at the whole swath of the Old Testament, the story could be divided into the story of two great oppressions: bondage in Egypt and exile at the hands of Assyria and Babylon.

Genesis to Exodus

In the first two chapters of the Bible, we have the people of God created, the fall, the flood, and then God starting over with a new chosen race of people. He makes a covenant with Abraham that would provide God's people with a blessing, offspring, and land. The promise was overwhelming. Not realized at the time was that this would come after 430 years of bondage in Egypt. This was not in their plan. Thousands of years removed, modern pilgrims talk about this bondage clinically. However, for Israel this was their reality for more than 400 years. They were not in bondage due to sin; they were in bondage due to God's fulfilling his promise to Abraham. In other words, the covenant had two sides: God's great completion and the suffering needed to accomplish it. Sometimes the completion of God's promises for us brings suffering to us. Covenant brings hardship and causes us to weep. Weeping is not always out of his will.

Joshua to Nehemiah

God kept his promise to give them a land, and they entered it under the leadership of Joshua. When they were finally in the land, they had the potential to prosper under the rule of godly leaders, but they ultimately fell into horrific idolatry under the rule of Solomon. This led to a divided kingdom and eventually to captivity and exile. The exile, unlike the bondage in Egypt, was self-inflicted.

Yet God graciously delivered them from both Egypt and exile. For Egypt there was Moses, and for the exiles there was Nehemiah.

In New Testament terms we could loosely compare this to the discipline of the Lord. In the same way God delivered his people to keep his covenant in Egypt, God still today helps his people through times that they are suffering through no fault of their own. The New Testament also teaches us that God still allows his children to suffer for things they have done. God still disciplines us.

We could refer to the first type of suffering as the *instructive discipline* of the Lord and the latter as the *corrective discipline* of the Lord. The instructive discipline of the Lord is when the Lord allows us to suffer for reasons that, whether we understand or not, he ultimately is going to use to glorify himself. The corrective discipline of the Lord is suffering the consequences of our sin.

Romans 8:28 helps us understand the instructive discipline of the Lord: all things will ultimately shape us into the likeness of Christ, even things we do not understand or do not enjoy. More precisely, the writer of Hebrews states in Hebrews 12:11, "No discipline seems enjoyable at the time, but painful. Later on, however, it yields the peaceful fruit of righteousness to those who have been trained by it." This is the best way to understand how God works in our lives. He works to train us. This is the instructive discipline of the Lord.

The Scriptures also teach that God disciplines us in response to our sin. The same chapter in Hebrews states that we are to "endure suffering as discipline: God is dealing with you as sons. For what son is there that a father does not discipline?" (Heb 12:7). So the discipline of the Lord can be instructive, but it can also be corrective.

Christians are so loved by the Father that they will be instructed and corrected. Neither of these is enjoyable. This is why they are called discipline. They are hard. They are the kind of trials that make you want to weep.

This leads us to the book of Lamentations.

In the Old Testament we have Egypt and exile. In the New Testament we have instruction and correction. They both lead to the keeping of the covenant promise, and they both demand lament.

Yet the tone of the book, not to mention the title (!), is off-putting. It discords with modern and postmodern thinking to suggest we should weep. Perhaps the reason this is so is because we tend to see suffering as immediately two-sided.

- Fall, then covenant
- Egypt, then promised land
- Cross, then resurrection
- Death, then heaven

This is gloriously true. Yet to so quickly understand them as couplets can subtly suggest an immediacy to suffering that is misleading. Sometimes lament is a life. It also suggests that we will see both sides in *this* life. The far reach of Western prosperity preachers and their perpetual distance from New Testament teaching should jolt the church back to the Scripture, where we see that suffering is part of life for the believer. Therefore, so is lament.

One of the features of this book, like the book of Jeremiah, is the remarkable verses that spring from the desperation. The book is so dark. It is genuinely depressing. At its worst there is no escape; the people have turned to desperate cannibalism, and Jeremiah, the one who is to be leading them out, feels like God is his enemy. It is altogether sad and depressing.

Yet in this desert the faithfulness of God shines through. In this darkness literary expression gives eyes to faith. Jeremiah writes,

> *Remember my affliction and my homelessness,*
> *the wormwood and the poison.*
> *I continually remember them*
> *and have become depressed.*
> *Yet I call this to mind,*
> *and therefore I have hope:*
> *Because of the Lord's faithful love*
> *we do not perish,*
> *for his mercies never end.*
> *They are new every morning;*
> *great is your faithfulness!*
> *I say, "The Lord is my portion,*
> *therefore I will put my hope in him."*
> *The Lord is good to those who wait for him,*
> *to the person who seeks him.*
> *It is good to wait quietly*
> *for salvation from the Lord.*
> *It is good for a man to bear the yoke*
> *while he is still young.* (Lam 3:19-27)

The words are both beautiful and haunting. How could something so comforting and beautiful come from a situation that is so dark? What is more interesting still is that these words have brought comfort to millions through the poetry of Thomas Chisholm when he wrote,

Great is Thy faithfulness, O God my Father;
There is no shadow of turning with Thee,
Thou changest not, Thy compassions they fail not,
As Thou hast been, Thou forever wilt be.
Chorus:
Great is Thy faithfulness!
Great is Thy faithfulness!
Morning by morning new mercies I see;
All I have needed Thy hand hath provided—
Great is Thy faithfulness, Lord unto me!

Summer and winter and springtime and harvest,
Sun, moon, and stars in their courses above;
Join with all nature in manifold witness,
To Thy great faithfulness, mercy, and love.

Pardon for sin and a peace that endureth,
Thine own dear presence to cheer and to guide;
Strength for today, and bright hope for tomorrow
Blessings all mine, with ten thousand beside. ("Great Is Thy
Faithfulness")

My prayer is that in these five short chapters you will find both a full
expression of lament and a hunger for the healing that is only provided
in the new covenant.

Prevention and Condemnation

LAMENTATIONS 1

Main Idea: To ignore God's prevention is to embrace God's condemnation.

I. The State of Jerusalem (1:1-7)
II. The Sin That Brought Them There (1:8-14)
III. The Sentence of God's Condemnation (1:15-22)

The millisecond after Kevin Hines jumped from the Golden Gate Bridge to the bay below, he felt instant regret.

"I said to myself, 'What have I done, I don't want to die, God please save me,'" recalls Hines, 34, of his suicide jump in September 2000. "The moment I hit freefall was an instant regret—I recognized that I made the greatest mistake in my life and I thought it was too late." (Herbst, "Man Who Survived Suicide")

Kevin Hines is one of the more than 1,000 people who have attempted suicide by jumping from the Golden Gate bridge. He is one of only twenty-five who have been known to survive. The stories of survivors are similar: they immediately regret the decision to attempt suicide. As he retells in his book *Cracked, Not Broken: Surviving and Thriving after a Suicide Attempt*, he did not want to die. He wanted to live, so he voiced a prayer to God to help him survive. The prayer, in its essence, was that God would reverse the consequences of his decision. In Hines's case, God seems to have intervened. However, he does not always do that. In fact, when we ignore God's laws, we face God's consequences. In other words, the natural consequences of our decisions are rarely reversed. This was certainly the case for Judah. They were committing spiritual suicide. They had violated God's law, and the consequences were rushing toward them.

Chapter 1 develops three themes woven throughout the chapter: the state of suffering the people find themselves in, the sin that caused the suffering, and God's response of condemnation—or, if you will forgive the alliteration, the state, the sin, and the sentence.

The State of Jerusalem
LAMENTATIONS 1:1-7

The opening line of poetry is haunting. "How she sits alone." Jerusalem was once lovely and vivacious, the center of the nation that was central to God's plan. Was there a more envied place in the whole world? She was God's bride! This is the place where David ruled with imperial, military gravitas. This is the place where Solomon built palaces so grand that the queen of Sheba came to visit. Jerusalem was spectacular, magnificent, marvelous! The beauty is important to remember because it makes Lamentations 1:1 more provocative. She went from epicenter to wasteland. One immediately thinks of once-thriving cities that are now a fraction of their former glory. But that metaphor would not be strong enough. This is Berlin after WWII. This is Atlanta after the Civil War. This is Aleppo after the Syrian civil war. This is NYC, Paris, or Prague reduced to a dumpster fire—but worse.

It reminds us, in a provocative way, that nothing lasts forever. Great people become bywords. Great churches become massive empty buildings whose presence stands as a monument to a bygone era. Great companies are subsumed. Great universities falter. Those beholden to formerly great institutions become intuitive historians. The old buildings of the former institutions stir hard memories—memories that make us smile so that, perhaps for a moment, we don't have to wince. As I am writing this, I am thinking of once-glorious institutions, leaders, movements, and churches that now remind us that nothing lasts forever. In fact, every great movement that is currently vital is ultimately fleeting. We do not normally sense it, but it is true. Nothing lasts forever. This is the sad tone of the first chapter of Lamentations.

Yet this city is like no other city. This is the city, the only city, that will descend from heaven. We Christians know the rest of the story: this is the city to which Christ will return. She will ultimately see the opposite of loneliness and despair. However, in Jeremiah's time that reality was light-years away. There is nothing like that at the moment. This was desperation and despair.

The Sin That Brought Them There
LAMENTATIONS 1:8-14

The sin that brought the residents of Jerusalem to this low point is rehearsed throughout the book of Jeremiah. This is not a case of suffering without reason. This is not like what happened to Job. This is a circumstance that they created. The evidence of this is the existence of the prophet Jeremiah. A prophetic voice is the evidence that God did not want this. He sent Jeremiah to help prevent it. But they passed up the possibility of prevention, and they learned the hard lesson that to ignore God's prevention is to embrace God's condemnation.

Jeremiah writes that Judah is suffering because of her sin (v. 5), and that is why she is despised by all (v. 8). She fell because she failed to consider the consequences of her actions (v. 9).

Suffering is inevitable. We think obedience is too much of a hardship. We don't want to obey, and we resent God for asking us to do so. Following God is not easy, but the price of obedience is a bargain compared to the price of rebellion. Prevention costs less than destruction. Avoiding sin costs less than repenting of sin.

Then, tragically, we see the result for those who will not put on the yoke of obedience: they are forced to suffer under the yoke of their sins, by which they are broken and defeated (v. 14). Zedekiah was asked to put his neck under the yoke of the king of Babylon. He refused. In chapter 3 Jeremiah will counsel us that it is good for a young man to bear his yoke in his youth. The yoke in both cases relates to discipline. To bear the yoke means to absorb the wrath that was intended. Yet notice how it is developed here. The yoke represents the sins of the nation. In this case it seems that God does not reverse the natural consequences for sin.

As in the story of Kevin Hines above, God did not immediately reverse the consequences of their sin. This was something they had to live with.

As we think about this in a new covenant context, we are reminded that we serve a God who will never leave us or forsake us. He gives us all the grace we need to face the challenges of this life and to overcome condemnation in the next life. Upon our salvation, he reverses the eternal consequences of our sin. Yet we must be careful to remind ourselves that God does not always reverse the temporal consequences of sin. Addictions must be fought with tenacity, relationships must be restored, and debts repaid. For the repentant God reverses the eternal consequences of sin, but he does not always reverse the temporal consequences of sin. For Judah, the consequences of sin become her yoke.

The Sentence of God's Condemnation
LAMENTATIONS 1:15-22

The reason they are in this position is no mystery. This is God's doing. While this theme is more fully developed in the following chapters, the people of Judah are in this position because of their own sin. Considering Jerusalem, Jeremiah writes that she will be crushed and trampled, her children will be desolate in defeat, and there will be no one to comfort her despite her pleas because God has turned against her (vv. 15-17).

As difficult as this is to read, we are reminded that Judah was warned on many occasions that it did not have to be this way. The presence of the prophet is the witness that it did not. They could have turned from sin and come back to God.

God is just because that has always been his essential nature. He is always consistent with his nature. Even though we might project him with a light, frothy attitude toward sin, we cannot change his character. He is against sin; he reacts against sin because that's who he is. Nothing about his character has changed since Jeremiah wrote these devastating words about the lonely city that sits on the hill.

Conclusion

The idea is clear: sin brings ruin. Sin ruins individuals; sin ruins families; sin ruins churches; sin ruins cities. The weight of destruction is heavier still in light of the warnings: the prophets, the metaphors, the miracles. All the things God did in the past to prevent this from happening are now clear.

Suffering brings clarity. It always does. The right thing to see when we suffer is that we have a pure heart like that of Job, of whom it was said that in all of his suffering he did not sin (Job 1:22). After all, what value is there when we suffer for our own wrongdoing? "For it is better to suffer for doing good, if that should be God's will, than for doing evil" (1 Pet 3:17).

Since all Scripture is given for our benefit (1 Tim 3:17), we have to ask what the benefit is of reading of the destruction of Jerusalem. Well, perhaps the reader should be warned. A nation disobeyed God after several warnings. God punished them.

God allows suffering as corrective discipline. However, this does not mean all suffering is corrective. Discipline, and sometimes suffering, can also be instructive. The question that inevitably surfaces is, Which is it? Is this trial a result of my disobedience or simply God's instruction to me? The question is not answerable. The answer, simply put, is that it's possible we will never know in this life. However, that does not matter. Our success in the trial is not dependent on our knowing what is going on behind the veil. The response is the same: we repent of sin and trust him. We trust him with our trials, and we hate the sin that brings ruin.

Reflect and Discuss

1. How does Jeremiah describe the state of Jerusalem?
2. Why is the city lonely? What does this imply?
3. Where else in Jeremiah and Lamentations does he use the metaphor of the yoke?
4. Why is the yoke metaphor a good one for Jeremiah?
5. Why is he now using the metaphor of the yoke on himself?
6. How does suffering bring clarity?
7. Can you give an example from history or experience where sin has brought ruin?
8. Can you explain the difference between God's corrective discipline and his instructive discipline?
9. Does God discipline his children? Is there a New Testament text that affirms this?
10. If God forgives all sin, does this mean he immediately reverses the natural consequences of our decisions?

The Dark Night

LAMENTATIONS 2

Main Idea: There is a dark night when the discipline of the Lord falls on us. When tragedy happens, we respond humbly because we don't know why it happens, and we soberly examine ourselves.

I. **Action: God's Rebuke (2:1-9)**
II. **Silence: Reacting to God's Rebuke (2:10-17)**
III. **Prayer: Responding to God's Rebuke (2:18-22)**

Walter Brueggemann observed that the Psalms move from orientation to disorientation to reorientation (*Spirituality of the Psalms,* passim). Life is oriented in a certain direction, and then tragedy brings disorientation. We want to go back to the original orientation. This is not how God works. Rather, ultimately he reorients us to a new reality. In this reorientation we often experience triumph—the end of the story, the reason all this has happened to us. We are sheep who walk through the valley of the shadow of death. But in the end God is no longer the shepherd; he is the host who prepares a table before us, and in a lavish display of abundance, our cup runs over.

Orientation, disorientation, and reorientation are familiar to us. It's the template of the gospel. This is the life of Christ and the life of Christ in us. Our lives are oriented toward God, we realize the disorientation caused by sin, and then God reorients our lives. This reorientation is the wonderful hope of the gospel. God's pattern of redemption is so familiar we might look for it, and even expect it, in Scripture. However, it's not here in Lamentations 2. If you are looking for a classic story structure that moves from plot and rising tension toward release of tension, Lamentations 2 only gives us the first two. And in this case two out of three is bad.

The Dark Night

Perhaps chapter 2 is the heaviest of all the poems in the book. It is heavy because, as verse 1 says, "The Lord has overshadowed Daughter Zion with his anger!" Judah feels the cold, dark night, and God casts the shadow. This is a shocking twist in the story. God the protector has become God the destroyer. The comfort of his presence is now cold.

The poetry itself is dark. The shadow of God's anger hangs over a city. When God directs his anger against a city, God is not, of course, angry at the latitude and longitude. God's anger is not aimed at a location but a people. A city *is* its people. God's anger is directed toward a people collectively. Thus, in contrast with the many passages that address personal sorrow, this is a chapter about corporate sorrow. The people are paying the price for bad decisions.

When we see a city broken, a people broken, we intuit that they are victims of their own bad decisions. This is the law of the harvest: they are reaping what they have sown. Paul applied the law of the harvest to the Galatians when in 6:7-8 he wrote,

> *Don't be deceived: God is not mocked. For whatever a person sows he will also reap, because the one who sows to his flesh will reap destruction from the flesh, but the one who sows to the Spirit will reap eternal life from the Spirit.*

This law is what David feared in Psalm 51 when, after sexual sin, he feared that he would be banished from God's presence, have the Holy Spirit taken from him, lose his joy, and not be sustained by God (Ps 51:11-12). A wicked seed grew a wicked weed. Sin has results. No sin is committed in a void of consequence.

In the same way, the people of Judah are reaping what they have sown. True enough, but that's not the focus here. The thrust of Lamentations 2 is what God is doing to them, not what they have done to themselves. The chapter is a working out of the anger of God against Zion. What is remarkable in Lamentations 2 is all the things that are attributed to God. Just think about the twenty-six action verbs attributed to God in the first nine verses (emphasis mine):

- He has *thrown down* Israel's glory (v. 1).
- He *did not acknowledge* his footstool (v. 1).
- The Lord *has swallowed up* (v. 2).
- He *has demolished* (v. 2).
- He *brought them to the ground* (v. 2).
- And *defiled* the kingdom and its leaders (v. 2).
- He has *cut off* every horn of Israel (v. 3).
- And *withdrawn* his right hand (v. 3).

- He has *blazed* against Jacob like a flaming fire (v. 3).
- He has *strung his bow* like an enemy (v. 4).
- He has *killed* everyone who was the delight to the eye (v. 4).
- He has *swallowed up* Israel (v. 5).
- He *swallowed up* all its palaces (v. 5).
- And *destroyed* its fortified cities (v. 5).
- He has *multiplied* mourning and lamentation (v. 5).
- He has *wrecked* his temple (v. 6).
- The LORD has *abolished* appointed festivals and Sabbaths in Zion (v. 6).
- He has *despised* king and priest (v. 6).
- The Lord has *rejected* his altar (v. 7).
- He has *repudiated* his sanctuary (v. 7).
- He has *handed* the walls of her palaces *over* to the enemy (v. 7).
- The LORD *determined to destroy* the wall (v. 8).
- He *stretched out* a measuring line (v. 8).
- And *did not restrain* himself from destroying (v. 8).
- He *made* the ramparts and walls *grieve* (v. 8).
- He has *destroyed and shattered* the bars on her gates (v. 9).

Philip Graham Ryken summarizes the tone well when he writes,

> What was amazing about these losses was that they were all the
> Lord's doing. To be sure, they were the result of Judah's sin.
> But the reality still had to be faced: God had turned against
> his own people. He had not simply allowed his own city to be
> defeated—he had helped to destroy it. . . . In a strange twist
> on the Old Testament motif of the divine warrior, God was
> not fighting for his people but against them. (*Jeremiah and
> Lamentations*, 749)

If it was not clear enough that God was responsible for the destruction, in verse 17 Jeremiah writes,

> *The LORD has done what he planned;*
> *he has accomplished his decree,*
> *which he ordained in days of old.*
> *He has demolished without compassion,*
> *letting the enemy gloat over you*
> *and exalting the horn of your adversaries.*

Verse 22 affirms the same idea: God has done this.

Jeremiah is lamenting the actions of God toward his people. Again, the driving idea of this chapter seems to be the overshadowing of God's anger against his people. They have provoked the anger of God, and now God is responding. The chapter is in the form of an acrostic poem, and thus the thoughts are not developed in a linear sequence. Yet Jeremiah 2 does have progression. The flow of the chapter could be expressed according to the outline above.

Action: God's Rebuke

LAMENTATIONS 2:1-9

The Lord has not acknowledged his footstool, which represents the city (Ps 132:7). In his anger he cut off the horn of Israel. The horn was the symbol of power. Now they have none—no horn, no power. The citadels are torn down, and the army is a wreck. Similarly, he has destroyed everything that "was the delight to the eye" (v. 4), meaning the best things about their nation are gone.

To make things worse, God plundered his own temple (v. 6) as if it were a shack in a field! What seemed unshakable was ransacked. The walls were a symbol of protection; they were a fortress and defense. However, the walls have been handed over to the enemy (vv. 7,9). This is a football team with no line, an army with no foot soldiers. Without walls this city will not stand a chance against her enemies. Even if the people now decided they wanted to learn what the Lord requires, they would not be able to because the prophets receive no more instruction (v. 9). The reaction that follows is fitting to the disaster.

We can all relate to a time when we thought we were untouchable. Like Jeremiah in chapter 1, we can relate to great movements or institutions that were formerly glorious but are no longer. This is not to suggest that in these cases we see it represents the rebuke of God. We simply cannot know that; it is in the mind of God. So when we see trouble somewhere, we are not to immediately assume God's rebuke. We do not do this with others, and we do not do it with ourselves. It may be clear to us that we are facing a difficult time as a response to some sin. But we are not Jeremiah, and we certainly are not God. We just cannot know with any certainty why bad things happen. We do not have the inspired certainty Jeremiah had.

Silence: Reacting to God's Rebuke
LAMENTATIONS 2:10-17

The familiar phrase *shock and awe* has its roots in military theory. The idea is to gain dominance over the enemy as quickly as possible. A nation that was awestruck by the power of another would more quickly surrender (Bromwich, "Meaning of Shock and Awe"). As the city of Jerusalem lay in devastation, Jeremiah records the reaction as silence (v. 10). They sit there unable to articulate what they are experiencing.

Jeremiah is weeping. This pathetic scene is almost too much to bear: children crying to their mothers for food while they die in their arms (v. 11). Jeremiah concludes that it is helpless. None can heal her. The nation is terminal. Dr. Jeremiah looks to the nation and says, "I'm so sorry. There's nothing else to be done." There is nothing left. Nothing.

What makes this tragedy so bad is that it could have been avoided. The sting of regret makes the moment worse. If only they had listened to the prophets, and if only the prophets had given them a clear word. Yet many of their prophets were deceptive inasmuch as they were unclear (v. 14).

The reaction from others compounds the suffering. Those who pass by scorn her. Taking credit for what God has done emboldens the enemies of this nation.

Anyone with any sympathy whatsoever is disturbed by this image of a city destroyed at the hands of God. What are we to make of this? How do we explain God's action? First, remember the uniqueness of this situation. This nation is *the* (singular, definite article) chosen people of God. They are unique. They were to have a love relationship with God like a bride to her groom. As such, God would use them to be a blessing to the nations and to fulfill all his covenant promises. Their rejection of their groom/God was serious because their responsibility to their God was great. Knowing this instructs us not to attach divine motives on national or natural disasters when they occur in other times or to other nations. Israel is unique, and so is her relationship with God. This uniqueness is clear in the summary verse quoted above (v. 17).

While we are cautious not to compare certain disasters to Judah's disaster in Lamentations 2, what is instructive is how we should respond to God in moments of crisis. This is found in the final section of the chapter.

Prayer: Responding to God's Rebuke
LAMENTATIONS 2:18-22

God is not an impersonal force. God is not an entity void of reason and relationship. We can communicate with him, and we are compelled to initiate communication with him. The people respond to God by crying out to him. The activity of prayer is at once reflexive and right. It is our impulse and our only hope. Some impulses can harm you; other impulses can save you.

In prayer, ironically perhaps, they are suggesting that the one who is destroying them is the only one who can save them. The one who is the enemy is now their only hope and salvation. Thus we see this beautiful cry come from this destitute wasteland.

Verse 18 is a powerful plea for a gut talk with God: do not let yourself rest until you have prayed all of this through. Pour yourself out like water to God. They had some specific topics to pray about: the lives of their children (v. 19), cannibalistic infanticide (v. 20), and the death of people of all ages (v. 21).

Unlike some passages this one does not end optimistically. Terror is on every side, no one has escaped, and Jeremiah is watching the demise of those people he has cultivated (v. 22).

When life is tragic, how do we respond? What are we to think about the relationship of evil and suffering? The only response is humility and sobriety.

Conclusion

The inevitable question is, What about now? This is a theodicy for a people, for a community. If today God's anger is provoked with a people—a community of believers—does he react in the same way? Does the coming of the Christ insulate us from corporate discipline?

First, Israel as a nation is unique. As mentioned above, Israel is the one and only people of God. There is no nation like her, nor will there ever be one comparable to her. As a Gentile Christian I know I am grafted into this nation and find mercy before God in that way (Rom 11:11-31). So again, when disaster happens in a community today, we should be slow to assume we know God had a motivation for allowing this.

Second, remember that the ways of God are higher than ours. Meaning, as was the point of the book of Job, we are not created with the capacity to

understand all that happens in the world. While this does not scratch
our itch of intellectual curiosity, I find it satisfying to know that even
with the greatest education, the greatest minds could not understand
why evil happens in the world. It is beyond our capacity to grasp.

*Third, God specifically warned the churches of the New Testament that he
reacts in demonstrable ways to disobedience.* Some examples would include
God's killing Ananias and Sapphira for lying about their gift (Acts 5:1-
11) and the threat of illness and even death for those taking the Lord's
Supper without discernment (1 Cor 11:27-32).

These are individual examples. So, what about a local church corporately? The final book of the Bible includes seven examples of Jesus's
addressing specifically the needs of a congregation. If for no other passages in Scripture, pastors should be motivated to lead their people in
purity against the backdrop of these warnings.

Ephesus lost her first love and was warned:

> *Remember then how far you have fallen; repent, and do the works you
> did at first. Otherwise, I will come to you and remove your lampstand
> from its place, unless you repent.* (Rev 2:5)

Pergamum was listening to false teaching and was warned:

> *So repent! Otherwise, I will come to you quickly and fight against them
> with the sword of my mouth.* (Rev 2:16)

Thyatira was guilty of tolerating false teaching and was warned:

> *I gave her time to repent, but she does not want to repent of her sexual
> immorality. Look, I will throw her into a sickbed and those who
> commit adultery with her into great affliction. Unless they repent of her
> works, I will strike her children dead. Then all the churches will know
> that I am the one who examines minds and hearts, and I will give to
> each of you according to your works.* (Rev 2:21-23)

Sardis was asleep and was warned:

> *Be alert and strengthen what remains, which is about to die, for I have
> not found your works complete before my God. Remember, then, what
> you have received and heard; keep it, and repent. If you are not alert,
> I will come like a thief, and you have no idea at what hour I will come
> upon you.* (Rev 3:2-3)

Laodicea was admonished to find again her first love:

I know your works, that you are neither cold nor hot. I wish that you were cold or hot. So, because you are lukewarm, and neither hot nor cold, I am going to vomit you out of my mouth. For you say, "I'm rich; I have become wealthy and need nothing," and you don't realize that you are wretched, pitiful, poor, blind, and naked. I advise you to buy from me gold refined in the fire so that you may be rich, white clothes so that you may be dressed and your shameful nakedness not be exposed, and ointment to spread on your eyes so that you may see. (Rev 3:15-18)

Then Jesus comes to a full stop. The summary in Revelation 3:19 is stunning and breathtaking: "As many as I love, I rebuke and discipline. So be zealous and repent." As many as Jesus loves. Does God discipline communities of faith? Yes, the ones he loves.

This, in a real sense, is glorious. The beginning of Revelation makes it so clear that God is not an impersonal force; he is a loving Father. A force, an abstract automaton, does not discipline. God loves people and God created churches. Each church, like a child, has strengths and weaknesses and areas that need affirming and challenging.

We began by asking the question about the reason behind suffering. This, in complete honesty, is the best answer we can give: For someone in Christ, God disciplines his children. And what God does individually, he still does corporately to local bodies of believers. Again, without the mind of God, we do not know when or how this happens, so we respond to tragedy with humility and sobriety. When tragedy happens, we respond humbly because we don't know why it happens, and we soberly examine ourselves.

Certainly, we don't look for equivalency in tragedies that happen to others. We don't say, "Hmm, I wonder what God is up to there." Israel, and her discipline, was unique. They were God's people. Yet, as those grafted in, we can't be dismissive about God's ways. God has not changed. He loves his local churches; and, as the letters to the seven churches testify, he relates to each church individually, he encourages each individually, and he disciplines each individually. God, have mercy!

Reflect and Discuss

1. What is meant by orientation, disorientation, and reorientation?
2. If you are comfortable doing so, discuss a time when God allowed your life to be disoriented.
3. How can we explain that God seems to be the agent acting against his people?
4. How do the promises of the covenant help us understand this?
5. How might you attempt to justify Jeremiah's apparent despondency?
6. How does God still bring corrective discipline in extreme cases against individuals?
7. What New Testament examples for punitive discipline on individuals do we have?
8. How does God still bring corrective discipline in extreme cases against churches?
9. What New Testament examples for punitive discipline on churches do we have?
10. How does God's discipline encourage us?

Great Faithfulness

LAMENTATIONS 3

Main Idea: Great is his faithfulness.

I. **Sometimes God Seems to Be the Enemy (3:1-18).**
   A. God is the enemy (3:1-6).
   B. God is a warden (3:7-9).
   C. God is a wild animal (3:10-11).
   D. God is a warrior (3:12).
   E. God is a hunter (3:13-14).
II. **When God Seems against You, Remember: Great Is His Faithfulness (3:19-33).**
III. **Sometimes We Are Drowning in Desperation (3:34-54).**
   A. What God has done (3:34-45)
   B. The response of the enemy (3:46-47)
   C. Jeremiah's response (3:48-54)
IV. **When We Are Drowning in Desperation, Remember: Great Is His Faithfulness (3:55-66).**

The brightest lights shine in the darkest nights. Like a desert rose, passages in Lamentations 3 are splendor in the midst of desolation. To appreciate the beauty, you have to see the ugly, the gore, that surrounds the passage. Grace glows in the dark.

Jeremiah is in a cavern without a light, the valley of the shadow of death without a shepherd—no light and no leadership, wholly dark. Lamentations 3 is not tied to a specific moment in this national crisis, yet the whole situation is desperate. The nation is captive. The leaders are gone. The life they knew is a memory and a bitter one at that. And, as discussed in previous chapters, it all could have been avoided. None of this had to happen. They did not have to be captives, they did not have to disobey, they did not have to follow foreign gods, they did not have to prostitute themselves, and they did not have to be unfaithful to God.

The wrath God poured out in chapter 2 as the primary actor in this tragedy was totally and completely avoidable. All sin is à la carte. You don't have to do it. Like people who had never even heard of God, Judah let the depravity within them and the nations around them control their actions. They followed their heart and broke God's heart. They chased their dreams of a life free from God's constraints and found a life free from God's protection. The collapsed walls of the city lay as a metaphor for the broken rubble of their lives.

In the midst of this moment, Jeremiah has the unenviable job of screaming to the nation that they are headed in the wrong direction. And that's not the bad part. While the nation is headed down, he has to ride along.

Like a conductor on a runaway locomotive, Jeremiah is called to pull the hand brake to no effect—400,000 pounds of iron, engineering, and inertia against his puny prophetic bicep on a brake. They were out of control, and Jeremiah was along for the ride. Every sin is indeed a choice, but the inertia of disobedience is real. This is why sin is so scary: it's hard to stop once it begins. Like a mutant alien from a bad sci-fi movie, it reproduces until it destroys.

So, as we read this depressing chapter, we might think Jeremiah is being a little dramatic. You know the type: that guy who is always down, the guy who can't force himself to be positive. Perhaps he is being too hard on himself and on others. Maybe. But this is not a silly glass-is-half-empty person. What he sees is real. The loss is real, the pain is real, the heartbreak is real, and the devastation is real. Real people lost their lives and their homes and their dreams of a whole covenant relationship with God. This is where God finds them, and this is where God works. God does in fact do maintenance, but what is thrilling is when he does a complete restoration. Sure, he does detailing to people who are already showroom quality. Yet what makes us stand up and notice is the restored rusted-out junker. When the odometer has turned over a few times, parts are missing, and the torn interior reeks of bad decisions, that's when God's abilities are more obvious. He is so faithful. He restores.

This is where Jeremiah is: broken. Yet there are cracks in Jeremiah's darkness from which light will stream in—full on, glorious, bright light. Here we have our hope: bright light, illuminating, warm, and waiting at the end of our darkness.

Structure

Unlike chapter 2, a measure of hope is seen here in the flow of the chapter. A repeated pattern of desperation and salvation is evident. This chapter has an undercurrent of hope. The chapter could be outlined this way:

God's Actions and Jeremiah's Desperation (vv. 1-18)
Hope (vv. 19-33)
Drowning in Desperation (vv. 34-54)
Salvation and Vindication (vv. 55-66)

Sometimes God Seems to Be the Enemy
LAMENTATIONS 3:1-18

As in chapter 2, God is the agent who is acting against his people. However, here it is personal. The actions directed toward Jerusalem are felt by Jeremiah. What's fascinating in this section are the metaphors. They are horrifying.

God Is the Enemy (3:1-6)

God has Jeremiah under the rod of his wrath. The same metaphor is in Psalm 2:9, the great passage on the Messiah and what he will do to his enemies. If Jeremiah is alluding to this psalm, then it is extremely fascinating. The Messiah was the principal figure of hope for the whole nation. The means of God's hope and national deliverance has turned on him. He is stricken with the rod or scepter of God. This is the famous rod mentioned in Psalm 23:4: "Your rod and your staff—they comfort me." The staff was for leadership and the rod for protection. The shepherd leads his sheep with his staff, and he beats the wolves with his rod. In Lamentations the God who should be Jeremiah's shepherd is treating him like a wolf. This is shocking!

God is no longer painting a beautiful picture. This is a twisted abstract painting that makes you stare in confusion. This is God as Picasso. The strangeness of this picture is seen in the twisted metaphors of verses 5-7. Like an enemy God has besieged Jeremiah and trapped him in a way that he cannot escape.

God Is a Warden (3:7-9)

God has walled Jeremiah in, and he can't get loose. There is no way out of this situation. His chains placed there by his warden are real. They are heavy. He would like to escape, but instead of a path he has a wall. Leadership has surrendered to obstruction. There is no escape.

God Is a Wild Animal (3:10-11)

The fear of wild animals is lost on many in modern times, but a bear or a lion was a real fear in Jeremiah's day. Largely, people were defenseless. To lions a man without defense is prey. They ravage.

God Is a Warrior (3:12)

Jeremiah feels as if he is a target for God's wrath.

God Is a Hunter (3:13-14)

This is perhaps the most vivid of all the metaphors. God is a hunter pursuing and stalking his prophet. He drives arrows into his kidneys, and since the prey cannot escape the stalker, he is a public spectacle.

He summarizes his plight in the telling words of verses 16-18. He concludes that the situation is utterly hopeless. There is nothing else he can do.

Some of these metaphors were also literally true. Jeremiah did have his life threatened, and he was a public spectacle. What are we to think of a God like this? The context of the text governs our conclusions, and these first verses fit into a larger context of this chapter. In the verses to follow, Jeremiah balances his desperation with stark beauty.

When God Seems against You, Remember: Great Is His Faithfulness
LAMENTATIONS 3:19-33

Now we come to one of the most beautiful passages in all Scripture. Jeremiah remembers that there is something he has previously forgotten: God's love. The hope that was lost (v. 18) is now recovered by the memory. To say it another way, Jeremiah confesses that all he just wrote was, in a sense, forgetful. It was penned in the lonely mental void of love, like a child sitting on the floor of a mansion weeping over a broken toy. There is more to the story than what was in his prefrontal cortex at that moment. His confession makes us more understanding of his hyperbole found in the first verses of the chapter.

God's mercies are new every morning, and he is good to those who wait on him. Another way to say this is that God is good to those who wait till morning. Those who do not wait do not see the mercy because new mercies come but not until the morning. "Despair" means awakening in the dark and assuming it's reality. Dark, for a believer, is pre-reality. Reality is coming. The Friday night before the Sunday. The disorientation before the reorientation. Therefore, if you give up before the sun rises, you miss the light of God's mercy. It comes in the morning.

I love rising early. The peaceful calm in the morning is, to me, the best time of the day. Everything else can wait. In the morning all that will come is still coming. In the hours before dawn everything is hope and expectation for the very reason that I know the sun *will* rise. The certainty of the sun makes the dark predawn glorious. And Jeremiah awakes to the thought that he is not in a black hole; he is in a black night that reminds him of the coming light. Those of us groggy in our suffering, waking before God's light, must not despair. The darkness is the evidence of the light in the same way that every morning is ushered in by light. It's the rhythm of our Father.

If my child were to awake in the night afraid, all would not be lost; he would simply come to me for comfort. Even a five-year-old knows that morning is coming. Children don't know why; they just know that resting on their father makes morning come. They don't need understanding to make it through the night; they need comfort, rest; then morning will come because it does. Our Father invented the order of day and night. The hard, utilitarian mechanism of the earth's rotation reflects this sweet sequence of his presence: dark before light. Always.

Jeremiah then gives us a means to the hope when he writes in verse 27 that it is good for a young man to bear the yoke. This is a strange passage indeed. Why is it good to bear the yoke in youth? The answer is that the young have a certain advantage of time. If they can bear the yoke of discipline now, they will be prepared in their later years to deal with whatever comes their way. Here is why: the yoke is not going away. We are not all young, but we are all younger than we are going to be. Embracing God's discipline now seems to lighten the load later. Why not, as has been said, do immediately what has to be done eventually?

There is a connection with Jeremiah 27:12. In the last days of the reign of Zedekiah, Jeremiah spoke to the king: "I spoke to King Zedekiah of Judah in the same way: 'Put your necks under the yoke of the king of Babylon, serve him and his people, and live!'" The yoke was a metaphor for surrender. Here is the irony. In order to live, he had to surrender. He had to surrender to the will of a king who hated God and wanted to destroy his people and take his land. Yet what Zedekiah could not see, would not see, is that this surrender was his salvation. This was discipline that was saving him from a worse fate later on. If he would surrender, he would live.

Of course, he did not. He was taken captive. His family was killed in front of him. His eyes were gouged out. Then he was hauled off to Babylon. God had wanted to spare him this suffering through discipline. He was to bear up under the yoke. When he rejected obedience to the Lord, he also rejected the protection of the Lord. All of this happened because he would not bear the yoke in his youth.

Among the greatest pieces of encouragement we could receive during hard times is verses 31-33. This passage is remarkably similar to Psalm 103:8-10. The psalmist said,

> The LORD is compassionate and gracious,
> slow to anger and abounding in faithful love.
> He will not always accuse us
> or be angry forever.
> He has not dealt with us as our sins deserve
> or repaid us according to our iniquities.

Jeremiah's point is slightly different from the psalmist's. He is not only drawing attention to God's character but also dealing with our response. The argument is that since the Lord will not cast off forever, since our suffering is not eternal, why not bear up under the yoke now and learn all that God wants to teach us?

Sometimes We Are Drowning in Desperation
LAMENTATIONS 3:34-54

After this pattern of desperation and salvation in the first half of the chapter, the pattern repeats itself from verse 34 to the end of the chapter.

What God Has Done (3:34-45)

Here we see that the actor in this drama is God, as we saw in chapter 2. God is the agent who is acting against his people (vv. 43-45). It would seem, outside of this context, accusatory, as if Jeremiah is blaming God. However, he deals with that in verses 34-42. The person who is poised to repent should not blame God for acting as God. God is the one who is acting, but his actions reflect a God who is responding to a people he has warned repeatedly.

The Response of the Enemy (3:46-47)

Judah's enemies respond by mocking them (v. 46). They seem to feel they are responsible for the defeat of the nation, and their gloating mocks the people and ignores the reality that God is sovereign over all. They just don't know it.

Jeremiah's Response (3:48-54)

Jeremiah is a broken man. The weeping prophet is weeping for his people (vv. 49-51). It is possible that Jeremiah is reflecting on his own experience. This was not metaphorical; he really was thrown into a pit (v. 53).

When We Are Drowning in Desperation, Remember: Great Is His Faithfulness
LAMENTATIONS 3:55-66

In the pit he calls on the Lord (v. 55). This is again a beautiful verse from a dark place. When preaching on sexual sin, I have borrowed the phrase *nothing good grows in the dark* to highlight that sins held privately need to be exposed in order to find healing. However, in a sense, the phrase does not apply here. The beauty of brokenness grows in the dark. Darkness does not stymie spiritual growth. The greenhouse of grace does not need the light of day, just the light of God.

These are the songs of lament, but they are also Jeremiah's journal. Note the change in tone. In the first six verses God was the enemy. God was both the wild animal and the hunter; Jeremiah was the victim and the prey. But look at the contrast! God is now the one who hears him, who comes near, and who champions his cause (vv. 55-58). God is no longer on the offense; God is the defender. This is a good reminder. When God seems a long way off and there seems to be no hope, keep writing in your journal. Jeremiah ends this chapter with a beautiful confession. In the last verse of this journal entry, God is no longer pursuing Jeremiah; he is pursuing Jeremiah's enemy.

Conclusion: Meaning, Mercy, Messiah

Throughout this chapter Jeremiah is borrowing from several lament psalms. It does not seem logical to picture him as a scholar with books strewn in his office, extracting quotes from here and there. That's not how he is alluding to the Hebrew songbook. Rather, it reads like a man trying to sleep at night and he can't. He is trying to find peace, trying to find rest, trying to find hope, trying to find a way to live. His survival skills don't lead him to quote some proto-Talmud. He does not quote the Torah. He is looking for new mercy, so he carefully selects psalms he has mentally archived for these types of situations—music as portable theology. He is desperate, and there are songs for that. He is desperate, hopeless, lost, and weak, but not alone. He had been needing help but finding none. This is when he reaches for his ancient songbook to meet his new problems. What he needs is the grace of new mercy. Grace comes with a melody.

Music is often the means of grace for new mercy—old songs for new mercies. The principle of pain teaches this. The Psalms help us understand what we are going through; they lead us to the meaning of new mercy. And the mercy we experience helps us understand the Psalms. In a sense the Psalms satisfy our hunger for comfort and make us hungry for knowledge. Both meaning and mercy come through music. In his dark place Jeremiah remembers, and he thinks, *I need to sing that one again*; or perhaps he thinks, *Now I know what that psalm means*. Music is both courier and linguist. Music brings grace to us and translates grace for us. And that's a new mercy available every morning. In this way Jeremiah relates to us. In this way he is our teacher. And in this way he teaches us about a greater life to come.

There was a time when the Son of God was under the wrath of God. There was a time when Jesus felt as if he was the hunted, the prey—like a lamb led to the slaughter (Isa 53:7). Jesus was the lamb. The Father was the one with the knife. This is because the wrath of the Father was pursuing him. He knew no sin, yet he did not even open his mouth.

In this moment of suffering and abandonment, Jesus turned to the Hebrew songbook and, quoting Psalm 22, cried out, "My God, my God, why have you abandoned me?" (Matt 27:46). And, as with Jeremiah in Lamentations 3, the direction of God's power changes. The Suffering Servant of Isaiah is eternally vindicated by God. The same pattern of suffering and song was in the life of our Lord. The same pattern of cosmic balance of light and dark was, in the moment when the world went dark, held up for us as a model of our own lives—when our lives move from light to dark, to light again. And we sing.

Reflect and Discuss

1. What do we do when we feel like God is the enemy?
2. Describe the poetic trajectory of this chapter. How does it move?
3. Discuss a time when you felt like God was thwarting you.
4. What are the poetic metaphors Jeremiah uses for God in verses 1-18?
5. What is the connection between Lamentations 3 and Psalm 103?
6. Jeremiah is broken. How, in light of the beatitudes, can that be a good thing?
7. Did you note a shift in the tone of Jeremiah's journal? Describe it.
8. How is music both a "courier and a linguist"?
9. How does this passage teach us more about Christ?
10. When did Christ quote a song of lament?

Everything Falls on Leadership

LAMENTATIONS 4

Main Idea: When leadership fails, the people are aimless.

Setting: The Siege of Jerusalem Was Horrific (4:1-12).
Setting: The Enemy Was Powerful (4:17-20).
I.   Leaders Can Fail Us Miserably (4:11-16).
II.   There Is Hope When Leaders Fail (4:21-22).

Throughout the history of the nation of Israel, three offices provided leadership. The office of **prophet** tethered people to the vision of God for a pure, distinct nation. The office of **priest** provided a mediating function. The priest served to facilitate access to the presence of God. The people had access to God's presence because the priest would act as a go-between, leading God's people into God's presence by following God's temple rites. The office of **king** facilitated military and civil leadership.

When these offices were in full force, it was a beautiful thing. When a king acted, for example, like King David, the people were safe from their enemies. There was political stability when David deferred to God's leadership. When a priest functioned like he was supposed to, the people had access to God and the temple was busy with ritual sacrifices. Remember, the sacrifice was not just a gift; it was a symbol. The spilled blood of the animal was a sermon, a tangible lesson on how God feels about sin. When priests functioned as true priests, the people understood this. They understood God. So much of the mind of God is represented symbolically in the temple. This is why the psalmist would sing, "May your priests be clothed with righteousness, and may your faithful people shout for joy" (Ps 132:9). When the prophets functioned like the prophet Samuel, the people had good leadership. Samuel was faithful to warn Saul of his ungodly presumption, to recognize the new King David, and to be a mouthpiece for God.

Historically, the offices served one another. When one office was out of kilter, another was on point. For example, Samuel spoke for God without hesitation when Saul was at his worst. At times the offices helped one another. For example, when Josiah became king, Hilkiah the priest rediscovered the law, and Josiah responded with brokenness and took down the high places where idols were worshiped. This triangle of leadership was not perfect, but it worked. Kings were held accountable by prophets, and the nation was blessed when the priests were leading the people well. Three offices kept the nation structurally sound; with them the nation was less wobbly.

And now we come to this dark hour—perhaps the darkest hour. The nation is facing a difficulty from which it will not, in many ways, ever recover. Lamentations 4 documents the downward slide of leadership in all three offices. Everything rises and falls on leadership. The nation is falling, so now everything is falling, including the leaders. This is a dark time with a small glimmer of hope.

- The princes who were strong are now emaciated (vv. 7-8).
- The prophets and priests shed innocent blood (v. 13).
- The priests and the elders are being chastised by God (v. 16).
- The king is captured (v. 20).

The threefold foundation of leadership is in ruins. The focus of this chapter is found in verses 13-15: when leadership fails, the people are aimless. Judah must face this reality and mourn. This really is something to cry about.

So here is a question: What is the future of a person, or a people, who are in ruins?

Setting: The Siege of Jerusalem Was Horrific (4:1-12)

The nation is at its lowest. Jeremiah sets the stage up poetically in verse 1: "How the gold has become tarnished, the fine gold become dull!"

Here is the irony: gold does not tarnish. Gold is called nonreactive because its properties do not allow oxygen, as an agent that reacts with metals, to cause corrosion. Yet the fine gold of the nation is tarnished. The point is simple: the untarnished is now tarnished; what seemed untouchable is now touchable.

The temple, the symbol of the nobility of the priesthood and the presence of God, is in ruins. The precious leaders of the nation, worth more than gold, are like common pots. Everything and everyone is vulnerable. There are leaders in my life that I look up to; they are precious to me. If they blew it morally or failed miserably, I would be crushed. They are relationships that are valuable to me. They are more valuable than precious metal. Yet all that I have I hold loosely. After all, Job teaches us that man's life is short and full of trouble, a fact that is complicated severely when we sin. So, just how bad is the situation in Israel?

There is always a price to disobedience. This one is tough and it is vivid. If this chapter were a news article on the website of a news outlet, it would come with a "graphic content" warning. It's disgusting. Lamentations 4 is not suitable for all audiences.

The situation is so bad that nursing babies are dying of starvation. Mothers in Jerusalem have become more cruel than wild animals, which at least don't neglect their young (vv. 3-4). Those who used to dine on the delicacies, epicureans with trained palates, are starving; those who were raised in royalty are dumpster diving (v. 5).

Jeremiah says in his hyperbole that it is worse than Sodom (v. 6), and maybe that's so. After all, Sodom was destroyed in a moment, while Judah's demise is excruciatingly slow (v. 9). Those slain don't suffer. They don't suffer like the women who turn cannibalistic (v. 10). It's not just that children died in their mothers' arms but that they died at their mothers' hands (Ryken, *Jeremiah and Lamentations*, 761).

Why did this happen? Jeremiah is quick to point out the truth (vv. 11-12). There are two players in this drama, and the action of neither can be overlooked. First, God exhausted his wrath. The only surprise is that he did not do it sooner. The people were warned in every conceivable way, by every means available, that the wrath of God was coming. Jeremiah preached it, communicated it to the leaders, and even used visual aids. The problem was not with the sender of the message or the message itself but with the receiver. Second, the other players here, the kings of the earth, were shocked as well. They could not believe it could happen. It's shocking. The nation was pure gold, and gold does not tarnish.

The liability of success is that feeling of invincibility. Scripture is full of examples: Moses, David, Saul, and even Peter. The most extreme example is Adam, who moved from endless life to inevitable death in one bite.

Paul sums up the application of this text when he tells us, "These things happened to them as examples, and they were written for our instruction, on whom the ends of the ages have come. So, whoever thinks he stands must be careful not to fall" (1 Cor 10:11-12).

The application from this text is simple: there is a high price of disobedience that we cannot see right now. It is so monumental. But the vista of future consequences is blocked by the pleasantness of today. Present pleasure blocks the view of future consequences. We feel immune to the cancer of sin; we are anesthetized with so many distractions. Here is Judah's lesson: no one is above God's law. Any one of us can fall—any person, any civilization, any movement. The most honest approach to life, if not the most daunting, is the lesson of Solomon in Ecclesiastes: simply to realize how fleeting and momentary we are. Every leader is merely setting the stage for the next one. Every parent is preparing children to leave home. Every movement we want so desperately to create, to be part of, is reaching a coveted tempest where, once reached, it will crest, fold into the sea, and create a way for the next one.

Since life is so short, we have to question choices that hurt us. Do we really want to disobey when we are not invincible? Since I am not above being a byword, a statistic, an also-ran, or worst of all simply forgotten, I have to ask myself, "Are there voices in my life that I am not listening to?" Like ignoring a vehicle warning light, am I slowly wearing down spiritually without even realizing it? As tragic as it would be, current success does not ensure invincibility from disobedience. In fact, success can hide our disobedience from ourselves. Like walking into traffic while looking at your phone, without realizing it, we can wander into dangerous places, alone, vulnerable, and blinded by current victories.

This sober warning is not the stuff of greeting cards, but this is a book of complaints, after all. Pain is an unwanted giver, but pain bequeaths honesty among its greatest gifts. And the truth is that disobedience is an equalizer. The rich and poor, high and low, immortal and unknown have all been her prey. So we read and weep. And we are warned.

Setting: The Enemy Was Powerful (4:17-20)

Jeremiah's song not only documents what God did but also the human means by which he did it. Verses 17-20 document just how powerful the enemy was. Judah watched in vain for help (v. 17). The time was up (v. 18).

The enemy was simply too powerful. They were too swift and pursued relentlessly (v. 19). Even the king was taken (v. 20).

So this is it. This is the desperate situation. The disobedience of the leaders motivated God to lay siege to the city, a city that could not do anything because the enemy was too powerful. So, what do you do? Now we come to an important point: they could do nothing. There was no exercise of military muscle. There were no political finesses that could save them. They were doomed. There was nothing left. They needed a savior.

Yet this is exactly what they did not have. In fact, the focus of this chapter is the failure of the leaders to help them at this point.

Leaders Can Fail Us Miserably
LAMENTATIONS 4:11-16

Leaders tell other people what to do. Of course, there is more to being a leader, and perhaps this is reductionist to the point of being naïve. Perhaps, but it's still true. Someone takes the shots because they called the shots. They set the direction the group is going. Ultimately, we do not captain by committee.

The best form of leadership, in a perfect world, is to have a perfect leader. If we do not have to question a leader's motives, capacity for leadership, or character, then we are all set. Since perfection is unattainable, we are left with a continuum of leadership. The more a leader defers to the good of an organization and less to self-interests, the better the organization. When leaders are supremely self-interested, the organization fails. The following section of Lamentations lets us know that the leadership has not kept them from disobedience; they have facilitated it. This is the focus of the chapter: the nation fell because of its leadership. The outcome is tragic.

God has poured out his wrath. He, again, is the agent who is acting. Things are so bad that the nations around Judah are awestruck at the fall of Jerusalem, a public fatality of the worst order. Other kings—actually the whole world—just gawked. So big. Impenetrable. Now it lies in ruins (vv. 11-12). So, why did this happen? Jeremiah explains,

> Yet it happened because of the sins of her prophets
> and the iniquities of her priests,
> who shed the blood of the righteous within her. (v. 13)

What was the great iniquity of the priests? It was not what they said but what they did not say. They failed to teach people the word of the Lord, a major theme for Jeremiah. In Jeremiah 5:30-31 he describes it like this:

An appalling, horrible thing
has taken place in the land.
The prophets prophesy falsely,
and the priests rule by their own authority.
My people love it like this.
But what will you do at the end of it?

Now we know what they will do. At the end of it all, they are stumbling in the streets. They have shed blood so they are unclean. Even among the pagan nations no one will touch them (vv. 14-15). The Lord has scattered them, and—this is the scariest part—the Lord no longer watches over them (v. 16).

When your leaders let you down, your world is in ruins, and the enemy is more powerful than you, you need a savior. So the chapter closes with a measure of hope.

There Is Hope When Leaders Fail
LAMENTATIONS 4:21-22

There is hope that God would punish the wicked. Just as Jeremiah prophesied in Jeremiah 49:7, Edom, who rejoiced at the destruction of the nation, would meet her end (Lam 4:21). It often seems extreme that God would be explicit that other nations, enemy nations, would suffer. Yet the nature of a covenant-keeping God is that he would bless those who blessed his people and curse those who cursed his people (Gen 12:3). Even when the relationship between God and his people has been complicated by so much sin and betrayal, he keeps his promise. The promise given in the initial events of the covenant are kept as the events of the Old Testament are ending. He is seeking wrath on those who hurt his people.

There is also hope for deliverance. A beautiful couplet of hope closes out the chapter (v. 22a). God does for them what they cannot do for themselves. What a remarkable end to this story! Can we wrap our minds around it? Here is the flow of the story Jeremiah is lamenting:

- God gives explicit instructions.
- His people disobey.
- He warns them repeatedly through Jeremiah.
- His people disobey.
- God gives some last chances.
- His people disobey.

- God punishes his people.
- God redeems his people from his own judgment.

In the end we learn that only God can save us from God.

Conclusion

So, in the end, what do we do if leaders fail us? There are so many natural responses that are wrong:

- Justify their sin because we are friends.
- Ignore their sin because we are affiliated with them in some way.
- Not deal with a public sin publicly.
- Use their sin as an excuse for our own sin.
- Fail to learn the lesson that all of us are vulnerable.
- Fail to see ourselves as a candidate for the same sin.
- Fail to use the moment of failure to warn us about our own sin.
- Fail to hold leaders accountable for their actions.
- Fail to restore the fallen leader with grace.

After the dust settles, we could simply wallow in despair and self-pity. But this is where the gospel enters.

There is so much about the gospel in this passage that it's hard to know where to start. This is a metaphor for life. People who disobey God are set on a certain path of destruction. Like the rogue nation, they cannot change trajectories, so God offers a way of escape from his pending judgment. God saves us from God. This is the good news of the gospel. God's wrath hangs over everyone in the world. All sins will be punished. Yet as the hand of judgment is falling, Christ stands up. He takes the blow for us. Charity Gayle encapsulates it beautifully in the song "Divine Exchange" when she writes,

On the cross hung my pain
And the guilt and the shame
Jesus bore my suffering
To the grave to make me free

Oh the blood that was shed
It now flows to cover sin
It washes, clean, and purifies
In its healing crimson tide

Jesus, He took my place in divine exchange Hallelujah!
Grace is mine.
Now I live by faith for the One who saves
He gave all to give me life.

There is a more subtle gospel note in Jeremiah's song. He complained, "The LORD's anointed, the breath of our life, was captured in their traps" (v. 20). This is a reference to their human king. Yet the Lord's anointed is more than a moniker for a human king; it was the title for the King of all kings.

Another song prophesies that in the end the whole world will set itself against the Lord's Anointed. When this happens, God will laugh (Ps 2). God is not threatened by anything. Nothing intimidates him the least bit or gives him pause.

The Anointed One is the Messiah, Jesus the Christ. He was never captured but gave his life so that those whose lives were in ruin, those whose enemy is stronger than they are, those who have leaders who let them down will never be captured again. We will be captured by grace and saved from judgment by the one anointed, the one chosen, to redeem us. The deliverance from my future problems is already provided.

This is the greater lesson—a lesson about present failure and future grace. The failure of present leaders makes us want a better Leader. This Leader we have in Christ. He is the Leader who never falters, never leaves us. Present failure feels like hitting a brick wall. God takes the bricks from our wall and creates a path.

Present failure is a window into a future. The reason God is such a good leader is due to his character and his nature. His character is as one who always does good. He lacks the capacity to give us anything but good leadership because he is so good to us. And his nature is all knowing. God leads us perfectly because he knows the future perfectly, and he wills good things for us. Wow! This is just amazing! Every failure of every leader creates a thirst for a leader who is all-knowing and all good. Praise God! He is so good!

Reflect and Discuss

1. Describe the offices of prophet, priest, and king.
2. How did Jeremiah feel now that all of those offices were in ruins?

3. How was it that this situation was worse than the destruction of Sodom (v. 6)?
4. How were the other nations shocked at the destruction of Jerusalem?
5. How does Jeremiah creatively use the metaphor of tarnished gold?
6. How does Paul explain how we should understand these Old Testament stories (1 Cor 12:11)?
7. How does the fact that we cannot currently see the price of disobedience warn us?
8. How did Christ fulfill all three offices of prophet, priest, and king?
9. Can you recall Scriptures that refer to Christ as filling all three offices?
10. How does this passage point us to the Anointed One of Psalm 2:2?

Turning Real Regret into Real Prayer

LAMENTATIONS 5

Main Idea: Prayer is greater than regret.

I. **We Pray Just to Survive (5:1-10).**
II. **We Pray When We Are Suffering (5:11-14).**
III. **We Pray When We Are Sorrowful (5:15-18).**
IV. **We Pray When We Are Searching for God (5:19-22).**

Recently I visited a prison and met with men in a program designed to help them re-enter society. The Pathway to Freedom reentry program is a prison ministry designed to teach men the ultimate form of release from bondage: release from spiritual bondage. What struck me most as I walked the bleached white halls of their prison was a pulsating joy—pristine, immaculate joy. These men were guilty, tried, and punished, yet the solitude of loneliness gave them the gift of reflection. They could ask questions about where they were going and what was next. In their darkness they became dazzled by the light. They were at once incarcerated and liberated, locked up and set free.

The statistics are not perfect, but the comparatively low number of repeat offenders coming from such programs gives even the deepest cynic pause and causes the believer to rejoice.

However, in the general population, the number of prisoners who are repeat offenders is high. Each man in prison has regrets. They wish they would not have done it, wish they were born to different circumstances, wish they could get free, and wish they had better friends or more opportunities. They have lives full of regret. Yet the number of those who return to prison reminds us that being sorry for something does not always evidence a changed life—not at all. Recidivism is the evidence that regret is not reform.

Remembering that prayer is something greater than regret, the book of Lamentations ends with a prayer. It is a prayer that expresses regret for all that has taken place in the rebellious nation. While there is a tinge of hope, this is a rehearsal of just how bad things were when Israel sought to do their own thing and walk their own way.

Prayer is greater than regret. The structure of the song is simply a telling of complaints ending with a tinge of hope. It does not seem there is a formal structure as much as a retelling of the regrets of the nation in the form of a prayer. However, Christopher Wright sees a four-fold division in the chapter, adapted in the outline above (*Message of Lamentations*, 149–66).

We Pray Just to Survive
LAMENTATIONS 5:1-10

This entire section is a prayer. The prayer is framed in remembrance as Jeremiah begins (v. 1). When he says, "Remember," he is not asking God to recall something God had forgotten. Rather, he is calling God to act on what he knows.

Verse 2 is the song in summary. The thrust of the lament is that other people have God's chosen people's inheritance. The theme of inheritance is a huge theme in Scripture. These people were God's inheritance. This is God's lot, meaning what God really wanted out of this relationship was them. He wanted their hearts turned back to him. Because God did not have his inheritance, the land, the inheritance of the people, was turned over to pagan people and their so-called gods.

There is something intensely practical here. In this simple prayer we see the power of a lament. We can think of laments as complaints; that is what they are. Yet the word *complaint* hints at something whiney, irrepressible, or insatiable, as you might hear from someone who could change his situation but refuses to do so. Instead, he whines. He gripes. There is also a hint of hopelessness in complaints. When my young children complain, often it is for things they could fix if they think about it.

This closing prayer is not whiney hopelessness. In fact, it is exactly the opposite. The lament prayer calls out to God in all their suffering and asks God to act.

Think about the power of this prayer. First, it assumes that God hears, that Jeremiah is not praying to the air, but that God perceives the situation. Second, this prayer assumes that God cares. There must be compassion in him. Finally, this prayer assumes that God can act. We often hole up in self-pity and self-loathing with worries and concerns that God could easily take care of. Prayer deflects the ultimate responsibility for the resolution of problems and places it on God. There is more to say about prayer here, but at this point it is enough to create distance between complaining and lament.

- Complaining is rooted in self-pity and is self-centered.
- Lament prayers are rooted in brokenness and are God focused.

God demands that we bring him all our problems. His expectation of every believer is that we will give everything to him in prayer. Head bowed. Palms open. Everything. Jeremiah 5 is a model of this: calling on God to do what we can't. In this way we honor him by the magnitude of our requests.

The resolution to the problems we are facing right now cannot be seen right now. As someone said, when we think our world is falling apart, it might just be falling in place. Many times I have thought some incident in my life was the death of a dream, the death of a hope that I had. The reality is that God was creating something far better than I could have imagined. I only needed to trust him in that moment. The greater reality lay on the other side of the great pain.

We Pray When We Are Suffering
LAMENTATIONS 5:11-14

The suffering that is described here is awful. The young women have been abused, the young men have been turned to slaves, and some were tortured and killed (vv. 11-13). The elders no longer gather to function like leaders (v. 14).

This is a difficult and dark day for this nation. Everything that once made them proud is disastrous. However, remember that this is a prayer. The point of recalling this back to God is not to inform him. The point is that God will act.

The suffering has led to great sorrow.

We Pray When We Are Sorrowful
LAMENTATIONS 5:15-18

They are bereft of joy. Their hearts are sick. The great Mount Zion is now taken over by jackals. The deep sorrow they feel is due to their own sin. This is something the nation has caused. They are having to deal with the sorrow of knowing that all of this pain is suffering at their own hand.

If you have ever had the spiritual life sucked out of you, then you understand the dilemma of Jeremiah. I know that joy is often a choice, and often it is a hard choice to make. We are rattled by the consequences of our own bad choices to the point that we cannot go on.

Winston Churchill, referring to the airmen who fought in the Battle of Britain, famously said, "Never in the field of human conflict was so much owed by so many to so few" ("Never"). Never have so many owed so much to so few. It could be said of Judah, "Never have so few lost so much for so many." Really, they were God's chosen people and are now the lonely city that sits on the hill. It's sad. Sin came at the price of lost joy. It always does.

We Pray When We Are Searching for God
LAMENTATIONS 5:19-22

Jeremiah is praising God for his exalted state (v. 19). Yet he asks a blunt question: Why has God forgotten them? This is a remarkable question and at first blush is nonsensical. God is the one he is praying to; therefore, he thinks God can do something about this. It would seem you do not ask for a deity to act in his omnipotence while you are jeering at his forgetfulness. The idea, of course, is not memory. God, as he expressed in chapter 2, seems to be against them. This is the meaning of "forget" here. Not that they are out of God's memory but out of God's mercy. Why is God treating them like this? This plaintive cry by the crushed prophet reminds us that God is not toppled by our questions.

What Jeremiah wants is expressed in verses 21-22. He wants to be completely restored back to God. He suggests that maybe this is not possible because God may have totally written them off. Yet this can't be true. Jeremiah already dealt with this in 3:31 when he wrote that the Lord will not reject them forever. His discipline is momentary and his mercies are new every morning.

Application/Conclusion

So, what does the New Testament say about regret? It's tempting to deal with regret in a cavalier way. We reckon that God's grace is real and we've got to move on, so we bury the regret deep down and try not to think about it. After all, there's nothing we can do to change the past. As Willie Nelson sang, "Nothing I Can Do about It Now."

Jesus teaches us something different. He teaches us that regret is not something to be buried but to be wielded for good. Perhaps the most outstanding reminder is found toward the end of the Gospel of Luke (18:18-23).

A wealthy young urbanite asked Jesus a simple question: "What must I do to inherit eternal life?" The answer Jesus gave is stunningly simple: he should keep the commandments. He replied that he had done that. Jesus then put his finger on the one area of his life where he was unwilling to yield: his finances. It seems he loved to keep the law, but he also loved money more than people. Money, as Jesus taught, was a resource to be invested. So, of course, Jesus goes there. When Jesus called for absolute obedience, the wealthy man went away sad. He had a heart full of regret. The regret was as real as it was useless.

It seems intentional that Luke would follow that story with the story of a man named Zacchaeus (Luke 19:1-9). That man regretted being a thief. And, seemingly immediately, he leveraged the regret to gain repentance. He restored what he had stolen. Jesus's observation was, "Today salvation has come to this house." The salvation was not evidenced by the regret but by the repentance.

Christians do in fact embrace grace. Wallowing in self-pity is not an option. The effectiveness of a believer is not marked by how little he sins but how quickly he repents. This is the point. The Christian position is not mindless self-denial but to leverage regret for the glory of repentance.

Regret is powerful. In a way it is almost too powerful. The power of regret, combined with the emotion of grief, is not unlike a knife. If we are tied up and have a knife, we can hurt ourselves or cut ourselves free. Repentance is using the knife of regret to cut the ropes. In this way repentance leaves regret and moves to freedom. Regret, a fearful master, can be the pathway to freedom. Remorse, on the other hand, coddles regret in self-inflicting wounds. Repentance liberates; remorse wounds.

It's strange really. Regret becomes a friend if it leads us to repentance. Regret for some is a dead end; for others, regret is the on-ramp to the road of repentance.

"For godly grief produces a repentance that leads to salvation without regret, but worldly grief produces death" (2 Cor 7:10).

Reflect and Discuss

1. Why is Jeremiah so down? What, in this chapter, is he lamenting?
2. Why is regret a fearful master?
3. Discuss how prayer is greater than regret.
4. Can you recall a time in your life when you were filled with regret? Were you tempted to let the regret lead you to despondency?
5. Does the fact that there is a high rate of repeat offenders after prison teach us that regret and remorse are not the same as genuine change?
6. What distinction was made between selfish complaining and lament?
7. Granted the distinction between complaint and lament is fine; still, does the distinction help us know how to focus our sorrow?
8. Jeremiah's sorrow was related to how far Jerusalem fell. Can you think of a time in your life when you have experienced great loss?
9. How does the story of the rich young man in Luke 18 relate to this chapter?
10. What are we to do with godly sorrow according to 2 Corinthians 7:10?

WORKS CITED

Adams, Peter. *Speaking God's Word*. Downers Grove, IL: Intervarsity, 1996.

Bromwich, David. "The Meaning of Shock and Awe." *Huffpost*. https://www.huffingtonpost.com/david-bromwich/the-meaning-of-shock-and-_b_2844688.html. Accessed January 18, 2018.

Brueggemann, Walter. *Spirituality of the Psalms (Facets)*, abridged edition. Minneapolis, MN: Fortress, 2001.

———. *To Build, to Plant: A Commentary on Jeremiah 26–52*. International Theological Commentary. Grand Rapids, MI: Eerdmans, 1991.

Chisholm, Thomas. "Great Is Thy Faithfulness." 1925.

Demoss, Nancy. "Proud People vs. Broken People." *FamilyLife.com*. http://www.familylife.com/articles/topics/faith/essentials/repentance/proud-people-vs-broken-people. Accessed July 30, 2018.

Dever, Mark. *The Message of the Old Testament: Promises Made*. Wheaton, IL: Crossway, 2006.

Dickens, Charles. *A Tale of Two Cities*. London: Capman and Hall, 1867.

Elliff, Bill. "The Sin That Prevents Revival." *Graceful Truth*. June 3, 2016. http://www.thesummitchurch.org/graceful-truth/the-sin-that-prevents-revival. Accessed July 28, 2018.

Gayle, Charity. "Divine Exchange." By Brandon Michael Collins, Charity Gayle, Jennie Lee Riddle, and Melanie Tierce. Self published: 2015. [Also released on *You Are My Song*, People & Songs label, 2018.] https://www.musixmatch.com/lyrics/Charity-Gayle/Divine-Exchange. Accessed January 30, 2017.

Hays, J. Daniel. *Jeremiah and Lamentations*. Teach the Text Commentary Series. Grand Rapids, MI: Baker, 2016.

Herbst, Diane. "Man Who Survived Suicide Jump from Golden Gate Bridge Shares His Story to Help Others: 'The Moment I Hit Freefall Was an Instant Regret.'" *People.com*. April 19, 2016. http://people.com/human-interest/kevin-hines-survived-suicide-jump-from-golden-gate-bridge. Accessed May 16, 2018.

Huey, F. B. *Jeremiah, Lamentations*. New American Commentary. Nashville, TN: B&H, 1993.

Kidner, Derek. *The Message of Jeremiah*. The Bible Speaks Today. Downers Grove, IL: InterVarsity, 1987.

Lansing, Alfred. *Endurance: Shackleton's Incredible Voyage*. New York, NY: Caroll and Graf, 1999.

Lehman, Frederick Martin. "The Love of God." 1917.

Lewis, Paul. "'Our Minds Can Be Hijacked': The Tech Insiders Who Fear a Smartphone Dystopia." *The Guardian.com*. October 6, 2017. https://www.theguardian.com/technology/2017/oct/05/smartphone-addiction-silicon-valley-dystopia. Accessed November 2, 2017.

McDonald, George. *Knowing the Heart of God*. Bloomington, MN: Bethany House, 1990.

McGonigal, Kelly. *Maximum Willpower: How to Master the New Science of Self-Control*. London: Macmillan, 2012.

Nelson, Willie. "Nothing I Can Do about It Now." On *A Horse Called Music*. Written by Beth Nielsen Chapman. New York, NY: CBS, 1989.

"Never in the Field of Human Conflict Was So Much Owed by So Many to So Few." *The Guardian*. August 21, 1940. https://www.theguardian.com/century/1940-1949/Story/0,,128255,00.html. Accessed May 28, 2018.

Ryken, Philip. *Jeremiah and Lamentations: From Sorrow to Hope*. Preach the Word. Wheaton, IL: Crossway, 2001.

Smith, Steven W. *Recapturing the Voice of God: Shaping Sermons Like Scripture*. Nashville, TN: B&H, 2015.

"Transplant Rejection." *MedlinePlus.gov*. U.S. National Library of Medicine. https://www.nlm.nih.gov/medlineplus/ency/article/000815.htm. Accessed June 16, 2016.

Wright, Christopher. *The Message of Jeremiah*. The Bible Speaks Today. Downers Grove, IL: InterVarsity, 2014.

———. *The Message of Lamentations*. The Bible Speaks Today. Downers Grove, IL: InterVarsity, 2015.

SCRIPTURE INDEX